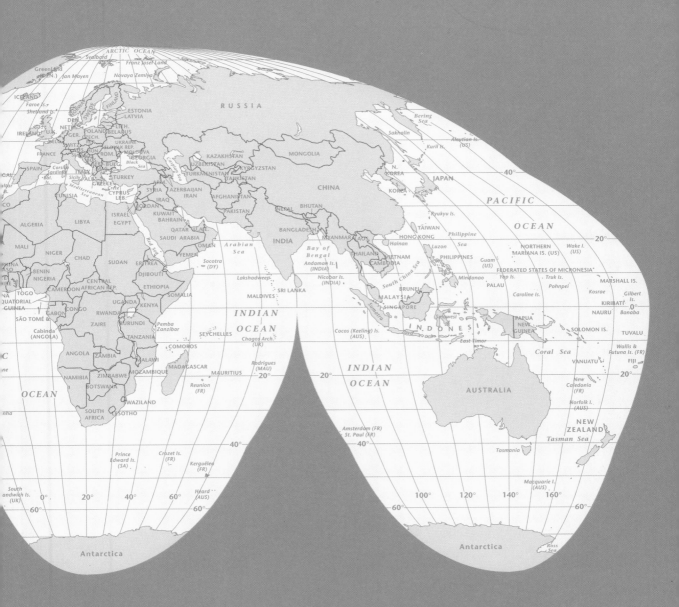

Junior
Worldmark
Encyclopedia
of the

Nations

VOLUME 6

Junior Worldmark Encyclopedia of the

Nations

VOLUME 6

Namibia to Portugal

An imprint of Gale Research
An ITP Information/Reference Group Company

Changing the Way the World Learns

NEW YORK • LONDON • BONN • BOSTON • DETROIT
MADRID • MELBOURNE • MEXICO CITY • PARIS
SINGAPORE • TOKYO • TORONTO • WASHINGTON
ALBANY NY • BELMONT CA • CINCINNATI OH

JUNIOR WORLDMARK ENCYCLOPEDIA OF THE NATIONS

Timothy L. Gall and Susan Bevan Gall, *Editors*
Rosalie Wieder, *Senior Editor*
Deborah Baron and Daniel M. Lucas, *Associate Editors*
Brian Rajewski and Deborah Rutti, *Graphics and Layout*
Cordelia R. Heaney, *Editorial Assistant*
Dianne K. Daeg de Mott, Janet Fenn, Matthew Markovich,
    Ariana Ranson, and Craig Strasshofer, *Copy Editors*
Janet Fenn and Matthew Markovich, *Proofreaders*
Maryland Cartographics, Inc., *Cartographers*

U•X•L Staff

Jane Hoehner, *U•X•L Developmental Editor*
Sonia Benson and Rob Nagel, *Contributors*
Thomas L. Romig, *U•X•L Publisher*
Mary Beth Trimper, *Production Director*
Evi Seoud, *Assistant Production Manager*
Shanna Heilveil, *Production Associate*
Cynthia Baldwin, *Product Design Manager*
Barbara J. Yarrow, *Graphic Services Supervisor*
Mary Krzewinski, *Cover Designer*
Margaret McAvoy-Amoto, *Permissions Associate (Pictures)*

Library of Congress Cataloging-in-Publication Data
Junior Worldmark encyclopedia of the nations / edited by Timothy Gall
    and Susan Gall.
        p.   cm.
    Includes bibliographical references and index.
    ISBN 0-7876-0741-X (set)
    1. Geography--Encyclopedias, Juvenile. 2. History--Encyclopedias,
Juvenile. 3. Economics--Juvenile literature. 4. Political science--
Encyclopedia, Juvenile. 5. United Nations--Encyclopedias,
Juvenile. I. Gall, Timothy L. II. Gall, Susan B.
    G63.J86 1995
    910'.3--dc20   95-36739
                                                     CIP

ISBN 0-7876-0741-X (set)
ISBN 0-7876-0742-8 (vol. 1)   ISBN 0-7876-0743-6 (vol. 2)   ISBN 0-7876-0744-4 (vol. 3)
ISBN 0-7876-0745-2 (vol. 4)   ISBN 0-7876-0746-0 (vol. 5)   ISBN 0-7876-0747-9 (vol. 6)
ISBN 0-7876-0748-7 (vol. 7)   ISBN 0-7876-0749-5 (vol. 8)   ISBN 0-7876-0750-9 (vol. 9)

U•X•L is an imprint of Gale Research Inc.,
an International Thomson Publishing Company.
ITP logo is a trademark under license.

CONTENTS

Guide to Country Articles

Every country profile in this encyclopedia includes the same 35 headings. Also included in every profile is a map (showing the country and its location in the world), the country's flag and seal, and a table of data on the country. The country articles are organized alphabetically in nine volumes. A glossary of terms is included in each of the nine volumes. This glossary defines many of the specialized terms used throughout the encyclopedia. A keyword index to all nine volumes appears at the end of Volume 9.

Flag color symbols

| Yellow | Red | Green | Blue | Orange | Brown | White | Black |

Alphabetical listing of sections

Agriculture	21	Income	18
Armed Forces	16	Industry	19
Bibliography	35	Judicial System	15
Climate	3	Labor	20
Domesticated Animals	22	Languages	9
Economy	17	Location and Size	1
Education	31	Media	32
Energy and Power	27	Migration	7
Environment	5	Mining	25
Ethnic Groups	8	Plants and Animals	4
Famous People	34	Political Parties	14
Fishing	23	Population	6
Foreign Trade	26	Religions	10
Forestry	24	Social Development	28
Government	13	Topography	2
Health	29	Tourism/Recreation	33
History	12	Transportation	11
Housing	30		

Sections listed numerically

1	Location and Size	19	Industry
2	Topography	20	Labor
3	Climate	21	Agriculture
4	Plants and Animals	22	Domesticated Animals
5	Environment	23	Fishing
6	Population	24	Forestry
7	Migration	25	Mining
8	Ethnic Groups	26	Foreign Trade
9	Languages	27	Energy and Power
10	Religions	28	Social Development
11	Transportation	29	Health
12	History	30	Housing
13	Government	31	Education
14	Political Parties	32	Media
15	Judicial System	33	Tourism/Recreation
16	Armed Forces	34	Famous People
17	Economy	35	Bibliography
18	Income		

Abbreviations and acronyms to know

GMT= Greenwich mean time. The prime, or Greenwich, meridian passes through Greenwich, England (near London), and marks the center of the initial time zone for the world. The standard time of all 24 time zones relate to Greenwich mean time. Every profile contains a map showing the country and its location in the world.

These abbreviations are used in references to famous people:
b.=born
d.=died
fl.=flourished (lived and worked)
r.=reigned (for kings, queens, and similar monarchs)

A dollar sign ($) stands for US$ unless otherwise indicated.

NAMIBIA

Republic of Namibia

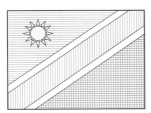

CAPITAL: Windhoek.

FLAG: Top left triangle is blue, center diagonal band is red, and the bottom right triangle is green. Colors are separated by narrow white bands. On the blue triangle is a golden sun with twelve triangular rays.

ANTHEM: *Namibia Land of the Brave*, music and words by Axali Doeseb.

MONETARY UNIT: The South African rand (R) of 100 cents is in use; notes and coins are those of South Africa. R1 = $0.2874 (or $1 = R3.4795).

WEIGHTS AND MEASURES: The metric system is in use.

HOLIDAYS: New Year's Day, 1 January; Independence Day, 21 March; Easter, 1–4 April; Workers' Day, 1 May; Casinga Day, 4 May; Ascension Day, 12 May; Africa Day, 25 May; Heroes' Day, 26 August; Day of Goodwill, 7 October; Human Rights Day, 10 December; Christmas, 25–26 December.

TIME: 2 PM = noon GMT.

1 LOCATION AND SIZE

Namibia covers 824,290 square kilometers (318,260 square miles), slightly more than half the size of the state of Alaska. It has a total boundary length of 5,424 kilometers (3,370 miles).

Namibia's capital city, Windhoek, is in the center of the country.

2 TOPOGRAPHY

Namibia is mostly a dry, elevated plateau. The coastal strip comprises the Namib Desert, and the eastern region is part of the Kalahari Desert.

All four permanent rivers form borders: the Kunene and Okavango in the north, the Zambezi in the northeast, and the Orange (Oranje) in the south.

3 CLIMATE

Namibia's climate is the driest in Africa, with sunny, warm days and cooler nights, especially during the winter months. The mean January temperature at Windhoek is 23°C (73°F). In winter, the mean temperature is 13°C (55°F). Much of Namibia experiences chronic drought. The annual rainfall, which mostly falls between December and March, generally averages only 2.5–15 centimeters (1–6 inches) in the south of the country, and some regions have gone 90 years without a drop of rain.

4 PLANTS AND ANIMALS

In Namibia's game parks and the neighboring grazing areas are found the tallest elephants in the world, along with rhinoceroses, lions, cheetahs, leopards, and ostriches. Also common are the giraffe, zebra, black-faced impala, and wildebeest. Birds of prey are numerous. Among the unique plants are many varieties of aloe.

5 ENVIRONMENT

Environmental problems in Namibia include water pollution and shortages of water. Ten percent of the nation's city dwellers and 63% of the people living in rural areas do not have pure water. Deforestation, soil erosion, and agricultural chemicals, such as DDT, are also a threat to the environment.

Twelve nature conservation areas cover 99,616 square kilometers (38,462 square miles). In 1994, 11 of Namibia's mammal species and 7 bird species were endangered, and 17 species of plants were threatened with extinction.

6 POPULATION

According to the 1991 census, the population of Namibia was 1,401,711. In 1994, the total population was estimated at 1,690,483. The projected population for the year 2000 is 1,964,000. Windhoek, the capital, had a 1991 population of 158,609.

7 MIGRATION

Namibia's migrant labor force exceeds 100,000. Ovambo people from northern Namibia have moved south since the 1920s to work in diamond mines near the coast and in cities and towns in the country's interior. As of 1986 there were 69,000 Namibian refugees in Angola and 7,000 in Zambia.

8 ETHNIC GROUPS

The largest group is the Ovambo, numbering about 665,000 in 1991, who live mainly in the north. The second-largest group is the Kavango (124,000). Other groups include the Damara (100,000) and the Herero (100,000). The majority of whites, called Afrikaners, are of Dutch descent and numbered 40,000 in 1991. There were also about 25,000 speakers of German and 5,000 English-speakers in the same year. In 1985, the Coloureds (peoples of mixed descent) numbered 48,000, and there were about 32,000 San (Bushmen) and 7,000 Tswana.

9 LANGUAGES

The official language of Namibia is English. Afrikaans and German are also spoken. However, Ovambo, in any of several dialects, is the language spoken by more Namibians than any other, and Herero is widely spoken in Windhoek.

10 RELIGIONS

Perhaps 90% of Namibians are Christians, including Lutherans, Roman Catholics, Anglicans, and Dutch Reformed. The rest practice traditional African religions.

11 TRANSPORTATION

Namibia has 2,341 kilometers (1,455 miles) of railway and 54,500 kilometers (33,867 miles) of roads. There were 109,940 registered vehicles in 1992. Walvis Bay is the main port for imports and exports. About 95% of all Namibian sea trade is handled there. The territory's international airport is near Windhoek.

NAMIBIA

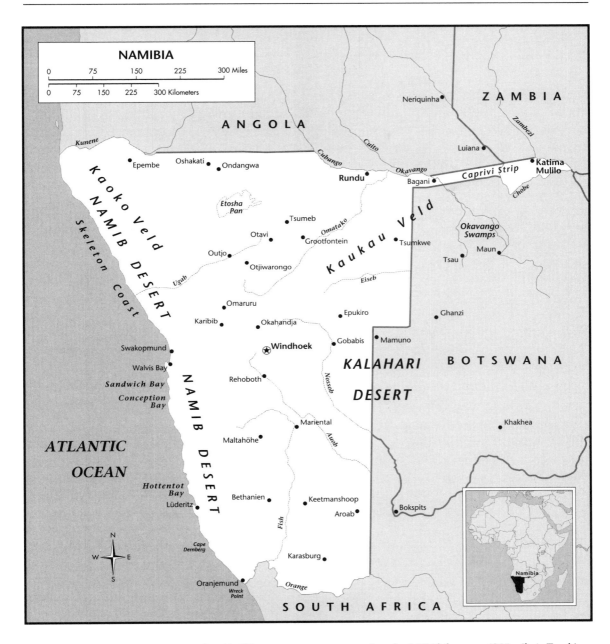

LOCATION: 11°44′ to 25°16′E; 16°58′ to 28°58′s. **BOUNDARY LENGTHS:** Angola, 1,376 kilometers (855 miles); Zambia, 233 kilometers (144 miles); Botswana, 1,360 kilometers (850 miles); South Africa, 966 kilometers (600 miles); Atlantic Ocean, including Walvis Bay, 1,489 kilometers (921 miles). **TERRITORIAL SEA LIMIT:** 12 miles.

Air Namibia flew 149,200 international and domestic passengers in 1991.

12 HISTORY

Paintings of animal figures on rock slabs are evidence that humans lived in Namibia at least 25,000 years ago. By the nineteenth century, the Damara, Ovambo, and Herero were the largest native ethnic groups. The Kavango and the Caprivians were also settled in the areas where they now live. There was competition for land, mostly between the Ovambo and the Herero. But then the invaders arrived. The Hottentots (now called Nama) won large areas of southern and central Namibia from the Herero and the Damara. The Germans came in 1883, first as traders and missionaries and then as soldiers. In the 1890s they established forts and dominated the Herero and Damara at Windhoek.

When World War I (1914–18) broke out, the South Africans invaded Süd-West Afrika, as the German colony of Namibia was then called. Between 1920 and 1946, the new League of Nations granted South Africa permission to govern the colony. South Africa took control of the territory but spent little money on social services and largely neglected (as had the Germans) the Ovambo-Kavango region in the north.

After World War II (1939–45), South Africa tried to turn Namibia into its own province. In the 1950s, senators from South West Africa sat in the South African parliament, and Windhoek was reduced to a provincial capital. The United Nations took South Africa before the International Court of Justice, but not until 1971 did the Court declare the South African occupation of Namibia illegal.

Meanwhile, in 1960, representatives of the native majority had formed the South-West Africa People's Organization (SWAPO) to seek independence and black majority rule. Beginning in 1966, but especially after 1977, SWAPO waged a guerrilla war. South Africa responded by building up its armed forces along Namibia's borders.

In 1978, South Africa accepted a Western-sponsored plan for an independent Namibia, but the plan proved difficult to implement in a way that satisfied all sides. It was not until April of 1989 that all sides finally agreed to a ceasefire and began the process of creating a new state.

Elections were held in November of 1989. SWAPO won 57% of the vote, the Democratic Turnahalle Alliance (DTA) received 29%, and a variety of ethnic-based parties received the rest. A new constitution was adopted on 9 February 1990, and Namibia became independent on 21 March 1990.

The SWAPO government (whose support comes chiefly from the Ovambo people of the north and from urban areas) has followed a policy of reconciliation with the white inhabitants and created a multiparty, nonracial democracy. In 1993, agreement was reached with South Africa to return Walvis Bay to Namibia, an act completed on 1 March 1994.

Photo credit: Cynthia Bassett

This woman, a member of the Herero tribe, sews traditional dolls.

13 GOVERNMENT

The Namibia constitution adopted on 21 March 1990 is considered a model of democratic government. It provides for a two-chamber legislature, consisting of a National Assembly and a National Council. The Assembly consists of 72 elected deputies and six members appointed by the president. The Council is comprised of two members from each of 13 regions.

The president is elected by direct, popular vote. The president serves as head of state and commander-in-chief of the Defense Force. The term of office can be for no more than two five-year terms.

14 POLITICAL PARTIES

The South-West Africa People's Organization (SWAPO) is the largest political party. There are a number of ethnic parties, including the South-West African National Union (SWANU), largely representing the Herero; the white-led Democratic Turnhalle Alliance (DTA); the SWAPO-Democrats, a small Ovambo-based group; the Damara Council; and the Namibia Christian Democratic Party (a Kavango group).

15 JUDICIAL SYSTEM

The formal court system is arranged on three levels: magistrates' courts, the High

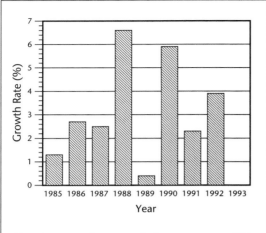

Yearly growth rate of the economy. This economic indicator tells by what percent the economy has increased or decreased when compared with the previous year.

which, together, account for nearly 90% of exports. The economy is highly integrated with that of South Africa. Years of white rule have resulted in one of the most unequal income distributions on the African continent. However, a democratically elected government is now committed to developing previously neglected regions of the country.

18 INCOME

In 1992 Namibia's gross national product (GNP) was $2,502 million at current prices, or about $1,820 per person. Although the per person GNP is relatively high for Africa, it covers up a tremendous income inequality between the black and minority white populations. For the period 1985–92, the average inflation rate was 10.2%, resulting in a real growth rate in GNP of 1.1% per person.

19 INDUSTRY

Namibia's industry is centered on meat and fish processing, with some production of basic consumer goods. There are furniture and clothing factories, metal and engineering works, assembly plants, and a cement plant. Historically, Namibia has been dependent on South African manufacturing.

20 LABOR

In 1992, agriculture supported 70% of the population, and the unemployment rate was about 25%. The principal trade union organization is the National Union of Namibian Workers (NUNW), a SWAPO-aligned federation of 7 industrial unions with 70,000 members.

Court, and the Supreme Court. The Supreme Court serves as the highest court of appeals and also exercises constitutional review of legislation. The traditional courts handle minor criminal offenses such as petty theft and violations of local customs.

16 ARMED FORCES

Postwar national forces number 7,400 men in 8 mixed battalions and 100 men in naval patrol forces. There is a small national police force. Defense spending is $66 million (1992).

17 ECONOMY

Namibia's economy is dependent on a few primary exports, including minerals (diamonds, uranium, copper, lead, silver), livestock (both meat and hides), and fish,

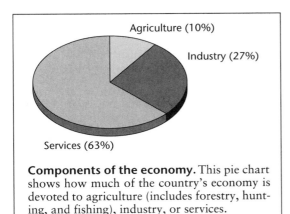

Components of the economy. This pie chart shows how much of the country's economy is devoted to agriculture (includes forestry, hunting, and fishing), industry, or services.

Children below the age of 14 may not work at any job. For mining, manufacturing, and construction work, the minimum age is 17. For underground work, the minimum age is 18. Despite the law, children under age 14 often work on family and commercial farms in the informal sector. Traditionally, boys in rural areas begin herding livestock at age 7.

21 AGRICULTURE

About 70% of the active population depends on agriculture directly or indirectly for their living. Colonialism left Namibia with a three-part agricultural production system: 4,000 commercial ranches; 20,000 livestock-raising households; and 120,000 mixed-farming operations. Corn production in 1992 amounted only to 13,000 tons (down from 50,000 tons in 1991). Recent droughts have created a dependency on grain imports. In 1992, 53,800 tons of corn were imported. Namibia is dependent on South Africa for corn, sugar, fruit, and vegetables.

22 DOMESTICATED ANIMALS

Livestock production is the major agricultural activity, making up more than 90% of that sector's output. In 1992, there were an estimated 2,100,000 head of cattle, 3 million sheep, and 1,972,000 goats. About 200,000 cattle and 1,208,000 sheep and goats were slaughtered in 1992.

23 FISHING

Fishing and fish processing are among the nation's best prospects for employment and economic growth. The government has predicted that by the year 2000, production could increase eight-fold, creating a $900 million industry. The total catch in 1991 was 204,517 tons.

24 FORESTRY

About 22% of Namibia consists of forests and woodland, all in the north and northeast. Most of the timber is used locally.

25 MINING

The most valuable minerals produced in 1991 included diamonds, uranium, copper, silver, lead, zinc, gold, pyrite, and salt. In 1991, the Namibian mining industry was the largest private employer. Namibia is among the world's premier producers of gem diamonds. Consolidated Diamond Mines, Ltd. (CDM), produced 1.2 million carats in 1991, their best year since 1981. In all, Namibia during 1991 produced an estimated 30,000 tons of mined copper, 11,800 tons of mined lead, 33,133 tons of zinc concentrates, and 67 tons of refined cadmium. Salt production was 98,222 tons.

Selected Social Indicators

These statistics are estimates for the period 1988 to 1993. For comparison purposes, data for the United States and averages for low-income countries and high-income countries are also given.

Indicator	Namibia	Low-income countries	High-income countries	United States
Per capita gross national product†	$1,820	$380	$23,680	$24,740
Population growth rate	2.7%	1.9%	0.6%	1.0%
Population growth rate in urban areas	5.9%	3.9%	0.8%	1.3%
Population per square kilometer of land	2	78	25	26
Life expectancy in years	59	62	77	76
Number of people per physician	4,315	>3,300	453	419
Number of pupils per teacher (primary school)	32	39	<18	20
Illiteracy rate (15 years and older)	62%	41%	<5%	<3%
Energy consumed per capita (kg of oil equivalent)	n.a.	364	5,203	7,918

† The gross national product (GNP) is the total dollar value of all goods and services produced by a country in a year. The per capita GNP is calculated by dividing a country's GNP by its population. The World Bank defines low-income countries as those with a per capita GNP of $695 or less. High-income countries have a per capita GNP of $8,626 or more. Less than 14% of the world's 5.5 billion people live in high-income countries, while almost 60% live in low-income countries.

n.a. = data not available   > = greater than   < = less than

Sources: World Bank, *Social Indicators of Development 1995,* Baltimore: Johns Hopkins University Press, 1995. Central Intelligence Agency, *World Fact Book,* Washington, D.C.: Government Printing Office, 1994.

26 FOREIGN TRADE

In 1991, minerals made up 33% of Namibia's exports. The level of both exports and imports increased over the year ending 1992, leaving Namibia with a $110 million trade surplus.

Main trading partners are South Africa, Switzerland, Germany, Japan, and the United States.

27 ENERGY AND POWER

Electric power production totaled 1,290 million kilowatt hours in 1991. All coal and petroleum products come from South Africa.

28 SOCIAL DEVELOPMENT

By many economic and social indicators, including population per physician and per telephone, Namibia is statistically better off than many black African countries. However, such figures are distorted by Namibia's relatively large white population (6.8% in 1985) which has a substantially higher standard of living. Such comparisons also hide the huge differences between rural and urban Namibia.

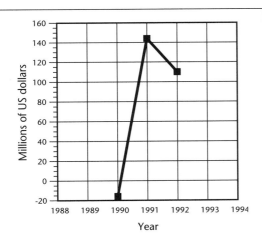

Yearly balance of trade measured in millions of US dollars. The balance of trade is the difference between what a country sells to other countries (its exports) and what it buys (its imports). If a country imports more than it exports, it has a negative balance of trade (a trade deficit). If exports exceed imports there is a positive balance of trade (a trade surplus).

29 HEALTH

In 1985 there were 64 hospitals and 130 clinics. In 1990, the population per physician was 4,315. Health services are provided through ethnically based government authorities, so the system is effectively segregated. In addition, most health care facilities are in the towns, which are largely white. In 1992, average life expectancy was 59 years, and 72% of the population had access to health care services.

30 HOUSING

There is a sharp contrast in housing standards between white and black Namibians. Most rural dwellings are self-constructed from local materials. In 1992 the backlog in housing units was estimated at 45,000 units.

31 EDUCATION

Education is compulsory for nine years between the ages of 7 and 16. In 1990, 313,528 Namibians were in primary and 62,976 pupils were in secondary schools. There is an Academy for Tertiary Education for adult students. In 1983, adult literacy was nearly 100% for whites and 28% for blacks. In 1991, there were 4,157 pupils and 331 teachers in all higher level institutions.

32 MEDIA

The five daily newspapers are published in Windhoek. The leading ones (with 1991 circulation) are: *The Times of Namibia* (16,200); *The Namibian* (15,000); *The Windhoek Advertiser* (10,000); and *Die Republikein* (12,000). The Namibian Broadcasting Corporation transmits radio programs in English, German, Afrikaans, and African languages. Television relays from South Africa began in 1981. In 1991 there were 188,000 radios and 31,000 television sets.

33 TOURISM AND RECREATION

Namibia's prime tourist attractions are game viewing, trophy hunting, and the scenic beauty of its deserts. In the west, Swakopmund is a resort town populated by Namibians of German descent. It is the center for tours of the nearby Namib dunes, and for visits to the wild Skeleton

Photo credit: Cynthia Bassett

A tribesman's hut, which is made from saplings covered with a mixture of mud and cattle dung.

Coast to the north. In the south, the Fish River Canyon, 85 kilometers (53 miles) long and 700 meters (2,300 feet) deep, ranks second in size to the Grand Canyon.

34 FAMOUS NAMIBIANS

Herman Toivo ja Toivo (b.1915?), the founder of SWAPO and the leader of Namibian nationalism, was imprisoned in South Africa from 1966 until 1984. Sam Nujoma (b.1929) has been leader of SWAPO since 1966.

35 BIBLIOGRAPHY

Cliffe, Lionel et al., *The Transition to Independence in Namibia.* Boulder: Lynne Rienner, 1994.

Laurè, J. *Namibia.* Chicago: Children's Press, 1993.

Sparks, Donald L. *Namibia: The Nation After Independence.* Boulder, Colo.: Westview Press, 1992.

NAURU

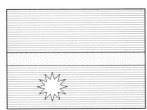

Republic of Nauru
Naoero

CAPITAL: There is no formal capital. The seat of government is in the district of Yaren.

FLAG: The flag has a blue background divided horizontally by a narrow gold band, symbolizing the equator. Below the band is a white 12-pointed star, representing the island's 12 traditional tribes.

ANTHEM: *Nauru Ubwema (Nauru, Our Homeland).*

MONETARY UNIT: The Australian dollar (A$) of 100 cents is the legal currency. A$1 = US$0.7008 (or US$1 = A$1.4269).

WEIGHTS AND MEASURES: Imperial weights and measures are used.

HOLIDAYS: New Year's Day, 1 January; Independence Day, 31 January; Angam Day, 26 October (a celebration of the day on which the population of Nauru reached the pre-World War II level); Christmas Day, 25 December; and Boxing Day, 26 December.

TIME: 11:30 PM = noon GMT.

1 LOCATION AND SIZE

Situated in the western Pacific, Nauru is the world's smallest independent nation, with an area of 21.0 square kilometers (8.1 square miles), about one-tenth the size of Washington, D.C. It lies between two island groups, the Solomons and the Gilberts and its nearest neighbor is Banaba (formerly Ocean Island, now part of Kiribati).

2 TOPOGRAPHY

Nauru, one of the largest phosphate-rock islands in the Pacific, is oval-shaped and fringed by a wide coral reef. It has no natural harbor or anchorage. A relatively fertile belt of land encircles the island. From this belt a coral cliff rises to a central plateau about 60 meters (200 feet) above sea level. Buada Lagoon covers some 120 hectares (300 acres) in the southeastern end of the plateau.

3 CLIMATE

The average annual rainfall is about 45 centimeters (18 inches), but the amount varies greatly from year to year, and long droughts have been a repeated problem. Temperatures remain steady, between 24° and 33°C (75–91°F) year round, and relative humidity is also constant at about 80%.

4 PLANTS AND ANIMALS

The plateau area contains large phosphate deposits that almost completely prevent any useful natural growth. Large areas of scrub and creeper, with occasional coconut and tamanu trees, grow in this region. On the coastal belt, coconut palms and pandanus thrive. Some hibiscus, frangipani, and other tropical flowers grow, but they do not flourish here as on other Pacific islands. Bird life is not plentiful, although noddies, terns, and frigate birds frequent the island. Fish life is abundant in the seas encircling Nauru, and good catches of tuna and bonito are made.

5 ENVIRONMENT

Nauru's phosphate mining industry has done significant damage to the land. Land in the coastal region however, has not been affected by the development of the country's mining industry. Vegetation in the coastal areas, such as pandanus and coconut palms, is plentiful.

6 POPULATION

The 1991 estimated population was 9,500. The annual population growth rate was estimated at about 3% in 1985–90. Most Nauruans live around the coastal fringes, in their traditional districts.

7 MIGRATION

Immigration to Nauru is strictly controlled by the government. Nauruans are free to travel abroad.

8 ETHNIC GROUPS

The Nauruan people (58% of the population in 1988) are the only native ethnic group on the island. They are of mixed Micronesian, Melanesian, and Polynesian origin, resembling the Polynesians most closely. Intermingling with Caucasian and Negroid lineage in the twentieth century, as well as frequent intermarriage with other Pacific islanders have changed the present-day features of Nauruans from those of their forebears.

There are Caucasians on the island (almost all Australians and New Zealanders), as well as Chinese, Filipinos, and immigrants from Kiribati and Tuvalu.

9 LANGUAGES

Nauruan, which is distinct from all other Pacific tongues, is the official language. However, English is still commonly used in the schools, in government, and in business transactions.

10 RELIGIONS

The Nauruans have accepted Christianity since the end of the nineteenth century. In 1993, the majority of the population was Protestant, with 37.5% Roman Catholics.

11 TRANSPORTATION

The public Nauru Pacific Line has a fleet of six ships. The government-owned Air Nauru flies regular air services to the Pacific islands, Taiwan, the Philippines, Hong Kong, Japan, Australia, and New Zealand. A 19-kilometer (12-mile) paved road encircles the island, accounting for 70% of the road system. Apart from a 3.9-kilometer (2.4-mile) railway (used to carry phosphates), a school bus service, and fewer than 2,000 registered motor vehicles, there is no local transport.

12 HISTORY

The first recorded discovery of Nauru by a Westerner was made by Captain John Fearn in 1798. From the 1830s to the 1880s, the Nauruans had a succession of visitors, including runaway convicts and deserters from whaling ships.

In accord with the British/German division of the Western Pacific, the German government took Nauru as a protectorate in 1888, although Christian missionaries who arrived in 1899 had a greater impact on the Nauruan culture than the German administration. Phosphate mining on Nauru began in 1907.

After the defeat of Germany in World War I (1914–18), the governments of Australia, New Zealand, and the United Kingdom agreed to administer Nauru jointly. The phosphate industry expanded greatly in the years between the two world wars (1919–38).

Nauru was flattened by Japanese bombings beginning in December 1941, and all its industrial plant and housing facilities were destroyed. The Japanese occupied the island from August 1942 until the end of the war three years later. Australian forces reoccupied Nauru in September 1945.

After World War II (1939–45), the island became a trust territory administered jointly by Australia, New Zealand, and the UK, who were to share the task of developing self-government on the island. On 31 January 1968, Nauru became the smallest independent republic in the world.

Since that time, Nauru has pursued a policy of isolation and nonalignment, although it does have a role in British Commonwealth affairs. In October 1982, Queen Elizabeth II visited the island, the

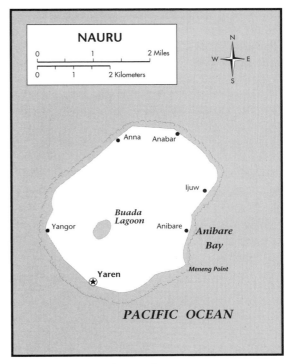

LOCATION: 0°32′s and 166°56′e. **TERRITORIAL SEA LIMIT:** 12 miles.

first British monarch to do so. Nauru filed a claim in 1989 for compensation from Australia at the International Court of Justice for the loss of nearly all its topsoil from phosphate mining during the League of Nations mandate and the United Nations trusteeship. Australia agreed to pay A$107 million (about US$73 million) in August 1993 to settle the case.

In June 1992, Nauru signed both the Climate Change and Biodiversity Conventions. In July it hosted the 24th South Pacific Forum heads of government meeting, which focused on environmental issues.

13 GOVERNMENT

Legislative power is held by the Parliament, composed of 18 members elected for a three-year term. Executive power is exercised by the president, who is also head of state.

14 POLITICAL PARTIES

The Democratic Party of Nauru, which aims to curb the power of the presidency, is the only political party in Nauru.

15 JUDICIAL SYSTEM

The constitution provides for a Supreme Court, with a chief justice presiding. Cases are also heard in the District Court or Family Court. The Supreme Court is the supreme authority on the interpretation of the constitution.

16 ARMED FORCES

Nauru has no armed forces. Although there is no formal agreement, Australia ensures its defense.

17 ECONOMY

The economy of Nauru has long been dependent on phosphates, which, according to recent estimates, will be exhausted by the early 2000s. By 1987, an estimated us$450 million had been set aside to support the country after the phosphates run out.

Aside from phosphates, Nauru has few domestic resources, and many food products and practically all consumer manufactures are imported.

18 INCOME

The gross national product (GNP) of Nauru was estimated to be $90 million in 1989. Phosphates have given Nauruans one of the highest per person incomes in the Third World.

19 INDUSTRY

The phosphate industry is the only industry on the island.

20 LABOR

In the mid-1980s, about 1,200 workers were employed in the state-owned phosphate industry. About 1,000 others were employed by the government and the Nauru Cooperative Society (NCP).

According to Nauruan law, the minimum age of employment is 17. However, this is honored only by the two largest employers—the government and the NPC. Some children under age 17 work in the few small family owned businesses.

21 AGRICULTURE

There is little commercial agriculture. The main crop is coconuts. In 1992, coconut production amounted to 2,000 tons.

22 DOMESTICATED ANIMALS

In 1992, there were an estimated 3,000 pigs.

23 FISHING

There is as yet no organized fishing industry on Nauru. Fish are plentiful and consumption is high, since almost all meat has to be imported from Australia. The total catch in 1991 was 190 tons.

24 FORESTRY

There are no forests on Nauru, and all building timber has to be imported.

25 MINING

Nauru's only natural resource is high-grade phosphate rock. As of 1990, over 61 million tons of phosphate had been mined with about 926,000 tons exported in 1990.

26 FOREIGN TRADE

Nauru's only export is phosphate rock, with about three-quarters of it going to Australia, New Zealand, and Japan. Imports consist mostly of machinery and construction materials for the phosphate industry and food, water, fuel, and other necessities. About half of the imports come from Australia, and almost all the rest from New Zealand, the United Kingdom, and Japan.

27 ENERGY AND POWER

Power requirements on the island are met by a diesel oil generator. In 1991, production was 29 million kilowatt hours.

28 SOCIAL DEVELOPMENT

Medical, dental, and hospital treatment and education are free. The government provides old age and disability pensions, and widows' and sickness benefits. Women face great social pressure to marry and raise families because Nauru's population was drastically reduced in World War II.

29 HEALTH

Tuberculosis, leprosy, diabetes, and vitamin deficiencies have been brought under control. Cardiovascular disease has become a major cause of illness and death. There are two modern hospitals, with a total of 207 beds and 10 doctors. Patients who need specialized care are flown to Australia.

30 HOUSING

Nearly all houses have electricity, and newer homes have a greater number of modern features.

31 EDUCATION

Attendance at school is compulsory for Nauruan children from 6 to 16 years old. In 1985 there were 1,451 students in seven government primary schools and 465 students in two secondary schools, with 142 teachers in all. There are scholarships available for higher education overseas, mainly in Australia and a university extension center connected to the University of the South Pacific.

32 MEDIA

The government publishes the weekly *Nauru Post* and fortnightly *Bulletin*, which report local news in Nauruan and English. There were about 2,000 telephones in 1989. Radio Nauru broadcasts in English and Nauruan; there were some 5,500 radios on the island in 1984.

33 TOURISM AND RECREATION

With its sandy beach, coral reef, tropical climate, and sea breezes, Nauru has the potential for the development of tourism.

34 FAMOUS NAURUANS

The best-known Nauruan is its first president, Hammer DeRoburt (1923–92), who led the Nauruan people to political independence.

35 BIBLIOGRAPHY

Baker, Mark. "The Dying Island." Melbourne: The Age Saturday Extra, February 28, 1987.

Petit-Skinner, Solange. *The Nauruans*. San Francisco: Macduff Press, 1981.

Trumbull, Robert. "World's Richest Little Isle." *New York Times Magazine,* March 7, 1982.

NEPAL

Kingdom of Nepal

Nepal Adhirajya

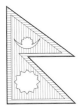

CAPITAL: Kāthmāndu.

FLAG: The national flag consists of two red adjoining triangles, outlined in blue and merging at the center; the points are at the fly. On the upper triangle, in white, is a symbolic representation of the moon; on the lower triangle, that of the sun.

ANTHEM: The national anthem begins "May His Majesty, solemn and supremely valiant, be prosperous forever."

MONETARY UNIT: The Nepalese rupee (NR) is a paper currency of 100 paisa. There are coins of 1, 2, 5, 10, 20, 25, and 50 paisa and 1, 2, 5, 10, 20, 25, 50, and 100 rupees, and notes of 1, 2, 5, 10, 20, 50, 100, 500, and 1,000 Nepalese rupees. NR1 = $0.0203 (or $1 = NR49.240).

WEIGHTS AND MEASURES: The metric system is in use, but some traditional Indian standards are also employed.

HOLIDAYS: National Unity Day, 11 January; Martyrs' Day, 30 January; Rashtriya Prajatantra Divas—National Democracy Day, 18 February; Nepalese Women's Day, 8 March; Navabarsha—Nepalese New Year's Day, mid-April; UN Day, 24 October; Queen Aishworya's Birthday, 7 November; Constitution Day, 9 November; National Day (King Birendra's Birthday), 28 December. Hindu and Buddhist religious holidays are based on the lunisolar calendar. Saturday is the general day of rest.

TIME: 5:45 PM = noon GMT.

1 LOCATION AND SIZE

A comparatively narrow strip of territory dividing India from China, landlocked Nepal has an area of about 140,800 square kilometers (54,363 square miles), slightly larger than the state of Arkansas, with a total boundary length of 2,926 kilometers (1,818 miles).

Nepal's capital city, Kāthmāndu, is located in the central part of the country.

2 TOPOGRAPHY

Nepal is made up of three strikingly contrasted areas. Southern Nepal, known as the Terai, is made up of both cultivable land and dense jungle. The second and by far the largest part of Nepal is formed by the Mahabharat, Churia, and Himalayan mountain ranges, extending from east to west. The third area is a high central region between the main Himalayan and Mahabharat ranges known as the Kāthmāndu Valley, or the Valley of Nepal, which supports a thriving agriculture.

Eight of the world's highest mountains are situated in the Himalaya range on the Tibetan border, including Mt. Everest, the world's highest peak at 29,028 feet (8,848 meters).

A Sherpa woman and her yak at a mountain lodge.

3 CLIMATE

Below the Kāthmāndu Valley, the climate is subtropical and, in the swamps and forests, extremely humid. Temperatures in Kāthmāndu in January range from an average minimum of 2°C (36°F) to an average maximum of 18°C (64°F). The July range is 20–29°C (68–84°F). Northward of the Kāthmāndu Valley, at altitudes above 4,300 meters (14,000 feet), the country is covered with snow during the long winter, and extreme cold is experienced in the upper Himalayas.

4 PLANTS AND ANIMALS

The wide range of climates accounts for marked contrasts between the native plants and animals in different regions of the country. Trees range from subtropical types in the south to conifers, hollies, and birches further north, and junipers in the extreme north. Ground orchids, lilies, yellow and blue poppies, and crimson anemones are prevalent in central Nepal. Wildflowers extend to very high altitudes, along with many kinds of alpine mosses and ferns.

Native animals include cats, squirrels, hare, deer, antelope, and black bear at middle altitudes and abundant wild sheep and goats higher in the mountains. Birds of Nepal include the green finch, dove, woodpecker, nuthatch, warbler, flycatcher, bulbul, and other species.

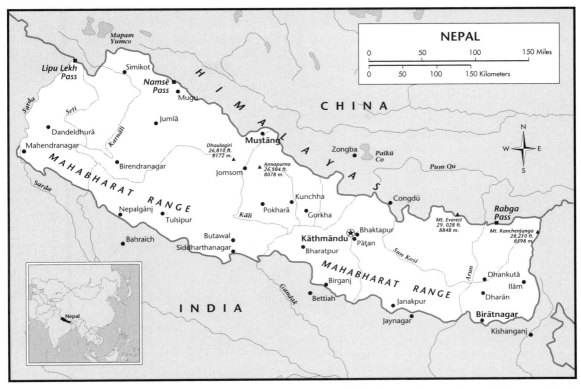

LOCATION: 26°20′ to 30°16′N; 80°15′ to 88°15′E. **BOUNDARY LENGTHS:** China, 1,236 kilometers (772 miles); India, 1,690 kilometers (1,046 miles).

5 ENVIRONMENT

By 1985, loss of forest land averaged 324 square miles per year, while reforestation was only 4,000 hectares (9,900 acres) per year. The United Nations Food and Agriculture Organization (FAO) estimates that at the present rate of depletion, the forests will be virtually wiped out by the year 2015.

Roughly one-third of the nation's city inhabitants and two-thirds of all rural dwellers do not have pure water. Untreated sewage is a major pollution factor: the nation's cities produce 0.4 million tons of solid waste per year.

In 1994, 22 of Nepal's mammal species and 20 of its bird species were endangered, as well as 33 plant species.

6 POPULATION

According to the 1991 census, Nepal had a population of 18,462,081, an increase of 22.9% from the 1981 census. The population for the year 2000 was projected at 24,858,000. The average estimated density in 1991 was 144 persons per square kilometer (373 per square mile). Kāthmāndu, the capital, had a 1991 population of 419,073.

7 MIGRATION

Hundreds of thousands of Nepalese were believed to be working in India in the 1980s, and over 100,000 Indians were working in Nepal. Some 86,000 ethnic Nepalese expelled from Bhutan were living in refugee camps at the end of 1993.

8 ETHNIC GROUPS

Nepal consists of two primary ethnic elements: Mongoloids, who migrated to Nepal by way of Tibet, Sikkim, Assam, and northern Bengal; and Indo-Aryans, who came from the Indian plains and from the sub-Himalayan hill areas to the west of Nepal. There are also small remnants of Dravidian tribes. Sherpas, a Himalayan people, have become well known as guides for mountain-climbing expeditions.

Photo credit: Susan D. Rock.

A holy man at Pātan's Durbar Square.

9 LANGUAGES

Nepali is the official language, although some 16 different languages, of the Indo-Aryan and Tibeto-Burman groups, and 36 main dialects are spoken. Nepali is the mother tongue of about 58% of the population and is the language for most inter-tribal communication. More than 11% of the people speak Maithili as their first language, 7.6% Bhojpuri, 4% Tharu, and about 3% each Newari and Tamang.

10 RELIGIONS

Although the royal family is Hindu—as is about 90% of the population—Hinduism and Buddhism exist side by side in Nepal and to some degree are intermingled. The importance of both in the national life is evident everywhere: more than 2,700 temples and shrines have been counted in the Kāthmāndu Valley alone. Bodhnath and Shambunath are famous Buddhist temples. Muslims constitute about 3% of the population. There are also small minorities of Christians, Baha'is, and Jains, amounting to less than 0.1% of the population.

11 TRANSPORTATION

Nepal's road mileage, in relation to its area and population, is among the lowest in the world. The principal means of land transport is by porters with pack animals.

In all, Nepal had 7,080 kilometers (4,400 miles) of roadway in 1991, of which 37% was paved. Nepal had a total of 62 kilometers (38 miles) of railways in 1990.

Much of Nepal is easily reached only by air. The leading air terminal is Tribhuwan airport at Kāthmāndu, which can handle medium-sized jets. Domestic flights are operated by the Royal Nepal Airlines Corp., which also schedules flights to Great Britain, Germany, India, and eight other Asian countries.

12 HISTORY

Reliable historical data date back to the conquest of Nepal by Harisinha-deva, rajah of Simraun in about AD 1324. Prithwi Narayan Shah, the ruler of Gorkha, a small state west of Kāthmāndu, established the modern kingdom of Nepal in AD 1768. Under his descendants, most of the present boundaries of Nepal were established and Hinduism was introduced from India as the official religion.

Nepal came in contact with the West in the late eighteenth century because of the British East India Company's conquest of India to its south. Britain and Nepal became engaged in a border dispute that threatened Nepal's independence. However, in 1816, Nepal and Britain signed an agreement that preserved Nepal's independence. In return Nepal gave Britain a large piece of territory and permission to establish a permanent British presence at Kāthmāndu. The 1816 agreement laid the groundwork for more than a century and a half of friendly relations between Britain and Nepal.

Rule by the Rana Family

In 1846 Shumshere Jung Bahadur (Rana) banished the king and became Nepal's ruler. He decreed that the office of the prime ministership could only be held by members of the Rana family. Under this system, the Rana family would go on to rule Nepal for the next 100 years. The Rana family kept Nepal's monarchs as virtual prisoners.

However, the end of World War II (1939–45) brought the end to British rule on the South Asian subcontinent and caused deep stirrings of change in Nepal. Resentment grew against the autocratic despotism of the Ranas. A political reform movement began in 1947 with the founding of the Nepali Congress Party.

With Indian support, rebels began operations against the Rana government. Ultimatley, with the guidance of Indian Prime Minister Nehru, a political compromise was reached that ended a century of hereditary Rana family rule and restored the monarchy. By late 1951 a new government took office, headed by Matrika Prasad Koirala, a founder of the Nepali Congress Party (NC).

Nepal after Rana Rule

The period after the fall of the Ranas was marked by a struggle between the government and the king for control of the country. In April 1959, King Mahendra Bir Bikram Shah proclaimed a democratic constitution providing for a constitutional monarchy, but suspended it and dissolved parliament less than 18 months later. In April 1962 he established an indirect, nonparty system of rule through a system of panchayats (councils) leading up to a National Panchayat. However, five years later, the king, under Indian pressure, began gradually liberalizing his government.

In January 1972, Mahendra died suddenly and was succeeded by his 27-year-old son, Birendra Bir Bikram Shah Dev. The young monarch, who had attended Harvard University in the United States, was committed to social reform. With the king promising further liberalization, the existing panchayat system was supported by 55% of the voters in May 1980. However, the king's failure to lift the ban on political parties angered his opposition.

Throughout the 1980s, opposition to the panchayat system, and to the ban on political parties, grew. After concessions by the king, a new constitution was adopted in November 1990. This constitution ended the panchayat era and restored multiparty democracy in a constitutional monarchy. In May 1991, the first open elections in 32 years were held. In the elections, the NC (Nepali Congress Party) won a majority in the new House of Representatives.

Nepal's foreign policies have remained generally neutral since World War II. It has maintained friendly relations with China and India, despite the occasional clash of policies on matters of trade. Nepal also has pursued friendly relations with the great powers and has received economic aid from India, the United States, the former USSR, and the World Bank.

13 GOVERNMENT

The 1990 constitution established a constitutional monarchy in which the legislature consists of the king and two houses of parliament, the lower house called the House of Representatives and the upper house, the National Council. The House of Representatives has 205 members and the National Council 60.

The country is divided into 14 zones and 75 districts.

14 POLITICAL PARTIES

The main party through Nepal's modern history has been the Nepali Congress Party (NC), which opposed and finally brought down King Mahendra's panchayat system of indirect government.

The Communist Party of Nepal (CPN), reorganized as the United Marxist-Leninists (UML) is the leading opposition party in the parliament.

The Rastriya Prajatantra Party (RPP) supports the monarchy.

Most of the remaining seats in the lower house are in the hands of minor left/communist parties, including the United People's Front–Nepal (UPF/N), the Nepal Sadbhavana Party (NSP), and the National Democratic Party (DDP).

15 JUDICIAL SYSTEM

Each district has civil and criminal courts, as well as a court of appeals and 14 zone courts. There are five regional courts to which further appeals may be taken. At the top is the Supreme Court in Kāthmāndu, which is empowered to issue writs of habeas corpus and decide on the constitutionality of laws. The Supreme Court is the court of last resort, but the King may grant pardons and suspend, commute or remit sentences of any court. There are separate military courts which deal only with military personnel.

16 ARMED FORCES

Nepal maintains a small standing army of 35,000 regulars organized in 8 brigades. It maintains 11 air transports and helicopters. The army is made up mostly of hill people known as gurkhas, who are among the world's most renowned fighting men with extensive service in all parts of the globe in both world wars and several United Nations actions of this century. In 1992, Nepal spent an estimated $34 million on defense.

17 ECONOMY

Nepal's per person national income was only $180 in 1991, and general living standards are low. The economy is based on agriculture, which engages about 90% of the labor force but is inefficiently organized and limited by a shortage of usable land in relation to population.

The industrial sector is still small and dominated by traditional handicrafts, spinning and weaving, and similar occupations. In 1989/90, Nepal weathered a major trade and transit dispute with India that suddenly placed potentially damaging tariffs on trade with its largest import supplier and external market.

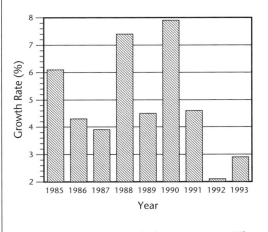

Yearly growth rate of the economy. This economic indicator tells by what percent the economy has increased or decreased when compared with the previous year.

18 INCOME

In 1992, Nepal's gross national product (GNP) was $3,285 million. The national income has averaged $190 per person since 1988. For the period 1985–92 the average inflation rate was 10.0%, resulting in a real growth rate in GNP of 2.1% per person.

19 INDUSTRY

The carpet, garment, and spinning industries are the three largest industrial employers, followed by structural clay products, sugar and jute processing. Sugar production was 41,400 tons in 1990/91; jute goods, 15,000 tons; and soap, 21.4 thousand tons. In 1988/89, 11,848 thousand meters of synthetic textiles and 7,057

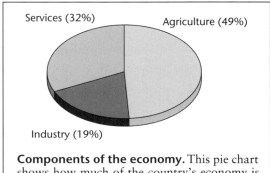

Services (32%)   Agriculture (49%)

Industry (19%)

Components of the economy. This pie chart shows how much of the country's economy is devoted to agriculture (includes forestry, hunting, and fishing), industry, or services.

hours of 6:00 a.m. and 6:00 p.m. Despite the law, many child workers are found in all areas of the economy. It is believed that as many as 57% of the children in Nepal may be employed, most in agriculture, with a growing number in the carpet making industry. In 1993, 23 Nepalese factories were fined for using child workers. Even so, enforcement of labor laws is inadequate.

21 AGRICULTURE

Rice, Nepal's most important cereal, is grown on more than half the cultivated land. In 1992, rice production totaled 2,509,000 tons. Production of maize, grown on the carefully terraced hillsides, was 1,164,000 tons in 1992. The output of wheat in 1992 was 779,000 tons; millet, 230,000 tons; and barley, 28,000 tons.

Cash crops (with 1992 output) included sugarcane, 1,291,000 tons; potatoes, 733,000 tons; linseed, 31,000 tons; jute, 10,000 tons; and tobacco, 6,000 tons. Sugarcane, jute, and tobacco are the major raw materials for Nepal's own industries. In 1990 and 1992, food exports totaled $19 million, representing 10.6% and 6.1% of total exports, respectively.

22 DOMESTICATED ANIMALS

Livestock, adapted to many uses, forms an essential part of the economy, accounting for about 30% of gross agricultural output. In 1992, Nepal had an estimated 6,246,000 head of cattle, 3,058,000 water buffalo, 912,000 sheep, 5,406,000 goats, and 599,000 hogs. There were about 7 million chickens in 1992, when 9,000 tons

thousand meters of cotton textiles were produced.

Production by heavy industries in 1990/91 included cement, 182,000 tons; iron goods, 42,500 tons; and stainless steel utensils, 237 tons. Output of bricks and tiles was 33,440 thousand pieces.

20 LABOR

As of 1992, over 90% of the 19.4 million population were farmers, while handicrafts, porterage, trade, military service, industry, and government work engaged the remainder. The 1990 Constitution grants the freedom to form and join unions and associations, and permits strikes except against public utilities.

The minimum age for employment in industry is 16. The minimum age for employment in agriculture is 14. Young people aged 14 to 18 are not allowed to work more than 6 hours per day or 36 hours per week. They are further prohibited from working except between the of poultry meat were produced. Traditionally, butter and cheese are among the leading exports of Nepal. Livestock products in 1992 included an estimated 612,000 tons of buffalo milk, 259,000 tons of cow's milk, 15,600 tons of butter and ghee (clarified butter), and 620 tons of wool.

23 FISHING

The commercial fish catch amounted to 15,595 tons in 1991 (up from 9,443 tons in 1986). Common fish species are carp, gar, and murrel.

24 FORESTRY

In the early 1990s, forests covered about 18% of Nepal's total area. That amount has been declining at a rapid rate because of overcutting and clearing for farmland. About 97% of the roundwood removals in the 1990s were for fuel. Approximately 4,000 cubic meters of roundwood were exported in 1991.

25 MINING

The country's mineral resources have not been used to advantage. There are known deposits of iron, copper, zinc, lignite, graphite, cobalt, mica, limestone, marble, talc, quartz, ceramic clays, and slate. Copper mining activity has increased in recent years. Copper production in 1991 amounted to 22 tons. Salt production rose sharply from 6 tons in 1988 to 7,300 tons in 1991.

26 FOREIGN TRADE

After a breakdown in treaty renewal negotiations between Nepal and India, Nepal's

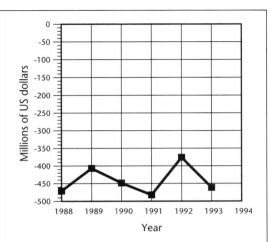

Yearly balance of trade measured in millions of US dollars. The balance of trade is the difference between what a country sells to other countries (its exports) and what it buys (its imports). If a country imports more than it exports, it has a negative balance of trade (a trade deficit). If exports exceed imports, there is a positive balance of trade (a trade surplus).

total exports dropped from $106.6 million in 1986/87 to $98 million in 1989/90. The signing of a new temporary agreement in 1990 prevented a prolonged crisis, helping to fuel a healthy recovery in export growth.

Carpets and garments presently account for 70% of all merchandise exports, far surpassing timber, rice, and jute. Major imports are heavy machinery, transport equipment, textiles, chemicals, fertilizers, metal manufactures, and petroleum products.

As the export of manufactured goods has expanded since the mid-1980s, Nepal has diversified its trading partners somewhat. The United States absorbs over 90%

Selected Social Indicators

These statistics are estimates for the period 1988 to 1993. For comparison purposes, data for the United States and averages for low-income countries and high-income countries are also given.

Indicator	Nepal	Low-income countries	High-income countries	United States
Per capita gross national product†	$190	$380	$23,680	$24,740
Population growth rate	2.6%	1.9%	0.6%	1.0%
Population growth rate in urban areas	7.2%	3.9%	0.8%	1.3%
Population per square kilometer of land	144	78	25	26
Life expectancy in years	54	62	77	76
Number of people per physician	16,106	>3,300	453	419
Number of pupils per teacher (primary school)	37	39	<18	20
Illiteracy rate (15 years and older)	74%	41%	<5%	<3%
Energy consumed per capita (kg of oil equivalent)	22	364	5,203	7,918

† The gross national product (GNP) is the total dollar value of all goods and services produced by a country in a year. The per capita GNP is calculated by dividing a country's GNP by its population. The World Bank defines low-income countries as those with a per capita GNP of $695 or less. High-income countries have a per capita GNP of $8,626 or more. Less than 14% of the world's 5.5 billion people live in high-income countries, while almost 60% live in low-income countries.

> = greater than   < = less than

Sources: World Bank, *Social Indicators of Development 1995,* Baltimore: Johns Hopkins University Press, 1995. Central Intelligence Agency, *World Fact Book,* Washington, D.C.: Government Printing Office, 1994.

of garment exports, while Germany and Belgium have become the main buyers of Nepali carpets. Still, India remains Nepal's largest export market and supplier of imported goods.

27 ENERGY AND POWER

Although Nepal's hydroelectric potential is great and development has been rapid in recent years, the kingdom still lacks an adequate power supply. In 1991, production was 981 million kilowatt hours, 91% of which was hydropower. The remainder was either imported from India or produced by diesel generators. Exploration for oil and natural gas deposits began in the mid-1980s.

28 SOCIAL DEVELOPMENT

The government maintains a countrywide village development service, which endeavors to meet the villagers' needs for food, clothing, shelter, health services, and education. The Employee Provident Fund administers a program of old age, disability, and death benefits for government and corporate employees.

The new Constitution has increased opportunities for women, including equal pay for equal work, but few women hold formal jobs.

29 HEALTH

Although protected by mountain barriers, Nepal is in frequent danger from epidemics, notably cholera. Common illnesses are black fever (kala-azar), amoebic dysentery, eye diseases, typhoid, and venereal diseases. Malnutrition, contaminated water, and inadequate sanitation cause widespread health problems. Improved health programs in rural areas have helped control malaria, leprosy, and tuberculosis. Nepal has an estimated 22,000 drug addicts. Average life expectancy in 1992 was 54 years for both women and men.

In 1990, there were 3 hospital beds per 100,000 inhabitants. The population per physician was 16,106. Health care expenditures were $141 million.

30 HOUSING

In the Kāthmāndu Valley, village houses are made of stone or mud bricks, with thatched roofs and raised eaves. Elsewhere, houses are often made of bamboo and reeds. Most houses have two stories, but some contain only two rooms, a sleeping room and a room for cooking. The well-constructed houses of the Sherpas are generally built of stone and timber, roofed with wooden slats. The latest available figures for 1980–88 show a total housing stock of 3,056,000 units with 5.6 people per dwelling.

31 EDUCATION

The number of literate persons, although small, is rising and was estimated in 1990

Photo credit: Susan D. Rock.

A Sherpa woman and her son.

at 26% of adults (males: 37.6% and females: 13.2%). In 1988, there were 13,514 primary schools with 2,108,739 pupils and 57,204 teachers. Secondary students numbered 612,943, with 21,132 teachers. In 1991, 110,239 students were enrolled in all higher level institutions with 4,925 teachers.

32 MEDIA

In 1991 there were some 67,000 telephones in use. Radio Nepal broadcasts in Nepali and English on both short and medium wavelengths. Television was introduced into the Kāthmāndu Valley in 1986, and the Nepalese Television Corporation broadcasts about 23 hours a week. In 1991, there were 670,000 radios and 40,000 television sets.

Dailies, weeklies, and monthlies in Nepali, Newari, Hindi, and English are published mainly in Kāthmāndu. In 1991, the country had 28 dailies, with a total circulation of about 122,000. The largest daily newspapers (with 1991 circulations) are the Nepali *Gorkha Patra* (40,000) and the English-language *Rising Nepal* (25,000).

33 TOURISM AND RECREATION

There were 292,995 foreign tourists in 1991; 118,065 came from Europe and 100,077 from Southern Asia. There were 5,206 hotel rooms. Earnings from tourism totaled $126 million.

For mountain trekkers, travel agencies in Kāthmāndu provide transportation to mountain sites, as well as Sherpa guides and porters.

34 FAMOUS NEPALESE

Siddhartha Gautama, who became known as the Buddha ("Enlightened One"), was born, according to most modern scholars, about 563 BC in the Terai, part of present-day Nepal.

Amar Singh Thapa, Nepalese military leader of the 19th century and rival of General David Ochterlony in the war between British India and Nepal, is a national hero. The most highly regarded writers are Bhanubhakta, a great poet of the 19th century, and the dramatist Bala Krishna Sama (Shamsher, b.1903).

King Mahendra Bir Bikram-Shah (1920–72) introduced the partyless political system, based on the Nepalese tradition of the village panchayat (council). Well-known political leaders include the brothers Matrika Prasad Koirala (b.1912), head of the Nepali Congress Party and the first post-Rana prime minister of Nepal (1951–52 and 1953–55), and Bisweswar Prasad Koirala (1915–82), head of the Nepali Congress Party and the first elected prime minister of Nepal (1959–60).

World renown was gained for Nepal by a Sherpa porter and mountaineer, Tenzing Norgay (Namgyal Wangdi, 1914–86), who, with Sir Edmund Hillary, a New Zealander, ascended to the summit of Mt. Everest in 1953.

35 BIBLIOGRAPHY

Carrier, Jim. "Gatekeepers of the Himalaya." *National Geographic,* December 1992, 70–89.

Chadwick, Douglas H. "At the Crossroads of Kathmandu." *National Geographic,* July 1987, 32–65.

Fraser, Mary Ann. *On Top of the World: The Conquest of Mount Everest.* New York: H. Holt, 1991.

Landon, Perceval. *Nepal.* New Delhi: Asian Educational Services, 1993.

Nagel, Rob, and Anne Commire. "Siddhartha." In *World Leaders, People Who Shaped the World.* Volume I: Africa and Asia. Detroit: U*X*L, 1994.

Rowell, Galen. "Himalaya Sanctuary." *National Geographic,* September 1989, 391–405.

THE NETHERLANDS

Kingdom of the Netherlands
Koninkrijk der Nederlanden

CAPITAL: Constitutional capital: Amsterdam. Seat of government: The Hague ('s Gravenhage; Den Haag).

FLAG: The national flag, standardized in 1937, is a tricolor of red, white, and blue horizontal stripes.

ANTHEM: *Wilhelmus van Nassouwen (William of Nassau).*

MONETARY UNIT: The guilder (gulden; abbreviated f, designating the ancient florin) of 100 cents is a paper currency with one official exchange rate. There are coins of 5, 10, and 25 cents and 1, 2 ½, 5, 10, and 50 guilders, and notes of 5, 10, 25, 50, 100, 250, and 1,000 guilders. f1=$0.5322 (or $1=f1.8790).

WEIGHTS AND MEASURES: The metric system is the legal standard.

HOLIDAYS: New Year's Day, 1 January; Queen's Day, 30 April; National Liberation Day, 5 May; Christmas, 25–26 December. Movable religious holidays include Good Friday, Holy Saturday, Easter Monday, Ascension, and Whitmonday.

TIME: 1 PM = noon GMT.

1 LOCATION AND SIZE

Situated in northwestern Europe, the Netherlands has a total area of 37,330 square kilometers (14,413 square miles), of which inland water accounts for more than 2,060 square kilometers (795 square miles). The land area is 33,920 square kilometers (13,097 square miles). Comparatively, the area occupied by the Netherlands is slightly less than twice the size of the state of New Jersey. The Netherlands has a total boundary length of 1,478 kilometers (918 miles).

The capital city of the Netherlands, Amsterdam, is in the western part of the country.

2 TOPOGRAPHY

The country falls into three natural topographical divisions: a long range of sand dunes on the western coast; the lowlands or "polders" (low-lying land reclaimed from the sea and from lakes and protected by dikes); and the higher eastern section of the country. Many dikes have been constructed along the lower Rhine and Meuse (Maas) rivers, as well as on a portion of the North Sea coast and along nearly the whole of the coast of IJsselmeer (the former Zuider Zee).

3 CLIMATE

The Netherlands has a maritime climate, with cool summers and mild winters. The average temperature is 2°C (36°F) in January and 19°C (66°F) in July, with an annual average of about 10°C (50°F). Average annual rainfall is about 765 centimeters (30 inches).

4 PLANTS AND ANIMALS

Plants and animals that thrive in temperate climates are found in the Netherlands. The most common trees are oak, elm, pine, linden, and beech. The country is famous for its flowers, both cultivated varieties (best known among them the Dutch tulip) and wildflowers such as daisies and buttercups. Birds are those characteristic of Western and Central Europe. Many kinds of fish are found along the North Sea coast and inland. Wild or large animals are practically nonexistent.

5 ENVIRONMENT

Air and water pollution are significant environmental problems in the Netherlands. Industry and agriculture have severely polluted the country's rivers. The Netherlands uses 34% of its water for farming and 61% for industrial purposes. Solid waste in the nation's cities amounts to 7.6 million tons yearly.

Since the mid-1970s, emissions of most major air pollutants from industrial use of fossil fuels have been substantially reduced. Efforts at controlling air pollution reduced sulphur dioxide emissions between 1980 and 1990 from 490,000 tons to 240,000 tons.

In 1994, 2 mammal species and 14 bird species were endangered and 7 plant species were threatened with extinction.

6 POPULATION

The Netherlands had an estimated population of 15,010,445 as of 1 January 1991, with a density of 406 persons per square kilometer (1,051 per square mile) of land, greater than that of any other West European country except Malta.

A population of 16,073,000 was projected for the year 2000. Major cities (with 1991 populations) include Amsterdam, 702,444; Rotterdam, 582,266; and The Hague, 444,242.

7 MIGRATION

Although the government has encouraged emigration to curb overpopulation, more people have migrated to the Netherlands than have left the country in recent years. Since the 1970s, the traditional pattern of migration from the countryside to the cities has been altered, and the trend has been largely from the larger cities to small towns and villages.

In 1990, 57,344 persons left the Netherlands, of which 36,749 were Dutch citizens. Of these, 56% went to other European countries, 8% to the United States, and 11% to the Netherlands Antilles or Suriname. In the same year, 81,264 immigrants arrived in the Netherlands, representing an increase of 24% over 1989. Of the total, 17% came from Suriname and the Netherlands Antilles, while about 13% were Turks.

Of the 692,000 aliens residing in the Netherlands in 1991 (4.6% of the population), 204,000 were Turkish nationals, 157,000 were Moroccan, 44,000 were

THE NETHERLANDS

NETHERLANDS

0   25   50 Miles

0   25   50 Kilometers

N
W   E
S

East Frisian Islands

West Frisian Islands
Terschelling
Ameland
Schiermonnikoog
Emden
Vlieland
Waddenzee
Texel
Leeuwarden
Princess Margriet Canal
Groningen
Veendam
Den Helder
Dam with locks
Heerenveen
Assen
Emmen
IJsselmeer
Hoogereen
Meppen
Northeast Polder
Alkmaar
Emlichheim
Noordzee-kanaal
Zaanstad
Lelystad
Zwolle
Haarlem
Flevoland Polder
Roalte
Rheine
Amsterdam
IJssel
Leiden
Apeldoorn
Enschede
Amersfoort
The Hague
Utrecht
Hengelo
Delft
Nederrijn
Arnhem
Winterswijk
Rotterdam
Lek
Borken
Dordrecht
Waal
Nijmegen
Maas
's-Hertogenbosch
GERMANY
Oosterschelde
Breda
Wilhelminakanaal
Zuid-Willemskanaal
Rhein
Middelburg
Tilburg
Westerschelde
Eindhoven
Maas
Düsseldorf
Antwerp
Mönchengladbach
Gent
BELGIUM
Heerlen
Aachen
Schelde
Brussels
Maastricht
Liege
FRANCE

North Sea

Amsterdam-Rijnkanaal

Netherlands

LOCATION: 50°45′ to 53°52′N; 3°21′ to 7°13′E. **BOUNDARY LENGTHS:** Germany, 577 kilometers (358 miles); Belgium, 450 kilometers (280 miles); North Sea coastline, 451 kilometers (280 miles). **TERRITORIAL SEA LIMIT:** 12 miles.

Photo credit: Susan D. Rock

A Dutch woman dressed in traditional clothing.

Germans, and 39,000 were British. At the end of 1992 there were 26,900 refugees.

8 ETHNIC GROUPS

The Dutch are an ethnically unified people descended from Frankish, Saxon, and Frisian tribes. Ethnic makeup changed slightly as a result of the arrival of some 300,000 immigrants and returning Dutch from Indonesia, and more than 140,000 from Suriname.

The influx of Turks and other workers from the Mediterranean area has further added to the ethnic mix.

9 LANGUAGES

Dutch, or Holland, is the official language in all of the 12 provinces. It is also the universal tongue, except in the north near the Frisian Islands, where most of the inhabitants speak the ancient Frisian language. Frisian, the native language of about 300,000 persons, is closely related to the Anglo-Saxon tongue but has many points in common with Dutch, which belongs to the Germanic language group. Many Netherlanders speak and understand English, French, and German, which are taught in secondary schools. Six Dutch dialects—notably Gelders and Groningen—are spoken in addition to Frisian.

10 RELIGIONS

Complete religious liberty is provided for by the constitution, and a tradition of tolerance is well established. As of 1993, an estimated 37% were Roman Catholics, and 30% belonged to six major Protestant groups. Minority religious groups in 1986 included an estimated 338,000 Muslims and 72,000 Hindus or Buddhists. There were 25,700 Jews in 1990.

Most Protestants belong to Calvinist churches. The largest of these is the Dutch Reformed Church (Hervormde Kerk), with about 17% of the population aged 18 or more. Others are the Gereformeerde Kerk and the Christelijke Gereformeerde Kerk. Lutherans and Baptists (Doopsgezinden) each comprise less than 1% of the population.

The largest growth has been among those professing no denomination, whose strength increased from 2.2% of the population in 1900 to nearly 35% in 1984.

11 TRANSPORTATION

Merchant shipping has always been of great economic importance to the seagoing Dutch. The Dutch merchant marine had 362 ships totaling 3,051,000 gross registered tons in 1991. In 1992, 383 million tons of freight were handled at Dutch ports. The inland water transport fleet handled 250 million tons of freight in 1992. Rotterdam is the Netherlands' chief port and the world's largest. In 1990, it handled nearly 30% of all the goods in the European Community transported by sea.

In 1991 there were 6,340 kilometers (3,940 miles) of navigable waterways and 3,037 kilometers (1,887 miles) of railroads. In 1992, rail transported 315 million passengers and 17 million tons of freight. In 1991 there were 108,360 kilometers (67,335 miles) of highways. Motor vehicles in use in 1992 included 5,658,267 cars and 644,929 commercial vehicles. The state finances the construction of urban and rural cycle paths.

Royal Dutch Airlines (Koninklijke Luchtvaart Maatschappij—KLM), which began regularly scheduled operations in 1920, serves some 115 cities in 70 countries. The major international airport is Schiphol, near Amsterdam, which handled 19.9 million passengers and 660,000 tons of freight in 1992.

12 HISTORY

In about 55 BC, Julius Caesar conquered a large part of the lowlands near the mouths

Photo credit: Susan D. Rock

A bridge opening over an inland waterway near Rotterdam.

of the Rhine and Meuse (Maas) rivers. The region was populated by Celtic and Germanic tribes, including Frisians. About 300 years later, powerful Germanic tribes invaded, and by the time of Charlemagne (742–814), the native Saxons and Frisians had been completely conquered by the West Franks.

Soon after the death of Charlemagne and the breakup of his empire, local leaders created several independent political divisions in the Low Countries (the Netherlands together with present-day Belgium and Luxembourg). As the Middle Ages drew to a close, individual cities such as Amsterdam, Haarlem, and Groningen became important, together with the Duchy of Gelderland.

In the fifteenth century, the dukes of Burgundy acquired most of the Low Countries. When Mary of Burgundy married Archduke (later Emperor) Maximilian I in 1477, the Austrian house of Habsburg gained control of the lands.

The Habsburgs

In 1547, Holy Roman Emperor Charles V decreed the formal union of the Netherlands and Austria, and in 1549, the union of the Netherlands and Spain. To bring the Low Countries under greater control, his son, Philip II, tried to stamp out the rising force of Protestantism and suppressed the political, economic, and religious liberties long cherished by the population. As a result, both Roman Catholics and Protestants rebelled against him under the leadership of William the Silent, Prince of Orange.

For 10 years, the 17 provinces making up the Low Countries united in a common revolt. Much of the area was freed in 1577, with William as the acknowledged ruler. In 1578, the southern region (now Belgium) began to turn against William. In 1579, the northern provinces formed the Union of Utrecht, which carried on the fight against Spain. Final recognition of Dutch independence by the Spanish government was not obtained until the Treaty of Westphalia (1648). Meanwhile, the southern provinces remained loyal to Spain and to the Roman Catholic Church, and were thereafter known as the Spanish Netherlands.

In the seventeenth century, the United Provinces of the north became the leading commercial and maritime power in the world. Its prosperity was nourished by Dutch settlements and colonies in the East Indies, India, South Africa, the West Indies, South America, and elsewhere. The Dutch were noted for their religious freedom. They welcomed religious refugees—Spanish and Portuguese Jews, French Huguenots, and English Pilgrims. Arts, sciences, literature, and philosophy flourished alongside trade and banking.

William III (r.1672–1702), grandson of the English King Charles I, and his English wife, Mary, were invited by the English Parliament to occupy the British throne in 1688, but they continued to take a close interest in Dutch affairs. The Dutch republic of which William had been governor survived for nearly a century after his death. Its position was continually threatened, however, by intense rivalries among and within the provinces. Four naval wars with Britain from the middle of the seventeenth century to the end of the eighteenth century also sapped Dutch strength. In 1795, a much weakened republic was overrun by revolutionary French armies.

After the Napoleonic period, the great powers of Europe at the Congress of Vienna (1814–15) set up a new kingdom of the Netherlands, composed of the former United Provinces and the former Spanish or Austrian Netherlands, and installed a prince of the house of Orange as King William I. In 1830, a revolt by the southern provinces resulted in the establishment of the kingdom of Belgium.

Photo credit: Susan D. Rock

A busy city street in Amsterdam.

After a decade of war and tension following Belgian independence, relations with Belgium gradually improved, and Dutch claims to the principality of Luxembourg ended with the death of William III in 1890.

The World Wars to 1994

The Netherlands successfully remained neutral during World War I (1914–18), and preserved its neutrality until the Germans overran the country during World War II (1939–45). Queen Wilhelmina (r.1890–1948) refused to surrender to the Germans, and instead fled to Britain with other officials of her government. Although Dutch resistance lasted only five

days, destruction was widespread. Nearly the whole of downtown Rotterdam was wiped out, and other cities suffered great damage. The Dutch withstood severe repressions until their liberation by Allied forces in May 1945. Wilhelmina gave up the throne in 1948 and was followed by her daughter, Juliana (r.1948–80).

The East Indies, most of which had been under Dutch rule for over 300 years, were occupied by Japanese forces in 1942. In 1945, a group of Indonesians proclaimed an independent republic and resisted Dutch reoccupation. After four years of hostilities and following United Nations intervention, the Netherlands recognized the independence of Indonesia in December 1949.

Suriname (formerly Dutch Guiana), controlled by the Netherlands since 1815, became an independent nation on 25 November 1975. The Netherlands Antilles and Aruba continue to be dependent areas.

Reform of the social security system has been the major political issue in the 1990s, along with efforts to reduce public spending. A number of radical social measures received parliamentary approval in recent years including conditions for administering euthanasia (causing death painlessly in terminal illnesses), legalization of prostitution, and laws banning discrimination.

Abdication of Queen Juliana

Queen Juliana gave up the throne in 1980 in favor of her daughter, Beatrix. In 1966, Beatrix married Claus von Amsberg, a German diplomat, whose title remained Prince of the Netherlands when Beatrix became Queen. Their first-born son, Prince Willem-Alexander, is heir to the throne.

13 GOVERNMENT

The Netherlands is a constitutional monarchy, under the house of Orange-Nassau. Executive power is exercised by the crown and the cabinet, which must have the support of a majority in the parliament. The monarch acts as an adviser to the cabinet, may propose bills, and signs all bills approved by the legislature.

The Council of State, begun in 1532, is appointed by and presided over by the crown. It considers all legislation proposed by the crown or the cabinet before it is submitted to the parliament.

Legislative power is exercised jointly by the crown and the States-General (*Staten-Generaal*), a two-chamber parliament. The upper house (*Eerste Kamer*) consists of 75 members elected for four years by the provincial representative councils. The lower house (*Tweede Kamer*) has 150 members elected for four years directly by the people. All Dutch citizens who have reached the age of 18 years and live in the Netherlands can vote.

As of 1994, the country was divided into 12 provinces, each governed by a representative provincial council (*Provinciale Staten*).

14 POLITICAL PARTIES

Religion plays an important role in the political life of the Netherlands, and religiously oriented parties exercise considerable influence. However, since the mid-1960s the general trend has been toward a division into conservative and progressive parties, and religious parties have lost voter support.

The religious political party with the largest membership is the Catholic People's Party (Katholieke Volkspartij— KVP), which favors democratic government and a middle-of-the-road social policy. The Labor Party (Partij van de Arbeid—PvdA) has appealed mainly to national interests rather than to socialist ones, although it does favor state economic planning. The conservative People's Party for Freedom and Democracy (Volkspartij voor Vrijheid en Democratie—VVD) has advocated free enterprise, separation of church and state, and individual liberties.

Smaller parties include the left-wing Pacifist Socialist Party (Pacifistisch Socialistische Partij—PSP), the Communist Party of the Netherlands (Communistische Partij van Nederland—CPN), the Farmers' Party (Boerenpartij—BP), and two very orthodox Calvinist groups: the State Reform Party (Staatkurdig Gereefoormeerde Partij—SGP) and the Reformed Political Association (Gereefoormeerd Politiek Verbond—GPV).

In 1991, the Communists formally dissolved and joined a new left-wing alliance known as the Green Left (Groen Links).

As no single party commands a majority in the States-General, the governing cabinet is made up of various party representatives, according to their numerical strength.

15 JUDICIAL SYSTEM

There is no jury system, and the state rather than the individual acts as initiator of legal proceedings. Administrative justice is separate from civil and criminal justice and not uniform in dispensation. The supreme judiciary body is the High Court of the Netherlands (Court of Cassation). Its principal task is to supervise administration of justice and to review the judgments of lower courts.

There are 5 courts of appeal (gerechtshoven). The 19 district courts (arrondisse-mentsrechtsbanken) provide first hearings of criminal cases and civil cases not handled by the 62 cantonal courts (kantongerechten), which handle petty criminal cases and civil cases involving sums of up to about $250. A single magistrate presides over most of these courts. There also are juvenile courts and special arbitration courts (for such institutions as the Stock Exchange Association and professional organizations).

16 ARMED FORCES

Universal military training has been in force since the beginning of the 20th century. All able-bodied men reaching the age of 20 (about 43,000 a year) are subject to military training for 12 to 15 months. A small percentage of draftees, who make a request under the Conscientious Objectors Act, are required to undertake alternative service.

In 1993, the army (68,000, half draftees) consisted of 6 mechanized infantry brigades, 3 armored brigades, and corps troops assigned to the North Atlantic Treaty Organization (NATO). The navy had 15,500 officers and men, including 2,400 marines. The air force of 12,000 men contained 8 combat squadrons and 12 air defense squadrons, as well as transport and special auxiliary groups.

The police force numbers 3,900. The reserves for all services total 144,300, about 30,000 on short recall. The US stations 2,300 troops in the Netherlands. The nation spent $7.2 billion on defense in 1991.

17 ECONOMY

An industrial nation with limited natural resources, the Netherlands bases its economy on the importation of raw materials for processing into finished products for export. Food processing, metallurgy, chemicals, manufacturing, and oil refining are the principal industries.

Because of its geographic position on the sea, outstanding harbor facilities, and numerous internal waterways, the Netherlands has traditionally been a trading, transporting, and brokerage nation. The economy, being dependent on international trade, is sharply affected by economic developments abroad—including changes in prices of primary goods—over which the Netherlands has little or no control.

Inflation has been low, averaging about 2% a year between 1986 and 1992. The unemployment rate fell from 10.5% in 1985 to 6.5% in 1993.

18 INCOME

In 1992, Netherland's gross national product (GNP) was $312 billion at current prices, or $20,950 per person. For the period 1985–92, the average inflation rate was 1.5%, resulting in a real growth rate in (GNP) of 2.1% per person.

19 INDUSTRY

Since World War II, the high rate of population growth and the severing of economic ties with Indonesia have made the further development of industry important. The metallurgical industry in particular has made tremendous progress. The Philips Electrical Company at Eindhoven has become the greatest electrical products firm in Europe as well as one of the world's major exporters of electric bulbs and appliances.

Royal Dutch/Shell owns and operates one of the world's largest oil refineries at Curaçao, near Venezuela, and Rotterdam's suburb of Pernis has the largest oil refinery in Europe. Total refinery output in 1992 (in millions of kilograms) included motor fuel, 3,775; naphtha, 10,314; gas and diesel oil, 18,404; and residual fuel oils, 14,922.

Selected industrial products in 1992 (in millions of kilograms) were crude steel, 5,439; pig iron, 4,849; and pharmaceutical products sold, 2,810. In 1992, the Netherlands also produced 81,440 million cigarettes and 2,062 million liters of beer. Canned fish, cocoa and cocoa products, sugar, candies, biscuits, and potato flour are among other leading food products.

20 LABOR

As of 1 January 1992, the civilian labor force numbered 6,610,000. Some 723,000 persons were self-employed or unpaid family workers, and about 490,000 persons were registered as unemployed on average in 1991. The unemployed represented about 8% of the work force in 1992, compared with 13% in 1985 and 1.2% in 1970.

Most labor unions are organized on the basis of a specific religious, political, or economic orientation and belong to a similarly focused central federation. Total

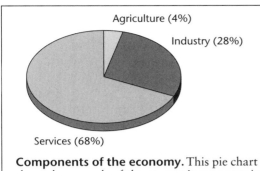

Components of the economy. This pie chart shows how much of the country's economy is devoted to agriculture (includes forestry, hunting, and fishing), industry, or services.

Agriculture (4%)

Industry (28%)

Services (68%)

membership of all labor unions in 1992 was 25% of those employed.

The minimum age for employment is 16. At that age, young people may work full time only if they have completed the mandatory 10 years of schooling. Those still in school at age 16 may not work more than 8 hours per week. People under the age of 18 are prohibited from working at night, working overtime, or working in areas which could be dangerous to their mental or physical development.

21 AGRICULTURE

More than 26% of the total land area of the Netherlands is under seasonal or permanent crop production. Most farms are effectively managed and worked intensively with mechanical equipment. Agriculture (including processed food and tobacco products) is an important export industry, contributing 24% of the total exports in 1992.

Gross agricultural output increased 4.2% in 1992, with crop output rising by 6%. Main crops and output in 1992 (in millions of kilograms) were sugar beets, 8,251; potatoes, 7,595; wheat, 1,017; barley, 204; oats, 19; and rye, 34. The Netherlands is famous for its flower bulbs grown for export, principally tulip, hyacinth, daffodil, narcissus, and crocus.

22 DOMESTICATED ANIMALS

World-renowned Dutch dairy products outrank all other agricultural produce. In 1992 there were 4.8 million head of cattle, 13.7 million pigs, 1.9 million sheep, and 105 million chickens. Milk production in 1992 totaled 10.8 billion kilograms. Meat production in 1992 was over 2.7 billion kilograms (pork and bacon, 1.5 billion; beef and veal, 630 million; poultry, 0.5 billion; mutton and horse meat, 17 million). Butter production was 150 million kilograms. Cheese production was 610 million kilograms.

Excellent grazing lands and a long growing season have greatly helped the northern dairy industry, whose main support is the famed Frisian strain of cows. The making of cheese is connected with such famous brands as those named for Edam and Gouda, towns in the province of South Holland.

23 FISHING

Fishing contributes substantially to the food supply. The total catch in 1991 was 443,097 tons, consisting primarily of plaice, mackerel, whiting, herring, cod, and mussels. Shrimp, oysters, sole, and other saltwater fish were also caught. Fishery exports have increased rapidly in recent years and amounted to $1.4 billion in 1992.

24 FORESTRY

One of the least forested countries in Europe, the Netherlands produces only about 8% of its wood requirements. Output of timber was approximately 1.3 million cubic meters from 1988 to 1991. Another 1.4 million cubic meters of roundwood are imported annually, and replanting has not kept pace with increasing consumption. Currently, Dutch wood fiber production is only 1.2 million cubic meters.

25 MINING

The only minerals of commercial importance are petroleum, natural gas, and salt. The production of salt from the mines at Hengelo is one of the oldest industries in the country. Magnesia is produced in a plant at Veendam from extracted salt brines.

26 FOREIGN TRADE

In recent years, the Netherlands has increased its trade in industrial products and decreased that in food products and foodstuffs. Principal Dutch exports today are manufactured goods, chemicals, petroleum products, natural gas, and foods. Chief imports are manufactures, crude petroleum, machinery, and chemicals.

Approximately 70% of Dutch trade is with other members of the European Union. Principal trade partners in 1992 were Germany, Belgium and Luxembourg,

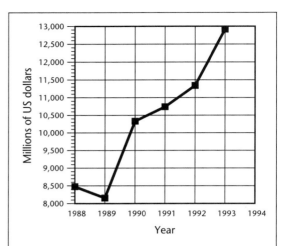

Yearly balance of trade measured in millions of US dollars. The balance of trade is the difference between what a country sells to other countries (its exports) and what it buys (its imports). If a country imports more than it exports, it has a negative balance of trade (a trade deficit). If exports exceed imports, there is a positive balance of trade (a trade surplus).

the United Kingdom, the United States, and Italy.

27 ENERGY AND POWER

The Netherlands, which has no water-power, depends on natural gas and petroleum as energy sources. Natural gas production in 1992 was fourth highest in the world, of which about half was exported.

The second main energy source is oil, which provided almost one-third of the Netherlands' energy needs in the early 1990s. Increased domestic production of crude petroleum (2.9 million tons in 1991) from offshore deposits in the North Sea still left the nation 80% dependent on

Selected Social Indicators

These statistics are estimates for the period 1988 to 1993. For comparison purposes, data for the United States and averages for low-income countries and high-income countries, are also given.

Indicator	Netherlands	Low-income countries	High-income countries	United States
Per capita gross national product†	**$20,950**	$380	$23,680	$24,740
Population growth rate	**0.7%**	1.9%	0.6%	1.0%
Population growth rate in urban areas	**0.8%**	3.9%	0.8%	1.3%
Population per square kilometer of land	**406**	78	25	26
Life expectancy in years	**77**	62	77	76
Number of people per physician	**412**	>3,300	453	419
Number of pupils per teacher (primary school)	**19**	39	<18	20
Illiteracy rate (15 years and older)	**<1%**	41%	<5%	<3%
Energy consumed per capita (kg of oil equivalent)	**4,533**	364	5,203	7,918

† The gross national product (GNP) is the total dollar value of all goods and services produced by a country in a year. The per capita GNP is calculated by dividing a country's GNP by its population. The World Bank defines low-income countries as those with a per capita GNP of $695 or less. High-income countries have a per capita GNP of $8,626 or more. Less than 14% of the world's 5.5 billion people live in high-income countries, while almost 60% live in low-income countries.

> = greater than   < = less than

Sources: World Bank, *Social Indicators of Development 1995,* Baltimore: Johns Hopkins University Press, 1995. Central Intelligence Agency, *World Fact Book,* Washington, D.C.: Government Printing Office, 1994.

imported petroleum. The Netherlands reexports two-thirds of all imported petroleum in the form of refined oil products.

Production of electric power in 1991 totaled 74,252 million kilowatt hours, of which thermal power plants using oil and coal as fuel supplied 95%, and nuclear power plants 5%. From 1988 to 1991, per person energy consumption increased by nearly 7%.

28 SOCIAL DEVELOPMENT

A widespread system of social insurance and assistance is in effect. Unemployment, accidents, illness, and disability are covered by insurance, which is compulsory for most employees and voluntary for self-employed persons. Maternity grants and full insurance for the worker's family are also provided, as are family allowances for children. There are also widows' and orphans' funds. A state pension is granted to all persons over 65. Women have equal legal status with men.

29 HEALTH

Under the Health Insurance Act, everyone with earned income of less than 50,900 guilders per year pays a monthly contribution in return for which they receive medical, pharmaceutical, and dental treatment and hospitalization. The state also pays for preventive medicine including vaccinations for children, and school dental services, medical research, and the training of health workers.

The general health situation has been excellent over a long period, helped by a rise in the standard of living, improvements in nutrition, hygiene, housing, and working conditions, and the expansion of public health measures. In 1992, average life expectancy was 77 years.

In 1985 there were 207 hospitals with 68,500 beds. In 1992, there were 4.1 hospital beds per 1,000 people. As of 1990, there were 37,461 physicians (about 1 for every 412 people).

Major causes of death in 1992 were categorized as follows, per 100,000 inhabitants: (1) communicable diseases and maternal/perinatal causes; (2) noncommunicable diseases; and (3) injuries. There were 339 deaths per 100,000 attributed to cardiovascular problems and 235 per 100,000 attributed to cancer.

30 HOUSING

During World War II, more than 25% of Holland's 2 million dwellings were damaged. From 1945 to 1985, nearly 4 million dwellings were built. In 1985 alone, 98,131 dwellings were built. Most of the new units were subsidized by the national government. Subsidies are granted to municipalities, building societies, and housing associations, which generally build low-income multiple dwellings. The total number of housing units in 1992 was 6,044,000.

31 EDUCATION

Illiteracy is nearly nonexistent in the Netherlands. School attendance between the ages of 6 and 16 is compulsory. Secondary school is comprised of three types: general secondary school; preuniversity—the athenaeum and the gymnasium, both lasting for six years; and vocational secondary school. Special education is provided to children with physical, mental, or social disabilities at special primary and secondary schools.

Vocational and university education is provided at the eight universities and five institutes (Hogescholen), which are equivalent to universities. These are funded entirely by the government. Facilities for adult education have been opened in various municipalities.

32 MEDIA

There are four radio networks. Broadcasting to other countries is carried on by the Netherlands World Broadcasting Service. There are three television channels. Shortwave programs are transmitted in Dutch, Afrikaans, Arabic, English, French, Indonesian, Portuguese, and Spanish. In 1991, television sets totaled 7,300,000 and radios 13,650,000. In the same year, there were 9,750,000 telephone connections, or 66 per 100 inhabitants.

The Dutch were among the first to issue regular daily newspapers. The oldest newspaper, the *Oprechte Haarlemsche Courant,* was founded in 1656 and is published today as the *Haarlemsche Courant*. The Dutch press is largely a subscription press, depending for two-thirds of its income on advertising. Sunday editions are not issued.

In 1991, the largest national and regional newspapers, with daily circulations, were *De Telegraaf* (720,000); *Algemeen Dagblad* (417,000); *De Volkskrant* (310,000); *NRC Handelsblad* (215,100); and *Haagsche Courant* (176,6000).

33 TOURISM AND RECREATION

The Netherlands is one of Europe's major tourist centers, and tourism is of great economic importance. Income from tourism totaled $4.07 billion in 1991. In 1991, the number of foreign tourists arriving in the Netherlands totaled 5,842,000, of whom 4,922,000 came from Europe and 552,000 from the Americas. There were 112,583 hotel beds with an occupancy rate of 37.9%.

Public railway, bus, and inland-waterway boat service is frequent and efficient. Principal tourist attractions include the great cities of Amsterdam, Rotterdam, and The Hague, with their famous monuments and museums, particularly the Rijksmuseum in Amsterdam; the flower gardens and bulb fields of the countryside; and North Sea beach resorts. Modern hotels and large conference halls in the large cities are the sites of numerous international congresses, trade shows, and other exhibitions.

Of a total population of 14 million, 4.3 million people belong to sport clubs. Pop-

Photo credit: Susan D. Rock

Windmills working in a recreated traditional village.

ular sports include soccer, swimming, cycling, sailing, and hockey.

34 FAMOUS NETHERLANDERS

The greatest Renaissance humanist was Desiderius Erasmus (Gerhard Gerhards, 1466?–1536). Baruch (Benedict de) Spinoza (1632–77), the influential philosopher, was born in Amsterdam.

The composers Jacob Obrecht (1453–1505) and Jan Pieterszoon Sweelinck (1562–1621) were renowned throughout Europe. Outstanding conductors of the world-famous Amsterdam Concertgebouw Orchestra include Bernard Haitink (b.1929), who also was principal conductor of the London Philharmonic from 1967 to 1979.

Hieronymus Bosch van Aken (1450?–1516) was a famous painter. Dutch painting reached its greatest heights in the 17th century, when Rembrandt van Rijn (1606–69) and Jan Vermeer (1632–75) painted their masterpieces. Two more recent painters—Vincent van Gogh (1853–90) and Piet Mondrian (1872–1944)—represent two widely divergent artistic styles and attitudes. Maurits C. Escher (1898–1972) was a skilled and imaginative graphic artist.

The outstanding figure in Dutch literature was Joost van den Vondel (1587–1679), poet and playwright. Distinguished historians include Johan Huizinga (1872–1945) and Pieter Geyl (1887–1966). Anne Frank (b.Germany, 1929–45) became the most famous victim of the Holocaust with the publication of the diary and other material that she had written while hiding from the Nazis in Amsterdam.

Jan Pieterszoon Coen (1587–1630), greatest of Dutch empire builders, founded the city of Batavia in the Malay Archipelago (now Jakarta, the capital of Indonesia). Peter Minuit (Minnewit, 1580–1638) founded the colonies of New Amsterdam (now New York City) and New Sweden (now Delaware). Peter Stuyvesant (1592–1672) lost New Netherland (now New York State) to the British.

Leading scientists include Anton van Leeuwenhoek (1632–1723), developer of the microscope. Among more recent scientists are Nobel Prize winners Frits Zernike (1888–1966), physics, 1953; Dutch-born Tjalling Koopmans (1910–85), who shared the 1975 prize for economic science; and Simon van der Meer (b.1925), co-winner of the physics prize in 1984. The 1911 Nobel Prize for peace was awarded to Tobias Michael Carel Asser (1838–1913).

The head of state since 1980 has been Queen Beatrix (b.1938).

35 BIBLIOGRAPHY

Andeweg, R. B. *Dutch Government and Politics.* New York: St. Martin's, 1993.

Barnouw, Adriaan Jacob. *The Dutch: A Portrait Study of the People of Holland.* New York: Columbia University Press, 1940.

Fradin, D. *The Netherlands.* Chicago: Children's Press, 1983.

Hoogenhuyze, Bert van. *The Dutch and the Sea.* Weesp: Maritiem de Boer, 1984.

King, Peter. *The Netherlands.* Santa Barbara, Calif.: Clio, 1988.

NEW ZEALAND

CAPITAL: Wellington.

FLAG: The flag has two main features: the red, white, and blue Union Jack in the upper left quarter and the four-star Southern Cross in the right half. On the blue state flag the stars are red outlined in white. On the red national flag, used by individuals or commercial institutions at sea, the stars are white.

ANTHEM: *God Save the Queen* and *God Defend New Zealand* have, since 1977, enjoyed equal status.

MONETARY UNIT: The New Zealand dollar (NZ$) is a paper currency of 100 cents; it replaced the New Zealand pound on 10 July 1967. There are coins of 5, 10, 20, and 50 cents and 1 and 2 dollars, and notes of 5, 10, 20, 50, and 100 dollars. NZ$1 = US$0.3982 (or US$1 = NZ$2.5113).

WEIGHTS AND MEASURES: Metric weights and measures are used.

HOLIDAYS: New Year's Day, 1 January; Waitangi Day, 6 February; Anzac Day, 25 April; Queen's Birthday, 1st Monday in June; Labor Day, 4th Monday in October; Christmas Day, 25 December; Boxing Day, 26 December. Movable holidays are Good Friday and Easter Monday. Each province has a holiday on its own anniversary day.

TIME: 12 midnight = noon GMT.

1 LOCATION AND SIZE

Situated in the southwest Pacific Ocean, New Zealand proper, with a total area of 268,680 square kilometers (103,738 square miles), consists of the North Island, including small islands nearby; the South Island; Stewart Island; and various minor, outlying islands.

Comparatively, the area occupied by New Zealand is about the size of the state of Colorado. New Zealand has a total coastline of 15,134 kilometers (9,404 miles).

New Zealand's capital city, Wellington, is located on the southern tip of North Island.

2 TOPOGRAPHY

The mountain ranges in the North Island include volcanic peaks. Mount Ruapehu and two others are still active. This volcanic system gives rise to many hot springs and geysers.

The South Island is significantly more mountainous than the North Island, but is without recent volcanic activity. The Southern Alps, running almost the entire length of the South Island from north to south, contain 19 peaks of 3,000 meters (9,800 feet) or above. The rivers are mostly swift-flowing and shallow, few of them navigable. There are many lakes. Those in the South Island are particularly noted for their magnificent mountain scenery.

3 CLIMATE

New Zealand has a temperate, moist ocean climate without major seasonal variations in temperature or rainfall. Mean annual temperatures at sea level range from about 15°C (59°F) in the northern part of the North Island to 12°C (54°F) in the southern part of the South Island. Mean annual rainfall ranges from around 300 centimeters (120 inches) near Dunedin to more than 800 centimeters (315 inches) in the Southern Alps.

4 PLANTS AND ANIMALS

As in other regions separated from the rest of the world for a long period, distinct native plants unique to New Zealand have developed. About 75% of the native plants are unique, and include some of the world's oldest plant forms. More than 250 species are common to both Australia and New Zealand. Undergrowth in the damp forests consists largely of ferns, of which there are 145 species.

Apart from seals and two species of bats, New Zealand has no native land mammals. Some of the land mammals introduced to New Zealand have become pests, such as the rabbit, the deer, the pig (now wild), and the North American opossum. Sea mammals include whales and dolphins.

There is a great diversity of birds, some 250 species in all. Among the flightless birds the most interesting is the kiwi, New Zealand's national symbol and the only

Photo credit: Susan D. Rock.

A fjord-like inlet on South Island.

known bird with nostrils at the tip of the bill instead of at the base. Other characteristic birds are the kea, a bird of prey, and the tui, a beautiful songbird. All but one type of penguin are represented in New Zealand.

5 ENVIRONMENT

Because of its relatively small population, New Zealand's natural resources have so far suffered less from the pressures of development than have those of many other industrialized nations. Air pollution from cars and other vehicles is an environmental concern in New Zealand. The use

NEW ZEALAND

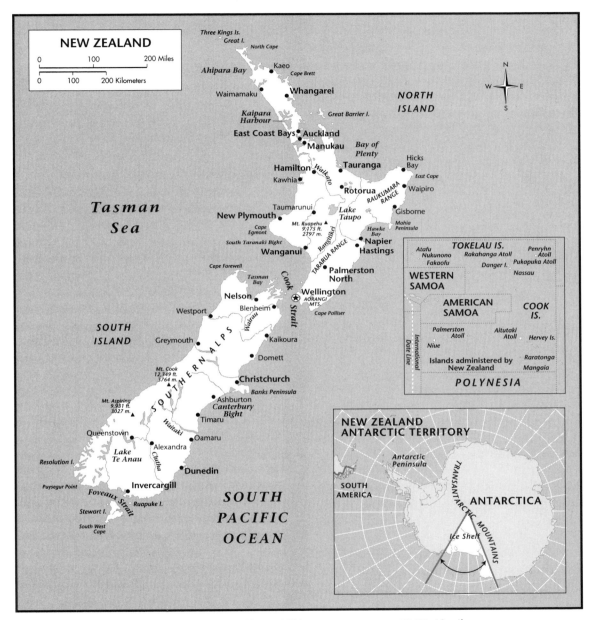

NEW ZEALAND

0 100 200 Miles
0 100 200 Kilometers

Three Kings Is.
Great I.
North Cape
Ahipara Bay
Kaeo
Cape Brett
Whangarei
Waimamaku
NORTH ISLAND
Kaipara Harbour
Great Barrier I.
East Coast Bays **Auckland**
Manukau
Bay of Plenty
Hicks Bay
Hamilton
Tauranga
East Cape
Kawhia
Rotorua
Waipiro
RAUKUMARA RANGE
Taumarunui
Lake Taupo
Gisborne
New Plymouth
Mahia Peninsula
Cape Egmont
Mt. Ruapehu
9,175 ft.
2797 m.
Hawke Bay
South Taranaki Bight
Napier
Wanganui
TARARUA RANGE
Hastings
Cape Farewell
Palmerston North
Tasman Bay
Cook Strait
Wellington
AORANGI MTS.
Nelson
Cape Palliser
Blenheim
Wairau
Westport
SOUTH ISLAND
Greymouth
Kaikoura
SOUTHERN ALPS
Domett
Mt. Cook
12,349 ft.
3764 m.
Christchurch
Banks Peninsula
Mt. Aspiring
9,931 ft.
3027 m.
Ashburton
Canterbury Bight
Waitaki
Timaru
Queenstown
Oamaru
Alexandra
Lake Te Anau
Chlutha
Resolution I.
Dunedin
Puysegur Point
Invercargill
Stewart I.
Foveaux Strait
Ruapuke I.
South West Cape

Tasman Sea

SOUTH PACIFIC OCEAN

TOKELAU IS.
Atafu
Nukunono
Fakaofu
Rakahanga Atoll
Penryhn Atoll
Danger I. Pukapuka Atoll
Nassau
WESTERN SAMOA
AMERICAN SAMOA
COOK IS.
Palmerston Atoll
Aitutaki Atoll
Hervey Is.
Niue
International Date Line
Raratonga
Islands administered by New Zealand
Mangaia
POLYNESIA

NEW ZEALAND ANTARCTIC TERRITORY
Antarctic Peninsula
SOUTH AMERICA
TRANSANTARCTIC MOUNTAINS
ANTARCTICA
Ice Shelf

LOCATION: 33° to 53°s; 162°E to 173°w. **TERRITORIAL SEA LIMIT:** 12 miles.

of fossil fuels also contributes to the problem.

Water pollution is also a problem due to industrial pollutants and sewage. The nation uses 44% of its water for farming activity and 10% for industrial purposes. Another environmental issue in New Zealand is how to pursue the development of resources—forests, gas and coal fields, farmlands—without serious cost to natural beauty and ecological balance.

In 1994, 1 of New Zealand's mammal species and 26 types of birds were endangered, as well as 232 plant species.

6 POPULATION

The population as of the census of 5 March 1991 was 3,434,950. A population of 3,710,000 was forecast for the year 2000. The population density in 1991 was 13 per square kilometer (33 per square mile), with nearly 75% of the population living on the North Island. The largest of the urban areas are Auckland (855,571 in 1991); Wellington, the capital (325,682); and Christchurch (307,179).

7 MIGRATION

Citizens of Fiji, Tonga, and Western Samoa may be admitted under special work permits for up to 11 months. There were a total of 57,088 permanent and long-term arrivals in 1991. Of the 25,437 people granted permanent residence in 1991, 5,322 came from Hong Kong and 3,875 from the United Kingdom. About 7,000 Indochinese refugees settled in New Zealand between 1975 and 1990. During 1991, New Zealanders departing, either permanently or long-term, numbered 45,472. Australia is the preferred destination.

8 ETHNIC GROUPS

About 80% of the population is classified as European. The overwhelming majority is of British descent. There are small groups of Dutch, Chinese, Indians, Arabs, Yugoslavs, Greeks, and Poles. The most significant minority group is the native Maori people, a Polynesian group with a distinctive culture and a well-ordered social system.

In March 1991 there were 321,396 Maoris or part-Maoris (those reporting a Maori ancestry of 50% or more). In all, there were 511,947 people with Maori ancestry, representing 14.9% of the census population. About 90% live on North Island. Many Maoris leave their tribal villages to seek job opportunities in the towns and cities. An estimated four-fifths of all Maoris live in urban areas.

The non-Maori Polynesian population in 1991 was 121,935, or 3.6% of the population. Chinese and Indians totaled 31,632 in 1986, or almost 1% of the population.

9 LANGUAGES

English is the universal language, although Maori, a language of the Polynesian group, still is spoken among the Maori population and is taught in Maori schools. It is the first language of about 50,000 Maori New Zealanders and became an official language in 1987, with the right of use in courts of law.

10 RELIGIONS

Most of the population in 1991 belonged to one of four main churches: the Church of England, 21.4%; the Presbyterian Church, 16.0%; the Roman Catholic Church, 14.8%; and the Methodist Church, 4.1%. There are numerous other Protestant denominations, two Christian sects (Ratana and Ringatu) that are native to New Zealand, and a small Hindu community. In 1990 there were an estimated 4,500 Jews.

11 TRANSPORTATION

The mountainous nature of New Zealand has made the development of rail and road communications difficult and expensive, particularly on the South Island. In 1991, 4,716 kilometers (2,931 miles) of state-owned railways were operative. Total length of maintained roadways as of 1991 was 92,648 kilometers (57,571 miles). Almost all roads were hard surfaced. As of 1992, registered motor vehicles included 1,557,951 passenger cars and 324,852 commercial vehicles.

With a registered merchant marine of only 180,000 gross tons in 1991, New Zealand is largely dependent on the shipping of other nations for its overseas trade. Auckland and Wellington, the two main ports, have good natural harbors with deepwater facilities and modern port equipment.

The government-owned Air New Zealand Ltd. operates air services throughout the Pacific region to Australia, Singapore, Hong Kong, Tokyo, Honolulu, and Los Angeles, among other destina-

tions. There are international airports at Auckland, Christchurch, and Wellington. In 1992, Air New Zealand carried 3,865,500 passengers on domestic and international flights.

12 HISTORY

The first European to discover New Zealand was Abel Tasman, a navigator of the Dutch East India Company, who sighted the west coast of the South Island in 1642. He did not land because of the hostility of the Maori inhabitants. According to Maori oral traditions, they migrated from other Pacific islands to New Zealand several centuries before Tasman's discovery, the chief migration having taken place about 1350. It seems likely, however, that ancestors of the Maoris had come to New Zealand from Southeast Asia by the end of the tenth century AD. No other Europeans are known to have visited New Zealand after Tasman until Captain James Cook of the British Royal Navy made his four voyages in 1769, 1773, 1774, and 1777.

In the 1790s, small European whaling settlements sprang up around the coast, and in 1814 the first missionary station was set up in the Bay of Islands near Cape Brett. In 1840, the Maori chieftains entered into a compact, the Treaty of Waitangi, whereby they turned over their independence to Britain's Queen Victoria while retaining territorial rights.

In the same year, groups of colonists began arriving from Britain to found the first settlements, which included Wellington (1840), Nelson (1842), Dunedin (1848), and Canterbury (1850). After the Maori Wars (1860–70), resulting largely

Photo credit: Susan D. Rock.

Maori men of Auckland in native costume.

from discontent with the official land policy, the colony of New Zealand rapidly increased in wealth and population. Discovery of gold in 1861 resulted in a large inflow of settlers.

The introduction of refrigerated shipping in 1882 enabled New Zealand to become one of the world's greatest exporters of dairy products and meat. The depression of the early 1930s revealed to New Zealand the extent of its dependence on this export trade and led to the establishment of more local light industry. New Zealand entered World Wars I (1914–18) and II (1939–45) on the side of the United Kingdom. New Zealand troops served in Europe in both wars and in the Pacific in World War II.

In 1907, New Zealand was made a dominion (a self-governing nation that recognizes the British monarchy) of the United Kingdom. In 1947, the New Zealand government formally claimed the complete independence available to self-governing members of the British Commonwealth. After World War II, New Zealand and US foreign policies were increasingly intertwined. New Zealand was a founding member of the Southeast Asia Treaty Organization (SEATO) in 1954. New Zealand troops fought with UN forces in the Korea conflict and with US forces in South Vietnam. The involvement in Vietnam touched off a national debate on foreign policy, however, and all New Zealand troops were withdrawn from the country by the end of 1971. New Zealand's military participation in SEATO was later terminated.

In 1984, a Labour government led by Prime Minister David Lange took office under a pledge to ban nuclear-armed vessels from New Zealand harbors. A United States request for a port visit by one of its warships was denied because of uncertainty as to whether the ship was nuclear-armed. The continuing ban put a strain on New Zealand's relations within the Australia-New Zealand-United States alliance (ANZUS), and in 1986 the United States suspended its military obligations to New Zealand under the ANZUS defense agreement. The United States also banned high-level contacts with the New Zealand government.

The native Maori people have claimed rights to all the country's coastline, 70% of the land, and half of the fishing rights. To answer these claims, a new Cabinet committee was formed in December 1989. The committee, including former Prime Minister Lange, worked with the 17-member Waitangi Tribunal, established in 1975 to consider complaints from Maoris.

The United States ended its ban on high-level contacts in March 1990.

13 GOVERNMENT

New Zealand is an independent member of the Commonwealth of Nations. Like the United Kingdom, it is a constitutional monarchy. The head of state, the governor-general, is the representative of the crown. The governor-general is appointed for a five-year term.

Government is democratic and modeled on that of the United Kingdom. The single-chamber legislature, the House of Representatives, has 97 members. Each is elected by universal adult vote for a term of three years. Although there have been coalition governments, the two-party system usually operates. The party with a majority of members elected to the House of Representatives forms the government, the other party becoming the Opposition.

On his appointment, the prime minister, leader of the governing party, chooses 20 other ministers to form the cabinet. Each minister usually controls several government departments. Ministers are responsible to the House of Representatives for the operation of their departments.

As of 1986, there were 22 regional councils, 90 county councils, 128 borough councils, 10 district councils, 15 district community councils, and 118 community councils.

14 POLITICAL PARTIES

New Zealand's major parties are the Labour Party, formed in 1916, and the National Party, formed in 1935. In October 1990 the National Party, led by Jim Bolger, won a general election victory. Bolger's government made major cuts in New Zealand's welfare programs. The National Party won reelection in the November 1993 general election, capturing 50 of 99 seats. The Labour Party won

45, and both the New Zealand First Party, led by Winston Peters, and The Alliance, led by Jim Anderton, won 2 seats. In December 1993 Helen Clark replaced Michael Moore as leader of the Labour Party, becoming the first woman to lead a major party in New Zealand.

15 JUDICIAL SYSTEM

Most civil and criminal cases are heard first in district courts. There is the right of appeal to the High Court, which is usually the court of first hearing for cases where a major crime or an important civil action is involved. Family courts were established in 1980 to hear cases involving domestic issues. The highest court, the Court of Appeal, rules on appeals only. There are also several special courts, such as the Arbitration Court, the Maori Land Court, and the Children and Young Persons Court. The judicial system is based on British common law. The judiciary is independent and impartial.

16 ARMED FORCES

Service in the New Zealand regular armed forces is voluntary, but some white males (18–21) may be required to have military training for service in the territorial force (5,650).

In 1993, the army had a full-time regular force of 4,800 and 1,650 reserves; the navy had 2,400 regulars (300 women) and 1,050 reserves; and the air force had 3,700 regulars (600 women) and 1,050 reserves. The army has one active brigade (unit of troops), the navy 8 small surface combatants (combat-ready units) and 7 helicopters, and the air force 41 combat aircraft.

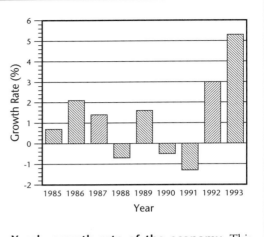

Yearly growth rate of the economy. This economic indicator tells by what percent the economy has increased or decreased when compared with the previous year.

Weapons are American and European. New Zealand has 35 service members working abroad in 6 different nations. The defense budget in 1992 was US$792 million.

17 ECONOMY

New Zealand's economy has traditionally been based on farming. The last decades, however, have seen the beginnings of heavy industry, and there has been a large expansion in light industries such as plastics, textiles, and footwear, mostly to supply the home market. In recent years there has been a trend toward the development of industries based on natural resources. The forest industry has greatly expanded. Pulp, log, and paper products are major exports.

The economy has been subjected to two major crises in 20 years: first, the loss of a large part of the British market for New Zealand's agricultural products when the United Kingdom joined the European Community in 1973; and, second, limits placed on overspending by the government in the early 1980s, which enforced a 10-year program of controls. Strict policies have slowed economic growth into the early 1990s. Unemployment from 1990 to June of 1992 ranged from 8.7% to 11%.

Components of the economy. This pie chart shows how much of the country's economy is devoted to agriculture (includes forestry, hunting, and fishing), industry, or services.

18 INCOME

In 1992, New Zealand's gross national product (GNP) was US$41,186 million at current prices. Since 1988, national income has averaged US$12,600 per person. For the period 1985–92, the average inflation rate was 6.6%, resulting in a real growth rate in GNP of –0.4% per person.

19 INDUSTRY

Industrial production has increased rapidly since the end of World War II. Plants include metal and petroleum processing, motor vehicle assembly, textiles and footwear, and a wide range of consumer appliances. The New Zealand Steel company manufactures billet slabs and ingots using domestically produced iron sands. Pacific Steel, which processes scrap metal, uses billets from New Zealand Steel. The Tiwai Point aluminum smelter, operated by an Australian-Japanese group, has an annual capacity of 244,000 tons.

The small but growing electronics industry produces consumer goods as well as commercial products such as digital gasoline pumps. Wool-based industries have traditionally been an important part of the economy, notably wool milling, the oldest sector of the textile industry. Other significant industrial areas include a diverse food-processing sector, tanneries, sheet glass, rubber, and plastics.

20 LABOR

In 1992, total civilian employment amounted to 1,467,000, including 159,000 in agriculture, 240,000 in manufacturing, 308,000 in wholesale or retail trade, and 416,000 in community or personal services. Unemployment was 10.6% in 1991.

In 1992, there were 160 registered trade unions, representing about 37% of the total labor force. In 1991, the minimum wage rate was about US$2.44 per hour. Minimum wages for men and women were equalized in 1977. The safety, health and welfare benefits, holiday provisions, hours of work, and overtime of all workers are closely regulated.

Children under the age of 15 may not work without special government approval, and must not work between the hours of 10 PM and 6 AM Laws are effectively enforced by the Department of Labor.

21 AGRICULTURE

Over 50% of the total area of New Zealand is devoted to agriculture and animal husbandry. About 75,000 tractors and 2,950 harvesters were in use in 1991.

In 1992, areas harvested to wheat totaled an estimated 42,000 hectares (103,780 acres), with a yield of 168,000 tons; 17,000 hectares (42,000 acres) yielded 65,000 tons of oats; and 79,000 hectares (195,210 acres) yielded 420,000 tons of barley.

In 1992, 848,000 tons of fresh fruit, (excluding melons) were produced. The kiwi, a fruit that has become popular in the United States, Japan, and elsewhere, represented 90% of fruit and vegetable exports. However, New Zealand is beginning to lose some of its market share in the production of kiwi, as other countries have started or expanded their own domestic kiwi production. In 1992, New Zealand produced 407,000 tons of apples, 16,000 tons of pears, 60,000 tons of peas, 160,000 tons of corn, and 300,000 tons of potatoes.

22 DOMESTICATED ANIMALS

Relatively warm temperatures, combined with ample rainfall, give New Zealand some of the world's richest pasturelands. In 1992, there were 5,250,000 head of beef cattle, 3,200,000 head of dairy cattle, 53,500,000 sheep, and 409,000 pigs. Some 24,000 farms stock mainly sheep, occupying over 11 million hectares (27.1 million acres), with an average flock of 1,800 head.

Products of animal origin account for more than half the total value of New Zealand's exports. New Zealand is the world's largest exporter of mutton and lamb, second largest exporter of wool, and a leading exporter of cheese. Wool production was 296,000 tons in 1992. Meat production in that year reached 1,226,000 tons. Mutton and wool accounted for 17% of gross agricultural output in 1992, when exports of pastoral products totaled US$4.3 billion. Butter production totaled about 286,750 tons. Cheese output was 139,500 tons. In 1992, 47,600 tons of eggs were produced.

With many more cows than people to milk them, New Zealand pioneered and relies on mechanical milking. Whole milk is pumped through coolers to vats where it is transferred to tanker trucks. In 1992, 8,140,000 tons of fresh milk was produced. Milkfat production averages about 330,000 tons annually, of which 13% is consumed as milk or fed to stock. The balance is used for dairy products.

23 FISHING

Although many kinds of edible fish are easily obtainable in New Zealand waters, the fishing and fish-processing industry has remained relatively small. The volume of fish caught in New Zealand was 609,031 tons in 1991. About 75% of the catch is exported (with a value of

US$460.7 million in 1991), mostly to the United States, Japan, and Australia. The main species caught included blue grenadier, mackerel, whiting, snoek, and orange roughy.

In addition, New Zealand fishermen in 1991 landed 2,997 tons of rock lobster, 4,497 tons of oysters, 43,600 tons of mussels, and 1,032 tons of scallops. The most valuable part of the catch is made up of orange roughy, hoki, squid, and rock lobster. Fish and seafood cultivation is also developing. Oyster and mussel farming are well established, with scallop, salmon, and abalone farming under consideration.

24 FORESTRY

The proportion of forest land in New Zealand has been reduced from about 70% of the land before settlement to about 28%. Much of the remaining natural forest is protected in national parks or preserves.

Total sawn wood production in 1991 was 2,198,000 cubic meters. Total paper and paperboard production amounted to 815,000 tons, including 321,000 tons of newsprint, 35,000 tons of other printing and writing paper, and 459,000 tons of other paper and paperboard. Wood-pulp production reached 1,350,000 tons in 1991. Wood-based paneling amounted to 687,000 cubic meters. In 1992, exports of forest products accounted for over 10% of total exports.

25 MINING

Many different minerals are found in New Zealand, but few have been extensively mined. Coal production is sufficient for domestic consumption, and a small amount is exported. In 1991 coal output was 2,550,000 tons. Estimated recoverable coal reserves amount to over 8.6 billion tons. Output from the gold deposits of the South Island, previously believed to have been exhausted, was 6,611 kilograms in 1991. Silver production was 11,000 kilograms in 1991.

Large quantities of iron-bearing sands are present, especially on North Island beaches; 2,300,000 tons of iron sands were extracted in 1991. Metal-bearing concentrates are produced for Japanese use from iron-sand deposits on the North Island's west coast. Output of building materials in 1991 included 5,000,000 tons of sand and gravel for building aggregate, and 1,400,000 tons of limestone for roads.

26 FOREIGN TRADE

New Zealand's trade per person and as a percentage of the country's income is among the highest in the world. Imports consist mainly of manufactured goods, petroleum and petroleum products, and raw materials for industry. Principal exports in 1991 were manufactured goods, meat, dairy products, forest produce, and fruits and vegetables.

Especially since the United Kingdom entered the European Community, New Zealand has expanded its trade relations with different countries. The proportion of total trade with the United Kingdom fell from 45% in 1959 to 6.6% in 1991. By 1991, Australia was the biggest market for New Zealand's exports (18.9%), while Japan was its biggest source of imports

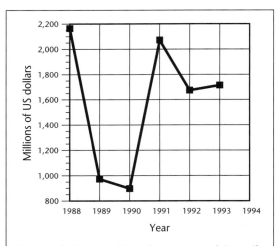

Yearly balance of trade measured in millions of US dollars. The balance of trade is the difference between what a country sells to other countries (its exports) and what it buys (its imports). If a country imports more than it exports, it has a negative balance of trade (a trade deficit). If exports exceed imports there is a positive balance of trade (a trade surplus).

(15%). The United States also now ranks ahead of the United Kingdom as a trading partner.

27 ENERGY AND POWER

New Zealand's per person consumption of electricity is among the highest in the world. A network of transmission lines links all major power stations, bringing electricity to 99% of the population. Of electricity generated for public supply in 1991, 74% was produced from hydroelectric resources, and 26% from steam. Future hydroelectric potential is limited, however, and thermal power based primarily on coal and natural gas is becoming increasingly important.

New Zealand now meets some 75% of its total energy requirements from native resources, the balance coming from imports of crude oil and refined petroleum products. Oil and gas exploration and development of native resources continue to be stressed, in efforts to reduce dependence on imports. Crude oil and natural gas liquid production levels in 1991 were estimated at 10 million and 1.6 million barrels, respectively. Proven reserves of natural gas totaled 100 billion cubic meters in 1992. Oil reserves were 200 million barrels.

28 SOCIAL DEVELOPMENT

All persons in New Zealand are now protected economically for retirement and in the event of sickness, unemployment, and widowhood. Monetary benefits under the Social Security Act are paid for retirement, unemployment, sickness, and emergencies; and to widows, orphans, families, invalids, and minors. Medical benefits include medical, hospital, and pharmaceutical payments. A 1982 plan provides compensation for all workers injured in an accident, even if the injury did not occur at work.

New Zealand was the first country to grant full voting rights to women, and it celebrated the 100th anniversary of that event in 1993 with conferences and other activities.

29 HEALTH

New Zealand's health care system has been undergoing a restructuring since the mid-1980s. Area health boards, formed to combine primary and hospital care facili-

Selected Social Indicators

These statistics are estimates for the period 1988 to 1993. For comparison purposes, data for the United States and averages for low-income countries and high-income countries are also given.

Indicator	New Zealand	Low-income countries	High-income countries	United States
Per capita gross national product†	**$12,600**	$380	$23,680	$24,740
Population growth rate	**1.2%**	1.9%	0.6%	1.0%
Population growth rate in urban areas	**1.5%**	3.9%	0.8%	1.3%
Population per square kilometer of land	**13**	78	25	26
Life expectancy in years	**76**	62	77	76
Number of people per physician	**608**	>3,300	453	419
Number of pupils per teacher (primary school)	**16**	39	<18	20
Illiteracy rate (15 years and older)	**<1%**	41%	<5%	<3%
Energy consumed per capita (kg of oil equivalent)	**4,299**	364	5,203	7,918

† The gross national product (GNP) is the total dollar value of all goods and services produced by a country in a year. The per capita GNP is calculated by dividing a country's GNP by its population. The World Bank defines low-income countries as those with a per capita GNP of $695 or less. High-income countries have a per capita GNP of $8,626 or more. Less than 14% of the world's 5.5 billion people live in high-income countries, while almost 60% live in low-income countries.

> = greater than   < = less than

Sources: World Bank, *Social Indicators of Development 1995,* Baltimore: Johns Hopkins University Press, 1995. Central Intelligence Agency, *World Fact Book,* Washington, D.C.: Government Printing Office, 1994.

ties for each region under a single administrative unit, were established in 1985. In 1991, the government announced plans to expand health care resources for those in financial need.

In 1993, there were 8,100 doctors (about 1 for every 608 people, with a nurse to doctor ratio of 0.1). Most physicians practice under the National Health Service, established by the Social Security Act of 1938, but private practice outside the scheme is permitted. In 1990, there were 344 hospitals with 30,000 beds (6.6 per 1,000 inhabitants).

Life expectancy at birth was 76 years in 1992. The principal causes of death are heart disease, cancer, and cerebrovascular diseases. There were about 10 reported cases of tuberculosis per 100,000 people in 1990. Alcoholism is a significant public health problem in New Zealand. Estimates of the number of chronic alcoholics range upward from 53,000, and another 250,000 New Zealanders may be classified as excessive drinkers.

30 HOUSING

About 18,000 houses and apartments were built in New Zealand in 1992, when

New Zealand's housing stock totaled 1,220,000. More than half the total housing stock has been constructed since 1957.

Most families own their own homes. The average private dwelling has three bedrooms, a living room, dining room, kitchen, laundry, bathroom, toilet, and garage. Most units are built of wood and have sheet-iron or tiled roofs.

31 EDUCATION

Education in New Zealand is compulsory for 10 years for children between 6 and 15, although most children attend school from the age of 5. The adult literacy rate is 99%. Most state schools are coeducational, but some private schools are not. New Zealand has 2,300 state primary schools and 60 privately owned schools. At the secondary level, there are 315 state-run schools and 15 private schools.

In 1990 there were 72,025 students in preschool institutions; 314,487 students in primary schools, and 335,456 students in secondary schools. For children in isolated areas, there is a public Correspondence School. In some regions there are special state primary and secondary schools for Maori children, but most Maori children attend public schools.

There are six universities: the University of Auckland, University of Waikato (at Hamilton), Massey University (at Palmerston North), Victoria University of Wellington, University of Canterbury (at Christchurch), and University of Otago (at Dunedin). All universities offer courses in the arts, social sciences, commerce, and science.

An agricultural institution, Lincoln College, is associated with the University of Canterbury. Law is offered at Auckland, Waikato, Victoria, Canterbury, and Otago, and medicine at Auckland and Otago. The Central Institute of Technology, near Wellington, is the leading institution in a network of 24 polytechnic institutions. There are evening classes for adults interested in continuing their education at secondary schools, institutes, and community centers. University tuition fees are low, and financial assistance is given to applicants who have passed special qualifying examinations.

32 MEDIA

The government is in the process of transferring the telecommunications sector to private ownership. In 1990, Telecom Corporation, which runs the country's telephone services, was sold to a group of companies led by American Information Technologies Corporation and Bell Atlantic. The number of telephones in 1991 was 2,402,619.

The Radio New Zealand network, a unified television service, operates the two national networks, TV1 and TV2, and one privately owned channel. As of 1991, there were 37 commercial community radio stations, 4 popular music stations, 26 non-commercial national stations, and 4 classical music stations. Color television was introduced in October 1973, and most households now have color sets. There were 1,515,000 television sets and 3,180,000 radios in 1991.

Aside from the usual British legal limits for libel, there is complete freedom of the

Photo credit: Susan D. Rock.

The skyline and harbor of Auckland.

press in New Zealand. The *Taranaki Herald*, founded in 1852, is New Zealand's oldest surviving newspaper. In 1991 there were 35 daily newspapers in New Zealand. The largest daily newspapers and their estimated 1991 circulation figures are the *New Zealand Herald* (252,000); *The Press* (95,900); the *Auckland Star* (86,200); and *The Dominion* (74,900).

33 TOURISM AND RECREATION

New Zealand draws many thousands of tourists to its shores because of the beauty, diversity, and compactness of its natural attractions and its varied sporting facilities. There are 10 national parks and 3 maritime parks. Urewera, noted for its forests and bird life, is the park in which early Maori culture is most strongly preserved; Tongariro includes two active volcanoes and is an important ski resort; and Mount Cook National Park includes Tasman Glacier, the largest glacier outside the polar regions.

New Zealand has numerous thermal spas, particularly in the Rotorua area, which also offers Maori villages where traditional arts and crafts may be observed. The Waitomo Cave, on the North Island, is lit by millions of glowworms and may be toured all year. Lake Taupo and its streams form one of the world's richest trout fishing areas. Christchurch is home to one of the world's finest botanical gardens. Skiing is available on both the North and South Islands, and there is good deep-sea fishing along the North Island coast. New Zealand has first-class golf courses. Spectator sports include horse racing, soccer, cricket, and rugby.

Tourism has slowed since 1989 due to the strengthening of the New Zealand dollar, rising costs, and international factors, including the 1991 Persian Gulf War. In 1991, there were 963,470 visitor arrivals, 35% from Australia, 14% from the United States, 12% from Japan, and 9% from the United Kingdom. In the same year, tourism receipts totaled US$1.02 billion. As of 1988, there were 39,327 rooms in hotels and motels.

34 FAMOUS NEW ZEALANDERS

Among New Zealand's best-known statesmen are Sir George Grey (1812–98), governor and later prime minister; Richard John Seddon (1845–1906), prime minister responsible for much social legislation; William Ferguson Massey (1856–1925); and Peter Fraser (1884–1950), World War II prime minister. Two outstanding leaders of the Maori people were Sir Apirana Ngata (1874–1950) and Sir Peter Buck (1880–1951).

William Pember Reeves (1857–1932), outstanding journalist, politician, and political economist, was the director of the London School of Economics. Frances Hodgkins (1869–1947) was a highly regarded painter. Katherine Mansfield (Kathleen Beauchamp Murry, 1888–1923) was a master of the short-story form. Other well-known authors include Sylvia Ashton-Warner (1908–84) and Maurice Shadbolt (b.1932).

Lord Ernest Rutherford (1871–1937), pioneer in atomic research and 1908 Nobel Prize winner for chemistry, was born in New Zealand. Other scientists include Sir Harold Gillies (1882–1960) and Sir Archibald McIndoe (1900–62), whose plastic surgery methods did much to rehabilitate war victims.

Prominent in the arts have been ballet dancers Alexander Grant (b.1925) and Rowena Jackson (b.1926); the singer and actor Inia Watene Te Wiata (1915–71); and the soprano Kiri Te Kanawa (b.1944). Sir Edmund Percival Hillary (b.1919) was the conqueror of Mt. Everest. The celebrated political cartoonist David Low (1891–1963) was born in New Zealand.

35 BIBLIOGRAPHY

Doublilet, David. "New Zealand's Magic Waters." *National Geographic,* October 1989, 507–529.
Fox, M. *New Zealand.* Chicago: Children's Press, 1991.
Hawke, G. R. *The Making of New Zealand.* Cambridge: Cambridge University Press, 1985.
Johnston, Carol Morton. *The Farthest Corner: New Zealand, a Twice Discovered Land.* Honolulu, Hawaii: University of Hawaii Press, 1988.
Jordan, Robert P. "New Zealand: the Last Utopia?" *National Geographic,* May 1987, 654–682.
Lealand, Geoffrey. *A Foreign Egg in Our Nest?: American Popular Culture in New Zealand.* Wellington: Victoria University Press, 1988.
McLauchlan, Gordon, ed. *The Illustrated Encyclopedia of New Zealand.* Auckland: D. Bateman, 1992.
Metge, Joan. *The Maoris of New Zealand.* London: Routledge & Kegan Paul, 1976.
Moffett, Mark W. "New Zealand's Insect Giants." *National Geographic,* November 1991, 101–105.
The Oxford Illustrated History of New Zealand. New York: Oxford University Press, 1990.

NICARAGUA

Republic of Nicaragua
República de Nicaragua

CAPITAL: Managua.

FLAG: The national flag consists of a white horizontal stripe between two stripes of cobalt blue, with the national coat of arms centered in the white band.

ANTHEM: *Salve a ti, Nicaragua (Hail to You, Nicaragua).*

MONETARY UNIT: The córdoba (c$) is a paper currency of 100 centavos. There are coins of 5, 10, 25, and 50 centavos and 1 and 5 córdobas, and notes of 1, 2, 5, 10, 20, 50, 100, 500, 1,000, 5,000, 10,000, 20,000, 50,000, 100,000, 200,000, 500,000, 1,000,000, 5,000,000, and 10,000,000 córdobas. c$1 = us$0.014 (or us$1 = c$70).

WEIGHTS AND MEASURES: The metric system is the legal standard, but some local units are also used.

HOLIDAYS: New Year's Day, 1 January; Labor Day, 1 May; Liberation Day (Revolution of 1979), 19 July; Battle of San Jacinto, 14 September; Independence Day, 15 September; All Saints' Day, 1 November; Christmas, 25 December. Movable religious holidays include Holy Thursday and Good Friday.

TIME: 6 AM = noon GMT.

1 LOCATION AND SIZE

Nicaragua, the largest of the Central American countries, has an area of 129,494 square kilometers (49,998 square miles), slightly larger than the state of New York. It has a total boundary length of 2,046 kilometers (1,271 miles).

Nicaragua's capital city, Managua, is located in the southwestern part of the country.

2 TOPOGRAPHY

The Caribbean coast, known as the Mosquito Coast or Mosquitia, consists of a low, flat, tropical jungle. The coastal lowland rises to a plateau covering about one-third of the country's total area and is broken by mountain ranges extending eastward from the main cordillera (mountain range). The Pacific lowlands region contains lakes Nicaragua and Managua (Lago de Nicaragua and Lago de Managua), connected by the Tipitapa River. Also found in this area is a belt of volcanoes. The principal waterways are the Coco (or Segovia) River and the San Juan River.

3 CLIMATE

Except in the central highlands, the climate is warm and humid. The mean temperature, varying according to altitude, is between 20° and 30°C (68° and 86°F). Average annual rainfall along the Mosquito Coast reaches 254–635 centimeters (100–250 inches). The highlands also have heavy rainfall. The Pacific coast averages over 200 centimeters (80 inches) a year.

4 PLANTS AND ANIMALS

The central highlands region has extensive forests of oak and pine on the slopes. The humid Caribbean coastal plain has an abundance of tropical forest. Wild rubber, cedar, ebony, mahogany, and rosewood trees are attractive for harvesting.

Wildlife includes the puma, deer, monkey, armadillo, alligator, parrot, macaw, peccary, and several species of snakes. Lake Nicaragua (Lago de Nicaragua) contains the only freshwater sharks in the world (as well as other varieties of saltwater fish). This resulted from a prehistoric geological movement that separated the lake from the Pacific Ocean, gradually changing the ocean water into fresh water.

5 ENVIRONMENT

Nicaragua lost 150,000 hectares (370,370 acres) of forest land in the year 1990–91 due partly to the use of wood for fuel. The purity of the nation's lakes and rivers is threatened by industrial pollutants. Dumping of sewage and chemical wastes has made Lake Managua (Lago de Managua) unsuitable for swimming, fishing, or drinking.

In 1994, eight of the nation's mammal species were endangered; seven bird species and 68 plant species were threatened with extinction.

6 POPULATION

The estimated population in 1991 was 3,999,231 and the projected population for the year 2000 was 5,169,000. In 1991, the population density for the nation was about 31 persons per square kilometer (81 persons per square mile). In 1985, the principal city and capital, Managua, had a population of 682,111.

7 MIGRATION

After the Sandinista leftists took power in 1979, thousands of Nicaraguans left the country. It was estimated in 1987 that 24,000 had fled to Honduras, 16,000 to Costa Rica, and over 200,000 to the United States, chiefly to Florida. After the defeat of the Sandinistas in the 1990 elections, some 200,000 Nicaraguans returned from abroad. Some 27,800 Nicaraguans were still refugees in Costa Rica at the end of 1992. At the same time, 14,500 Central American refugees were in Nicaragua.

8 ETHNIC GROUPS

The Nicaraguan population is basically mestizo, a mixture of white and Amerindian. There are no census data on racial composition, but 1980 estimates placed the mestizo component at 69% and the white population at 14%, while blacks account for 13% and Amerindians for the remaining 4%.

9 LANGUAGES

Spanish is the official language and is spoken by the overwhelming majority of the population. Some Nahuatl and other Amerindian words and phrases are in common use.

NICARAGUA

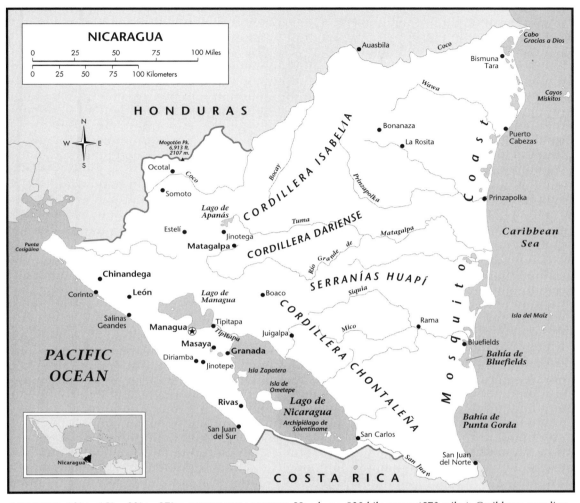

NICARAGUA

| 0 | 25 | 50 | 75 | 100 Miles |
| 0 | 25 | 50 | 75 | 100 Kilometers |

LOCATION: 10° to 15°N; 83° to 87°W. **BOUNDARY LENGTHS:** Honduras, 922 kilometers (573 miles); Caribbean coastline, 478 kilometers (297 miles); Costa Rica, 300 kilometers (186 miles). **TERRITORIAL SEA LIMIT:** 200 miles.

10 RELIGIONS

Roman Catholicism is the predominant religion, claiming the allegiance of about 89.3% of the population. The Protestant community numbered about 400,000 in 1986. There are also small communities of Baha'is, followers of Amerindian tribal religions, Buddhists, and Jews.

11 TRANSPORTATION

The national road network in 1991 totaled 25,000 kilometers (15,535 miles). In 1991, there were 70,000 registered motor vehicles.

Pacific Railways of Nicaragua has a length of 373 kilometers (232 miles).

Ten year old Marta Gonzalez (middle) and her dog, Rita, sit at the altar at a local church in Monimbo, to celebrate Dogs' Day. Thousands of Nicaraguans and their dogs gathered in the town some 20 miles east of Managua to honor Saint Lazaro, the patron saint of dogs, and give thanks for the good health of their pets.

The merchant fleet in 1991 consisted of two vessels totaling 2,161 gross registered tons. Corinto, Nicaragua's only natural harbor on the Pacific coast, is the major port, handling about 60% of all waterborne trade. A new state-owned airline, Aerolíneas de Nicaragua (AERONICA), provides services to El Salvador, Costa Rica, Panama, and Mexico. There is an international airport at Las Mercedes, near Managua.

12 HISTORY

Nicaragua derives its name from that of the Amerindian chief Nicarao who once ruled the region. The first European contact came with the explorer Christopher Columbus in 1502. At that time, the country was inhabited by the Sumo and Miskito Amerindians.

The first Spanish settlements in Nicaragua were founded by the conquistador Gil González de Ávila in 1522. During the next 300 years—most of the colonial period—Nicaragua was ruled as part of the Spanish captaincy-general of Guatemala. On 15 September 1821, the independence of the five provinces of Central America, including Nicaragua, was proclaimed by Spain. After a brief period under the Mexican empire of Augustín de Iturbide (1822–23), Nicaragua joined the United Provinces of Central America. On 30 April 1838, Nicaragua declared its independence from the United Provinces, and a new constitution was adopted.

Nicaragua was not immediately a unified nation. The Spanish had never controlled all of Nicaragua. The Mosquito Coast at the time of independence was an Amerindian and British area.

Beyond that, Nicaragua was torn apart by a bitter internal struggle between liberals and conservatives. In 1853, liberals revolted and invited the American military adventurer William Walker to aid them. Walker invaded Nicaragua in 1855, and had himself elected president in 1856. However, he ruled for only one year before being ousted. Conservatives seized control in 1863 and ruled until 1893. The 30-year conservative reign brought increases in coffee and banana production.

Liberals successfully revolted in 1893, and José Santos Zelaya became president. Zelaya's dictatorship lasted 16 years, during which he absorbed most of the Mosquito territory into Nicaragua, developed railroads and lake transportation, and enlarged the coffee plantations.

From 1909 until 1933, US influence in Nicaragua grew. American banks extended a large amount of credit to the bankrupt Treasury, and American marines and warships arrived in 1912 in support of president Adolfo Díaz. After this, American forces remained active in Nicaraguan politics, and administered the country directly or through handpicked rulers.

Somoza Family in Power

The guerrilla hero General Augusto César Sandino began organizing resistance to the American marine occupation force in 1927. American President Franklin D. Roosevelt created a foreign policy known as the "good neighbor" policy in 1933. The marines were pulled out for the last time. However, they left a legacy, having built the Nicaraguan National Guard, headed by Anastasio ("Tacho") Somoza García.

Officers of the National Guard shot Sandino after offering to negotiate a settlement with his forces. The National Guard was now unchallenged in Nicaragua, and three years later, Somoza unseated the liberal president Juan B. Sacasa and assumed the presidency. Somoza and his family were to rule Nicaragua directly or indirectly for the next 42 years.

Except for a three-year period between 1947 and 1950, Somoza was president until he was assassinated in 1956. His son, Luis Somoza Debayle, was president of congress and immediately became president under the constitution. In spite of a 1962 law attempting to limit the Somozas' hold on the government, the presidential election of February 1967 returned the Somozas to power after a four-year break. The victory for Anastasio Somoza, the younger brother of Luis, was overwhelming.

After drawing up a new constitution and declaring nine opposition parties illegal, Somoza won the September 1974 elections and remained president. While Somoza consolidated his hold on Nicaragua, a rebel organization, the Sandinista National Liberation Front (Frente Sandinista de Liberación Nacional—FSLN) began to agitate against his rule. Throughout the 1970s, opposition to Somoza grew, and American support began to dissolve.

By 1979, loss of support from the Church and the business community left Somoza without domestic allies. To make matters worse, the administration of President Jimmy Carter cut off military aid. In May 1979, the Sandinistas launched a final offensive. By July, Somoza had fled the country. By this time, an estimated 30,000–50,000 people had died in the fighting.

The Sandinistas engaged in an ambitious program to develop Nicaragua under leftist ideals. They dissolved the National Guard. However, the Guard did not go away. In 1982 a number of anti-Sandinista guerrilla groups (broadly referred to as the "contras"), consisting of former Guard members and Somoza supporters, began operating from Honduras and Costa Rica. As antigovernment activity increased, a state of emergency, proclaimed in March 1982, extended into 1987.

U.S. Aids the Contras

In April 1981, the administration of President Ronald Reagan began aiding the contras with funds channeled through the Central Intelligence Agency (CIA). Reagan was angered by the Sandinistas' support of the leftist guerrillas in El Salvador. However, the US Congress proved reluctant to fund the Nicaraguan resistance. In 1986, it was revealed that US government funds had been secretly diverted to provide aid to the contras. This was in violation of a US congressional ban on such aid.

On the domestic scene, the Sandinistas' economic policies had not proven effective. The inflation rate reached 33,000% in 1988, and price controls led to serious food shortages. The Sandinistas continued to seek negotiated settlements for their internal strife.

In August 1987, Nicaragua signed the Arias peace plan for Central America. Nicaragua promised a cease-fire with the contras, a reduction in the armed forces, and amnesty for the rebels. In exchange, the Nicaraguans were to receive guarantees of nonintervention by outside powers.

The 1990 elections had a surprise winner—Violeta Chamorro, widow of a prominent newspaper publisher slain in 1978. Politically, Chamorro's situation was unstable. The Sandinistas were still in control of the military. Some former contras took to the field again, resuming their previous guerrilla tactics. Chamorro's own coalition, the National Opposition Union (UNO), proved shaky, and withdrew support from her government in 1993 after she attempted to call for new elections. The besieged government persisted, but by 1994 the outlook was bleak.

13 GOVERNMENT

The 1984 electoral reforms by the Sandinista government created an executive branch with a president elected for a six-year term by popular vote and assisted by a vice-president and a cabinet. Legislative power is vested in a 96-member single-chamber National Constituent Assembly elected under a system of proportional representation for six-year terms. In July 1982, the nation's 16 departments were consolidated into 6 regions and 3 special zones.

14 POLITICAL PARTIES

When the Sandinista government came to power in July 1979, all political parties except those favoring a return to Somoza rule were permitted. Under the junta, Nicaragua's governing political coalition was the Patriotic Front for the Revolution (Frente Patriótico para la Revolución—FPR), formed in 1980.

The National Opposition Union (UNO) coalition headed by Violeta Chamorro includes the Conservatives and the Liberals, as well as several parties formerly aligned with the Sandinistas.

15 JUDICIAL SYSTEM

The Supreme Court in Managua, whose justices are appointed by the National Assembly for six-year terms, heads the judicial branch. The judicial system consists of both civilian and military courts.

16 ARMED FORCES

In 1993, the regular armed forces, a fusion of the Sandinista and Contra armies, numbered 15,000. The army had 13,000 personnel, the navy 500, and the air force 1,200 (with 16 combat aircraft). Nicaragua spent $40 million for defense in 1992.

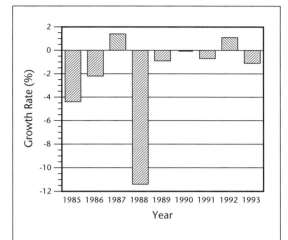

Yearly growth rate of the economy. This economic indicator tells by what percent the economy has increased or decreased when compared with the previous year.

17 ECONOMY

When President Violeta Chamorro took office in April 1990, she inherited a country in desperate economic trouble. It had the highest per-capita foreign debt in the world, and inflation was climbing uncontrollably. The Chamorro administration introduced a strict economic stabilization program and worked to reestablish private enterprise (including the return of properties confiscated during the Sandinista era).

After two years in office, the Chamorro government had successfully halted inflation, which amounted to only 3.9% in 1992, down from 13,490% in 1990 and 775% in 1991.

18 INCOME

In 1992, Nicaragua's gross national product (GNP) was $1,325 million at current

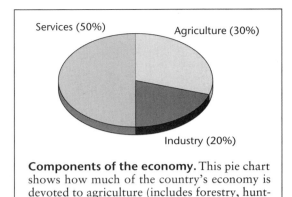

Components of the economy. This pie chart shows how much of the country's economy is devoted to agriculture (includes forestry, hunting, and fishing), industry, or services.

Child labor is outlawed by the constitution; nonetheless, it is estimated that more than 100,00 children work as much as 12 hours per day.

21 AGRICULTURE

From 1983 to 1987, the contras sought to destabilize Nicaraguan agriculture by damaging agricultural machinery, destroying crop storage sheds, and intimidating farm workers. After eight years of steady decline, agriculture grew by a modest 1% to 2% in 1992, mostly due to the largest coffee harvest since 1984.

Coffee production rose to 47,000 tons in 1991. In 1992, banana output reached 135,000 tons, cottonseed production was 36,000 tons, and 2,563,000 tons of sugar were produced, largely for export. Major food crops in that year were corn, 231,000 tons; rice, 158,000 tons; beans, 79,000 tons; and sorghum, 74,000 tons.

Sorghum, cacao, yucca, tobacco, plantains, and various other fruits and vegetables are produced on a smaller scale for the local markets

prices, or about $340 per person. For the period 1985–92 the average annual inflation rate was 2,534%, resulting in a real growth rate in per person GNP of –7.8%.

19 INDUSTRY

Nicaraguan industry expanded during the 1970s but was severely disrupted by the civil war. In 1980, the manufacturing sector began to recuperate, and modest growth continued through 1984. Manufacturing is concentrated primarily in the areas of food and tobacco processing, beverages, petroleum refining, and chemicals.

20 LABOR

In 1990, the official estimate of the total economically active population was 1,386,300, which was distributed as follows: services, 39.6%; agriculture, 30%; and industry, 16.4%. Officially, unemployment was at 14% in 1991. However, according to some estimates, more than 50% of the work force remains unemployed or underemployed.

22 DOMESTICATED ANIMALS

Nicaragua, the second largest cattle-raising country of Central America (after Honduras), had 1,673,000 head of dairy and beef cattle in 1992. There were also 172,000 horses, 700,000 hogs, and 91,000 mules and donkeys. Total meat production in 1992 was 63,000 tons. Milk production in 1992 totaled 160,000 tons; eggs production, 26,000 tons.

23 FISHING

Commercial fishing in the lakes and rivers and along the seacoasts is limited. In 1991, the total catch amounted to 5,709 tons. About 80% of the marine catch comes from the Atlantic coast.

Exports of shrimp and lobster rose to $16 million in 1991. The commercial fishing industry is trying to diversify its catch to include more red snapper, grouper, and flounder.

24 FORESTRY

About 28% of Nicaragua is still forested. The country has four distinct forest zones: deciduous hardwood, mountain pine, lowland pine, and evergreen hardwood. Nicaragua is the southernmost area of natural North American pine lands. In 1991, roundwood production totaled 4.18 million cubic meters, and sawn wood production was about 222,000 cubic meters.

25 MINING

The extent of Nicaragua's mineral resources remains largely undetermined. In the late 1970s, gold, silver, copper, lead, and zinc were being mined. Gold output in 1991 was 1,154 kilograms; silver, 1,543 kilograms.

26 FOREIGN TRADE

Nicaragua's export earnings fell by 16.4% in 1992, mainly reflecting lower prices of coffee, cotton, banana, and sugar. At the same time, the country's imports increased by 14.2% to $757 million. Petroleum imports rose by 5.2% and consumer goods imports jumped by 31.3%. At year

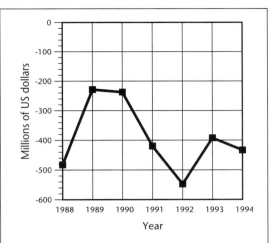

Yearly balance of trade measured in millions of US dollars. The balance of trade is the difference between what a country sells to other countries (its exports) and what it buys (its imports). If a country imports more than it exports, it has a negative balance of trade (a trade deficit). If exports exceed imports, there is a positive balance of trade (a trade surplus).

end 1992, Nicaragua's major export-trading partners were Canada, Germany, Japan, the United States, and Central American Common Market (CACM) nations. Its major import-trading partners included the United States, CACM nations, Japan, and Mexico.

27 ENERGY AND POWER

Production of electricity increased to 1,043 million kilowatt hours in 1991. In August 1983, a geothermal electrical generating plant was opened at the foot of the Momotombo volcano; its generating capacity of 70,000 kilowatts supplied about 17% of Nicaragua's electricity needs in 1991.

Selected Social Indicators

These statistics are estimates for the period 1988 to 1993. For comparison purposes, data for the United States and averages for low-income countries and high-income countries are also given.

Indicator	Nicaragua	Low-income countries	High-income countries	United States
Per capita gross national product†	**$340**	$380	$23,680	$24,740
Population growth rate	**3.8%**	1.9%	0.6%	1.0%
Population growth rate in urban areas	**4.8%**	3.9%	0.8%	1.3%
Population per square kilometer of land	**31**	78	25	26
Life expectancy in years	**67**	62	77	76
Number of people per physician	**1,492**	>3,300	453	419
Number of pupils per teacher (primary school)	**37**	39	<18	20
Illiteracy rate (15 years and older)	**13%**	41%	<5%	<3%
Energy consumed per capita (kg of oil equivalent)	**241**	364	5,203	7,918

† The gross national product (GNP) is the total dollar value of all goods and services produced by a country in a year. The per capita GNP is calculated by dividing a country's GNP by its population. The World Bank defines low-income countries as those with a per capita GNP of $695 or less. High-income countries have a per capita GNP of $8,626 or more. Less than 14% of the world's 5.5 billion people live in high-income countries, while almost 60% live in low-income countries.

> = greater than   < = less than

Sources: World Bank, *Social Indicators of Development 1995,* Baltimore: Johns Hopkins University Press, 1995. Central Intelligence Agency, *World Fact Book,* Washington, D.C.: Government Printing Office, 1994.

28 SOCIAL DEVELOPMENT

A social insurance law enacted in 1956 provides for national compulsory coverage of employees against risks of maternity, sickness, employment injury, occupational disease, unemployment, old age, and death. Family allowance legislation enacted in 1982 provides benefits for children under the age of 15.

Women tend to hold traditionally low-paid jobs in the health, education, and textile sectors while occupying few management positions in the private sector.

29 HEALTH

Slow progress in health care was made from the 1960s through the 1980s. In 1992, average life expectancy was 67 years. However, malnutrition and anemia remained common, poliomyelitis and goiter were endemic, and intestinal parasitic infections (a leading cause of death) afflicted over 80% of the population.

In 1990, there were 1.8 hospital beds per 1,000 inhabitants. In 1992, there was about one doctor for every 1,492 people, and 83% of the population had access to health care services.

Photo credit: AP/Wide World Photos

A Nicaraguan youngster clutches two handfuls of food at a market in Managua.

30 HOUSING

Both urban and rural dwellers suffer from a dire lack of adequate housing. As a result of the 1972 earthquake, approximately 53,000 residential units were destroyed or seriously damaged in the Managua area. The Sandinistas launched housing-construction programs, but were hampered by a shortage of hard currency to pay for the construction equipment required.

31 EDUCATION

The Sandinista government claimed that the adult illiteracy rate had been reduced to 13% in the 1980s; however, the Population Reference Bureau said that the illiteracy rate was 42% in 1985.

Primary and secondary education is free and compulsory between the ages of 6 and 13. In 1990, there were 632,882 pupils in 4,030 primary schools, with 19,022 teachers. There are about 37 students per teacher in primary schools. There are 168,888 students in secondary schools, with 4,865 teachers; and 30,733 students in 16 institutions of higher learning, with 2,289 teachers.

Universities include the National Autonomous University of Nicaragua with campuses in Léon and Managua, the Central American University, and the Polytechnic University of Nicaragua.

32 MEDIA

Telephone service is limited to the heavily populated west coast and, except for Managua (where there is an automatic dial system), is inadequate. In 1992 there were 45 AM radio stations, no FM stations, and 7 TV stations. In 1991, an estimated 997,000 radios and 249,000 television sets were in use. In 1991, important dailies included the *Nuevo Diario*, with 30,000 circulation, and the *Barricada*, with 38,000. *La Prensa*, a harsh critic of Somoza rule and of the Sandinista regime, had a 1991 circulation of 45,000.

33 TOURISM AND RECREATION

Nicaragua has beaches on two oceans, magnificent mountain and tropical scenery, and the two largest lakes in Central America. But a decade of military conflict slowed the development of the tourist industry. However, tourism has gained momentum since the advent of the Chamorro government. In 1991, 145,872 tourists arrived in Nicaragua, 118,312 from the Americas and 22,969 from Europe. Tourist revenues reached $17 million in that year. Baseball is the national sport. Basketball, cockfighting, bullfighting, and water sports are also popular.

34 FAMOUS NICARAGUANS

Poet and short-story writer Rubén Darío (Félix Rubén Garcia-Sarmiento, 1867–1916) created a new Spanish literary style. Santiago Arguëllo (1872–1940) was a noted poet and educator. Luis Abraham Delgadillo (1887–1961), a writer, educator, and musical conductor, was also Nicaragua's leading composer.

The Somoza family, which ruled Nicaragua from 1934 to 1979, included Anastasio Somoza (1896–1956), his eldest son, Luis Somoza Debayle (1922–67); and a younger son, Anastasio Somoza (1925–80). The Sandinistas, who overthrew the Somoza dynasty, take their name from the nationalist General Augusto César Sandino (1895–1934). José Daniel Ortega Saavedra (b.1946) emerged as the leading figure in the junta that governed Nicaragua from 1979 to 1990.

35 BIBLIOGRAPHY

Borge, Tomás, et al. *The Sandinistas Speak: Speeches and Writings of Nicaragua's Leaders.* New York: Path, 1982.

Haverstock, Nathan A. *Nicaragua in Pictures.* Minneapolis: Lerner Publications Co., 1987.

Norsworthy, Kent. *Nicaragua: A Country Guide.* 2nd ed. Albuquerque, N.M.: Inter-Hemispheric Education Resource Center, 1990.

NIGER

Republic of Niger
République du Niger

CAPITAL: Niamey.

FLAG: The flag is a tricolor of orange, white, and green horizontal stripes, with an orange circle at the center of the white stripe.

ANTHEM: *La Nigérienne.*

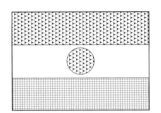

MONETARY UNIT: The Communauté Financière Africaine franc (CFA Fr) is a paper currency with one basic official rate based on the French franc (CFA Fr = 1 French franc). There are coins of 1, 2, 5, 10, 25, 50, 100, and 500 CFA francs, and notes of 50, 100, 500, 1,000, 5,000, and 10,000 CFA francs. CFA Fr1 = $0.0018 (or $1 = CFA Fr571).

WEIGHTS AND MEASURES: The metric system is the legal standard.

HOLIDAYS: New Year's Day, 1 January; Anniversary of 1974 military takeover, 15 April; Labor Day, 1 May; Independence Day, 3 August; Proclamation of the Republic, 18 December; Christmas, 25 December. Movable religious holidays include 'Id al-Fitr, 'Id al-'Adha', and Milad an-Nabi.

TIME: 1 PM = noon GMT.

1 LOCATION AND SIZE

A landlocked country, the Republic of the Niger is the largest state in West Africa, with an area of 1,267,000 square kilometers (489,191 square miles), slightly less than twice the size of the state of Texas. It has a total boundary length of 5,621 kilometers (3,492 miles). Niger's capital city, Niamey, is located in the southwestern part of the country.

2 TOPOGRAPHY

Niger is four-fifths desert, and most of the northeast is uninhabitable. The southern fifth of the country is tropical grassland, suitable mainly for livestock raising and limited agriculture. The Niger River flows for about 550 kilometers (342 miles) through southwestern Niger. A portion of

Lake Chad is located in the southeastern corner of the country.

3 CLIMATE

Niger, one of the hottest countries in the world, has three basic climatic zones: the Sahara desert in the north, the semidesert region to the south of the desert, and the Sudan in the southwest corner stretching across Niger and Chad.

The intense heat of the Saharan zone often causes the slight rainfall to evaporate before it hits the ground. At Bilma, in the east, annual rainfall is only 2 centimeters (0.79 inches). At Niamey, the average maximum daily temperature fluctuates from 31°C (88°F) in August to 41°C (106°F) in April.

4 PLANTS AND ANIMALS

The northern desert has vegetation only after rare rainfalls. The savanna, or tropical grassland, includes a vast variety of vegetation, with such trees as bastard mahogany, baobab, and the shea tree (karité). There are antelope, lion, waterbuck, leopard, hyena, monkey, warthog, and countless varieties of bird and insect life. In the Niger River are crocodiles, hippopotamuses, and sometimes manatee.

5 ENVIRONMENT

In Niger, serious reduction of vegetation has been caused by these human activities: burning of brush and grass to prepare for the planting of crops; excessive grazing; and tree cutting for fuel and construction. With Benin and Burkina Faso, Niger administers "W" National Park, of which 334,375 hectares (826,254 acres) are in Niger along the Niger River near the borders with Burkina Faso and Benin. There are also several game reserves, but as of 1994, the nation's wildlife was still endangered by unlawful hunting. Fifteen of Niger's mammal species and one of its bird species are endangered.

6 POPULATION

According to the 1988 census, the population of Niger was 7,250,383. By 1994, it had risen to an estimated 9,031,163. A population of 10,640,000 is projected for the year 2000. Only about 200,000 people live in the northern half of the country. In 1990, Niamey, the capital, had about 580,000 people.

Photo credit: Corel Corporation.
A market vendor in Agadez, Niger.

7 MIGRATION

Most of the northern area of Niger is inhabited by migratory peoples who follow their flocks and herds through the countryside. During the 1968–75 drought, many nomads migrated to urban areas in order to keep from starving, and as many as 500,000 people may have moved to Nigeria. Since 1983, many thousands have returned after being expelled by Nigeria. At the end of 1992 there were 3,400 refugees from Chad in Niger.

8 ETHNIC GROUPS

The Hausa are the largest ethnic group, forming 53% of the total population. The

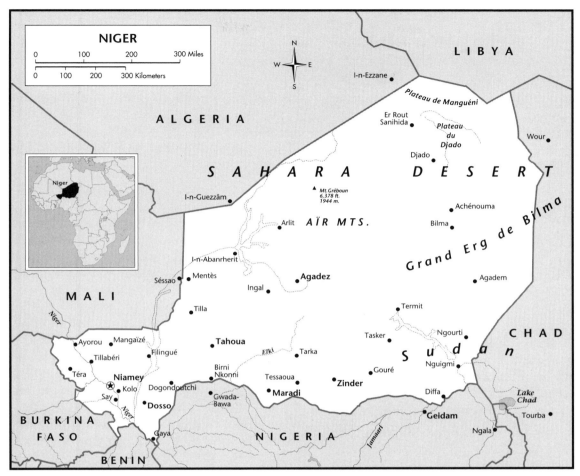

LOCATION: 12° to 23°30′N; 0°30′ to 15°30′E. **BOUNDARY LENGTHS:** Libya, 354 kilometers (220 miles); Chad, 1,175 kilometers (730 miles); Nigeria, 1,497 kilometers (930 miles); Benin, 190 kilometers (118 miles); Burkina Faso 628 kilometers (390 miles); Mali, 821 kilometers (510 miles); Algeria, 956 kilometers (594 miles).

Djerma-Songhai, the second-largest group, make up 22% of the population. Nomadic livestock-raising peoples include the Fulani, or Peul (10%), the Tuareg (10%), and the Kanuri (4%).

9 LANGUAGES

French is the official national language, but it is spoken by only a small minority of the people. The various ethnic groups use their own local languages, and Hausa is spoken all over the country as the language of trade.

10 RELIGIONS

An estimated 88% of the population is Muslim, 11.5% belongs to traditional tribal religions, and 0.5% is Christian.

[11] TRANSPORTATION

Landlocked Niger relies heavily on road and air transportation. As of 1991 there were 39,970 kilometers (24,840 miles) of roads and 36,000 registered motor vehicles. Niger's most important international transport route is by road to the rail terminus at Parakou, Benin. The international airport is at Niamey. It handled 85,000 passengers and 6,200 tons of freight in 1991.

[12] HISTORY

Archaeological evidence indicates that humans have been present in northern Niger for over 600,000 years. By at least 4000 BC, a mixed population of Libyan, Berber, and Negroid peoples had created an agricultural economy in the Sahara. Written history begins only with Arab chronicles of the tenth century AD. By the fourteenth century, the Hausa ethnic people had founded several city-states along the southern border of today's Republic of the Niger. These were taken over in about 1515 by the Songhai Empire of Gao (now in Mali), which, in turn, fell to Moroccan invaders in 1591. Probably during the seventeenth century the Djerma settled in the southwest. Bornu, Hausa, and Fulani groups competed for power during the 19th century.

Niger Under French Rule

The French entered Niger at the close of the nineteenth century and pushed steadily eastward, encircling Lake Chad with military outposts by 1900. In 1901, they established Niger as a military district, part of a larger unit known as Haut-Sénégal et Niger. After putting down a Tuareg rebellion that began during World War I (1914–18), the French made Niger a colony in 1922. It had a governor but was administered from Paris. World War II (1939–45) barely touched Niger, since the country was too isolated to be of use to the French anti-Nazi forces.

Independence

On 19 December 1958, Niger's Territorial Assembly voted to become an independent state within the French Community. On 3 August 1960, the Republic of the Niger was proclaimed, and Hamani Diori became its first president.

Diori was able to stay in power throughout the 1960s and early 1970s. However, unrest developed as Niger suffered from the drought of the early 1970s. On 15 April 1974, the Diori government was overthrown by a military takeover led by Lieutenant Colonel Seyni Kountché, the former chief of staff. Kountché then assumed the presidency. The former president was put under house arrest from 1974 to 1980. Kountché died of a brain tumor in November 1987, and Colonel 'Ali Seybou (now Brigadier General), the army chief of staff, was appointed president.

The National Movement for the Development of Society (MNSD) was created in 1989 as Niger's sole political party. Since then, however, there have been demands for multiparty democracy. The president agreed to the calling of a National Conference (July–October 1991) to prepare a new constitution. An interim government, headed by Amadou Cheiffou, was appointed. After the adoption of the new constitution in December 1992, a series of elections were held. In the elections, Mahamane Ousmane was elected president with 54% of the vote.

The new government has attempted to control a Tuareg rebellion in the north. It accuses Libya of encouraging the Tuaregs. Others accuse the Niger government of showing favoritism for members of the Zarma (or Djerma), one of the five major ethnic groups in Niger. High level talks, under the joint mediation of Algeria, Burkina Faso, and France, were resumed in February 1994.

13 GOVERNMENT

A national conference from July to October 1991 drafted a new, multiparty democratic constitution that was approved on 26 December 1992. It established the Third Republic with a National Assembly of 83 deputies chosen by popular and competitive elections, a president likewise elected, and a prime minister elected by the Assembly. The new government was sworn in on 23 April 1993.

14 POLITICAL PARTIES

After the constitutional referendum of December 1992 introduced multiparty democracy, several new parties were formed.

Although the National Movement for the Development of Society (MNSD) is the largest party in the legislature (29 of 83 seats), it did not form the government. A coalition of nine parties known as the Alli-

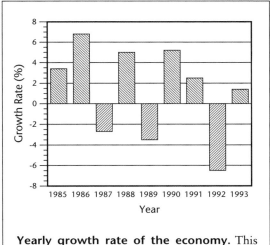

Yearly growth rate of the economy. This economic indicator tells by what percent the economy has increased or decreased when compared with the previous year.

ance of the Forces of Change (AFC) now controls the National Assembly and the presidency.

AFC members include the Social Democratic Convention (CDS); the Nigerien Party for Democracy and Socialism (PNDS); the Nigerien Alliance for Democracy and Progress (ANDP); and the Nigerien Progressive Party-Reunion for Democracy in Africa (PPN-RDA).

15 JUDICIAL SYSTEM

The 1992 constitution calls for an independent judiciary. The Supreme Court is now the final court of appeals. Special courts deal with civil service corruption. There are also magistrates' courts, eight labor courts, and justices of the peace in 19 administrative districts. Traditional and customary courts hear cases involving divorce or inheritance. Customary courts are presided over by a legal practitioner with basic legal training who is advised about local tradition by a local official.

16 ARMED FORCES

Niger's army numbered 3,200 in 1993. There were 100 personnel in the air force. France provides military advisers and is the chief source of military equipment. Niger spends $27 million on defense (1989).

17 ECONOMY

Niger is a dry, landlocked country with much of its territory located in the Sahara desert. The economy depends mainly on uranium mining, foreign aid, livestock raising, and farming. Oil and gold may contribute to the economy by the middle of the 1990s.

18 INCOME

In 1992 Niger's gross national product (GNP) was $2,466 million at current prices, or $270 per person. For the period 1985–92 the average inflation rate was −1.6%, resulting in a real growth rate in GNP of −1.5% per person.

19 INDUSTRY

Manufacturing consists mainly of the processing of agricultural products and includes a groundnut (edible root) oil plant, rice mills, flour mills, cotton gins, and tanneries. A textile mill and cement plant are in operation, and light industries produce beer and soft drinks, processed meats, baked goods, soaps and detergents,

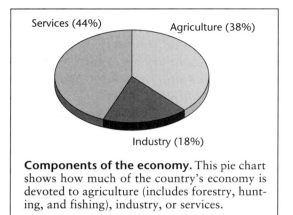

Components of the economy. This pie chart shows how much of the country's economy is devoted to agriculture (includes forestry, hunting, and fishing), industry, or services.

perfume, plastic and metal goods, farm equipment, and construction materials.

20 LABOR

About 90% of the population in 1990 was engaged in agriculture and livestock raising. About 60,000 people earned salaries in 1992. Those in government service numbered 24,131 in 1991, mostly in public utilities (18.4%) and social services (16.6%). The Union of Workers' Syndicates of Niger (Union des Syndicats des Travailleurs du Niger—USTN) is the only trade union.

The law allows children to work in nonindustrial jobs under certain conditions. Children under the age of 14 must obtain a work permit, and those aged 14 to 18 may work no more than 4.5 hours per day. The law requires employers to maintain basic minimum sanitary conditions for child workers and women. In the formal business sector, child labor is practically nonexistent, but many children

Camels for sale at a market in Niger.

work on family farms or businesses, or can be found begging on urban streets.

21 AGRICULTURE

The most plentiful rains in 30 years fell during the 1992–93 season, pushing agricultural production up by 64%. Over 90% of the active population is engaged in some form of agriculture. However, farming techniques in Niger are still old-fashioned.

In 1992, millet production was 1,784,000 tons, sorghum was 393,000 tons, and rice was 70,000 tons. Other crops (with their estimated output) include cassava (218,000 tons), sugarcane (140,000 tons), onions (170,000 tons), and sweet potatoes and yams (35,000 tons). Peanut production was reported at 40,000 tons and seed cotton at 2,000 tons.

22 DOMESTICATED ANIMALS

In 1992, there were an estimated 1,800,000 head of cattle, 8,800,000 sheep and goats, and 363,000 camels. Meat production, which had dropped to 38,000 tons in 1973, was an estimated 110,000 tons in 1992. Production of milk from goats and cows came to 87,000 and 152,000 tons, respectively. Cattle hides came to about 4,360 tons in 1992; sheepskins, 1,500 tons; and goatskins, 3,340 tons.

23 FISHING

Most of the total annual catch of 3,150 tons in 1991 was from the Niger River and its tributaries. A small amount is from the Lake Chad region.

24 FORESTRY

Roundwood production was estimated at 5,116,000 cubic meters in 1991, almost all for fuel. Small amounts of gum arabic used in the manufacture of inks, adhesives, and other products, are extracted from acacia trees. Some tree planting has been undertaken, mainly with acacia species, but deforestation remains a serious problem.

25 MINING

Niger ranked seventh in the world in uranium production in 1991. The country has proven reserves, at several sites, estimated at 360,000 tons, the fifth largest uranium reserves in the world. Two mines produced 3,330 tons of uranium in 1991. Salt production was about 3,000 tons in 1991. Cassiterite (tin ore) is mined near Agadez. Cassiterite production was 20 tons in 1991. About 1,000 tons of phosphates were produced in 1985.

26 FOREIGN TRADE

Trade figures show that uranium accounts for 78.9% of exports by value. Exports of live animals and hides represent 13.8% of exports. Imports are led by cereal grains (23.3%) and miscellaneous manufactured goods (18.2%). France takes the majority of Niger's exports, followed by Nigeria. Of Niger's imports, 30% come from France, and 11% from the United States.

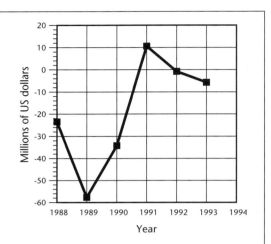

Yearly balance of trade measured in millions of US dollars. The balance of trade is the difference between what a country sells to other countries (its exports) and what it buys (its imports). If a country imports more than it exports, it has a negative balance of trade (a trade deficit). If exports exceed imports, there is a positive balance of trade (a trade surplus).

27 ENERGY AND POWER

Niger depends on petroleum imports for most of its production of electrical energy. Coal production was 156,542 tons in 1991. In 1991, 168 million kilowatt hours of electricity was produced, while an estimated 188 million kilowatt hours was imported from Nigeria.

28 SOCIAL DEVELOPMENT

The National Fund of Social Security provides pensions, family allowances, and workers' compensation for employees in the private sector. Civil servants participate in a national insurance fund and also receive family allowances.

Selected Social Indicators

These statistics are estimates for the period 1988 to 1993. For comparison purposes, data for the United States and averages for low-income countries and high-income countries, are also given.

Indicator	Niger	Low-income countries	High-income countries	United States
Per capita gross national product†	**$270**	$380	$23,680	$24,740
Population growth rate	**3.3%**	1.9%	0.6%	1.0%
Population growth rate in urban areas	**5.6%**	3.9%	0.8%	1.3%
Population per square kilometer of land	**7**	78	25	26
Life expectancy in years	**47**	62	77	76
Number of people per physician	**35,141**	>3,300	453	419
Number of pupils per teacher (primary school)	**38**	39	<18	20
Illiteracy rate (15 years and older)	**72%**	41%	<5%	<3%
Energy consumed per capita (kg of oil equivalent)	**38**	364	5,203	7,918

† The gross national product (GNP) is the total dollar value of all goods and services produced by a country in a year. The per capita GNP is calculated by dividing a country's GNP by its population. The World Bank defines low-income countries as those with a per capita GNP of $695 or less. High-income countries have a per capita GNP of $8,626 or more. Less than 14% of the world's 5.5 billion people live in high-income countries, while almost 60% live in low-income countries.

> = greater than   < = less than

Sources: World Bank, *Social Indicators of Development 1995*, Baltimore: Johns Hopkins University Press, 1995. Central Intelligence Agency, *World Fact Book*, Washington, D.C.: Government Printing Office, 1994.

29 HEALTH

In 1992, there were about 3 physicians per 100,000 people. There were 38 medical centers throughout the country. Health care expenditures in 1990 were $126 million. Only 41% of the population had access to health care services in 1992, and the average life expectancy was 47 years.

30 HOUSING

Most government buildings and many houses in the metropolitan centers are essentially French in style. The Tuareg nomads live in covered tents, while the Fulani live in small collapsible huts made of straw mats.

31 EDUCATION

The adult literacy rate stood at 28% in 1990 (males: 40.4% and females: 16.8%). Schooling is compulsory for children aged 7–15. In 1990, there were 2,807 primary schools with 9,703 teachers and 368,732 pupils. On average, there are 38 primary students per teacher. In 1990, there were 76,758 pupils in secondary schools. In 1989, 4,506 students were enrolled in higher institutions, including the National School of Admin-

Photo credit: Corel Corporation.

Nigerien children at market.

istration in Niamey, the University of Niamey, and the Islamic University of West Africa at Say.

32 MEDIA

The Voice of the Sahel and Télé-Sahel, the government's radio and television broadcasting units broadcast in French, Djerma, Hausa, and several other languages. There were an estimated 480,000 radios and 37,000 television sets in 1991, and there were 11,824 telephones in use. Major publications include the daily *Le Sahel*, with a circulation of about 5,000, and the

weekly *Sahel Dimanche*. A monthly, the *Journal Officiel de la République du Niger,* is also published. All are government publications.

33 TOURISM AND RECREATION

The "W" National Park along the Niger River offers views of a variety of fauna, including lions and elephants. Other tourist attractions include Agadez's 16th-century mosque, one of the oldest in West Africa; villages built on piles in Lake Chad; the annual six-week gathering of nomads near Ingal; the Great Market and Great Mosque in Niamey, and the Sahara desert.

There were about 16,000 tourist arrivals in 1991, 43% from Africa and 42% from Europe. Tourist receipts were estimated at $16 million. There were 1,524 hotel rooms with a 33% occupancy rate. Nigeriens engage in fishing, swimming, and a variety of team sports.

34 FAMOUS NIGERIENS

Hamani Diori (b.1916) was president of the Republic of the Niger until April 1974, when he was deposed by a military takeover. Seyni Kountché (1931–87) became head of state after the takeover of 1974 and ruled the country until his death.

35 BIBLIOGRAPHY

Fugelstad, F. *A History of Niger, 1850–1960*. London: Oxford University Press, 1984.
Miles, William F. S. *Hausaland Divided: Colonialism and Independence in Nigeria and Niger*. Ithaca: Cornell University Press, 1994.

NIGERIA

Federal Republic of Nigeria

Nigeria

CAPITAL: Abuja

FLAG: The national flag consists of three vertical stripes. The green outer stripes represent Nigerian agriculture. The white center stripe represents unity and peace.

ANTHEM: *Arise, All Compatriots.*

MONETARY UNIT: On 1 January 1973, the Nigerian pound (N£) was replaced by the naira (N) of 100 kobo at a rate of N2 = N£1. There are coins of ½, 1, 5, 10, 25, and 50 kobo and 1 naira, and notes of 5, 10, 20, and 50 naira. N1 = $0.24 (or $1 = N4.141).

WEIGHTS AND MEASURES: As of May 1975, the metric system is the official standard, replacing the imperial measures.

HOLIDAYS: New Year's Day, 1 January; National Day, 1 October; Christmas, 25 December; Boxing Day, 26 December. Movable Christian religious holidays include Good Friday and Easter Monday; movable Muslim religious holidays include 'Id al-Fitr, 'Id al-'Adha', and Milad an-Nabi.

TIME: 1 PM = noon GMT.

1 LOCATION AND SIZE

Located at the extreme inner corner of the Gulf of Guinea on the west coast of Africa, Nigeria occupies an area of 923,770 square kilometers (356,670 square miles), slightly more than twice the size of the state of California. It has a total boundary length of 4,900 kilometers (3,045 miles). Nigeria's capital city, Abuja, is located in the center of the country.

2 TOPOGRAPHY

Along the entire coastline of Nigeria lies a belt of mangrove swamp forest. (Mangroves are tropical shrubs or trees that send out many roots.) Beyond the swamp forest lies a zone of tropical rainforest. The country then rises to a plateau known as the Jos Plateau, with a maximum elevation of 2,042 meters (6,700 feet). The Niger River, the third-largest river of Africa, enters Nigeria from the northwest running in a southeasterly direction and then flowing south to the Gulf of Guinea.

3 CLIMATE

Although Nigeria lies completely within the tropical zone, its climate varies widely. Near the coast, temperatures rarely exceed 32°C (90°F). Inland, during the dry season (November to March) midday temperatures exceed 38°C (100°F). Average rainfall varies from around 130 centimeters (50 inches) over most of central Nigeria to about 430 centimeters (170 inches) in certain parts of the east. Two principal wind currents affect Nigeria: the southwest

Photo credit: Corel Corporation.

A baobob tree located in northern Nigeria near Gumel.

wind, and the harmattan, a hot, dry wind from the northeast that carries a reddish dust from the desert and causes high temperatures during the day.

4 PLANTS AND ANIMALS

Along the coast, there are mainly mangrove trees (trees that send out a dense root system), while immediately inland is freshwater swamp forest, which is somewhat more varied and includes palms and mahogany. North of the swamp forest lies the rain forest, whose trees reach as much as 60 meters (200 feet) in height. Important trees include the African mahogany, iroko, African walnut, and the most popular export wood, the obeche.

Few large animals are found in the rain forest, although gorillas and chimpanzees in decreasing numbers are present, as well as baboons and monkeys. Reptiles abound, including crocodiles, lizards, and snakes of many species. Nigeria possesses two dozen species of antelope, but they are rarely seen in large numbers. The hippopotamus, elephant, giraffe, leopard, and lion now remain only in a few locations and in decreasing numbers. Wildcats, however, are more common and widely distributed. Nigeria is rich in bird life, a great number of species being represented.

5 ENVIRONMENT

In 1992, United Nations reports identified soil erosion as Nigeria's most pressing environmental concern. The amount of timber cut has been greater than the number of trees replanted. By 1985, deforestation claimed 1,544 square miles of the nation's forest land, an average of 5% per year.

Oil spills, the burning of toxic wastes, and urban air pollution are problems in more developed areas. Water pollution is also a problem due to improper handling of sewage. In 1994, twenty-five of Nigeria's mammal species were threatened. Ten types of birds and nine plant species are also endangered.

6 POPULATION

Nigeria is the most populous nation in Africa. The 1991 census reported a total of 88,514,501 people. There are about

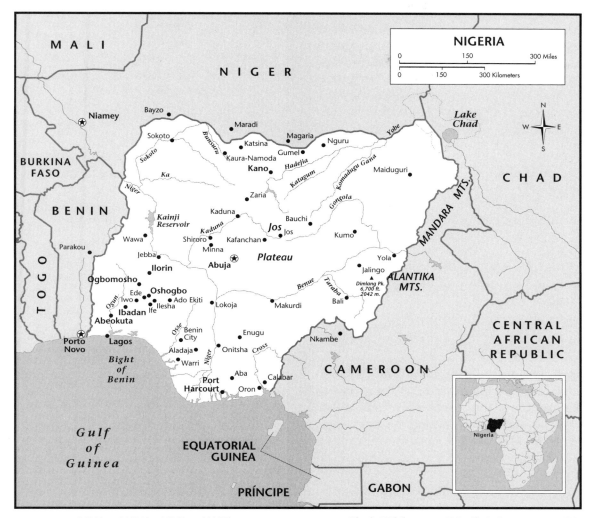

LOCATION: 2°30′ to 14°30′E; 4°30′ to 14°17′N. **BOUNDARY LENGTHS:** Chad, 87 kilometers (55 miles); Cameroon, 1,690 kilometers (1,050 miles); Atlantic coastline, 853 kilometers (530 miles); Benin, 773 kilometers (480 miles); Niger, 1,497 kilometers (930 miles). **TERRITORIAL SEA LIMIT:** 30 miles.

110 people per square kilometer (285 per square mile). The United States Census Bureau's estimate for 1995 was 101,232,251. The United Nations projected a population of 147,709,000 for the year 2000. Lagos, the former capital and still the largest city, had a population of 7,998,000 in 1991 and the highest population density of any major African city.

7 MIGRATION

Immigrants are drawn from neighboring nations by economic opportunity. In the 1980s, Nigeria expelled nearly 1 million resident aliens, most from Ghana. These aliens were straining Nigeria's economy. There were small numbers of refugees at the end of 1992, including 2,900 Liberians and 1,400 Chadians.

8 ETHNIC GROUPS

The main racial group is West African Negroid. Non-Negroid peoples include the Fulani (Fulbe), of Mediterranean descent, and the Semitic Shuwa Arabs.

The main ethnic groups, distinguished by different languages, are the Yoruba, the Ibo (Igbo), the Hausa, and the Fulani. The Hausa have been officially estimated to constitute 21% of the population; Yoruba, 20%; Ibo, 16.1%; and Fulani, 12%.

9 LANGUAGES

The official language is English, although there are over 300 distinct native tongues. Hausa and Yoruba are widely used.

10 RELIGIONS

The northern states are mostly Muslim. The southern states are predominantly Christian. According to 1993 estimates, about 48% of the total population is Muslim, and 34% Christian; 10% belonged to traditional African religions.

11 TRANSPORTATION

Lagos remains Nigeria's principal port, handling more than 75% of the country's general cargo. The Nigerian National Shipping Line operated a fleet of 28 ships of 418,000 gross tons between West Africa and Europe in 1991. The Nigerian

Photo credit: Corel Corporation.

Cleaning grain, Gumel, northern Nigeria.

railway system consists of 3,510 kilometers (2,181 miles) of single track, and is the fifth largest in Africa. Nigeria in 1991 had about 120,000 kilometers (74,570 miles) of roads. In 1991, 1.4 million vehicles were registered, including 785,000 passenger cars.

Air traffic has been growing steadily. International service is provided from Lagos, Port Harcourt, and Kano airports by more than two dozen international airlines. In 1991, 555,700 domestic passengers and 374,300 international passengers were carried.

12 HISTORY

Archaeological evidence shows that an Iron Age culture was present in the area that is now Nigeria sometime between 500 BC and AD 200. Agriculture and livestock raising probably existed long before then. About the eleventh century AD, Yoruba city-states developed in western Nigeria. Islamic influence was firmly established by the end of the fifteenth century. Until the arrival of the British, northern Nigeria was economically oriented toward the north and east, and woven cloth and leatherwork were exported as far as the Mediterranean.

European Influence

In the fifteenth century, the Portuguese were the first Europeans to establish close relations with the coastal people. Their trade monopoly was broken after a century by other European nations participating in the growing slave trade, which was abolished by the British in 1807.

In 1861, the British took control of the island of Lagos, an important center of palm oil trade, and afterward they gradually extended their influence over the nearby mainland of Yorubaland. In 1887, the British established the Oil Rivers Protectorate, which was gradually extended inland and became the Niger Coast Protectorate in 1894. British rule over northern Nigeria was confirmed by the establishment of the Protectorate of Northern Nigeria in 1900.

Although supposedly unified, the separate regions of Nigeria—North, East, and West—were administered separately under the British colonial system known as indirect rule.

Independence

After World War II (1939–45), increasing pressures for self-government resulted in a series of short-lived constitutions. On 1 October 1960, Nigeria became a fully independent member of the British Commonwealth, and on 1 October 1963 it became a republic. Nnamdi Azikiwe was elected the first president of the Federal Republic of Nigeria.

Disagreements between regions led to a military takeover on 15 January 1966 and another takeover later that year which brought Lieutenant Colonel Yakubu Gowon to power as head of the military government. On 28 May 1967, Colonel Gowon assumed emergency powers as head of the Federal Military Government and announced changes in state borders throughout the country.

Rejecting the new arrangement, Eastern Region leaders announced on 30 May the independent Republic of Biafra. On 6 July, the federal government declared war on the new republic. By the time the war ended, on 12 January 1970, Biafra had been reduced to about one-tenth of its original area of 78,000 square kilometers (30,000 square miles), and a million or more persons had perished, many of disease and starvation.

In 1970, with the civil war ended, General Gowon promised a return to civilian rule, but then postponed it indefinitely. This helped lead to his overthrow on 29 July 1975. His successor, Brigadier Mur-

A common dugout canoe on the Niger River.

tala Ramat Muhammad, strongly pursued government reform but was assassinated in the course of a failed rebellion. He was replaced as head of the government by the former chief of staff of the armed forces, Lieutenant General Olusegun Obasanjo. In March 1976, Obasanjo established a 19-state federation. Political party activity was again permitted, and a new constitution took effect on 1 October 1979 and Alhaji Shehu Shagari became president. In August 1983, Shagari won reelection to a second term as president. In late December, however, he was removed from office in a military takeover.

The new military government, led by Major General Muhammadu Buhari, attracted growing public dissatisfaction and another takeover on 27 August 1985 brought Major General Ibrahim Badamasi Babangida to power. He assumed the title of president. Babangida promised a return to full civilian rule by 1992, local elections on a nonparty basis, the creation of a governing assembly, the establishment of no more than two political parties, state elections, a national census, and finally presidential elections.

Civil Unrest

The change from military rule to a democratic civilian Third Republic was scheduled to be completed in 1992, but was blocked by crisis after crisis. Clashes between Muslims and Christians in 1991 and 1992 spread through northern cities. Hundreds were killed in the rioting and by the army seeking to control the riots.

Nonetheless, by January 1992, Nigerians geared up for the national presidential and legislative elections scheduled for later in the year. On 20 May 1992, the government banned all political, religious, and ethnic organizations other than the two approved political parties. Legislative elections were conducted on 4 July, but the ruling military council would not allow the people elected to the legislature to take office. Presidential elections were to follow, but again the military stood in the way. Political violence and charges of election fraud followed. In response, the military banned all 23 of the presidential candidates from future political competition.

The presidential election finally took place in 1993 amid controversy and great voter confusion. Chief M.K.O. Abiola apparently defeated his nearest rival 58.4% to 41.6%. But the military annulled the election a week later because of supposed irregularities, poor turnout, and legal complications.

Abiola, backed largely by the Yoruba people, demanded to be certified as president-elect. Civil unrest, especially in Lagos, followed. However, the military would not give up power. Under its latest strongman, Gereral Sani Abacha, the corrupt military government has crippled the Nigerian economy and driven the country into debt.

13 GOVERNMENT

The 1979 constitution established a federal system resembling that of the United States, with a directly elected president and vice-president and separate executive, legislative, and judicial branches. The military government that took command after the December 1983 takeover suspended the 1979 constitution, and it was still suspended after Abacha seized power on 17 November 1993. A military-dominated Provisional Ruling Council (PRC) rules by decree, and a 32-member Federal Executive Council manages government departments.

14 POLITICAL PARTIES

All existing political parties were dissolved after the December 1983 takeover, and two parties were permitted: a right-of-center National Republican Convention (NRC) and a left-of-center Social Democratic Party (SDP). In November 1993, the new military rulers suspended all party and political activity.

15 JUDICIAL SYSTEM

The Supreme Court, its members appointed by the president, is the highest court in Nigeria. It hears appeals from the Federal Court of Appeals, which in turn hears appeals from the Federal High Court and state high courts. The Supreme Court also has original jurisdiction over constitutional disputes between the federal government and the states or between states. Customary and area courts exist to administer local laws and customs. In the northern states, Muslim law (Shari'ah) is

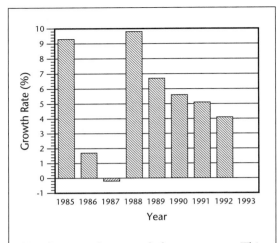

Yearly growth rate of the economy. This economic indicator tells by what percent the economy has increased or decreased when compared with the previous year.

for economic growth. However, poor economic policy, political instability, and too much reliance on oil exports have created severe problems in the economy. A crippling blow to the economy came in mid-1994 when oil workers in the southeast went on strike. With daily crude oil output down 25% because of the strike, the government's lack of income forced it to stop paying most of its $28 billion external debt. Fuel has become scarce. Agriculture remains the basic economic activity for the great majority of Nigerians.

administered in most courts. Decisions can be appealed to state courts.

16 ARMED FORCES

The Nigerian armed forces are the largest in sub-Saharan Africa after South Africa, with 76,000 members in 1993. The army, with 62,000 members was divided into 10 brigades. The navy, with a total strength of 4,500, possessed two warships, and 51 smaller craft. The air force, composed of 9,500 members, had 95 combat aircraft. Nigeria contributes about 5,000 troops to seven different peacekeeping operations, the majority in Liberia. Nigeria spent $300 million on defense in 1990.

17 ECONOMY

The Nigerian economy, with a wealth of natural resources, offers great potential

18 INCOME

In 1992 Nigeria's gross national product (GNP) was $32,944 million at current prices, or about $300 per person. For the period 1985–92 the average inflation rate was 28%, resulting in a real growth rate in GNP of 3.4% per person.

19 INDUSTRY

The textile industry has shown the greatest growth since independence, and the country is practically self-sufficient in printed fabrics, blankets, and towels. Other areas of expansion include cement production (3,500,000 tons in 1990), tire production, and furniture assembly. Other important industries include sawmills; cigarette factories; breweries; sugar refining; rubber, paper, soap, and detergent factories; footwear factories; pharmaceutical plants; tire factories; paint factories; and assembly plants for radios, record players, and television sets. Nigeria has six state-owned motor-vehicle assembly plants for Volkswagen, Peugeot, and Mercedes products.

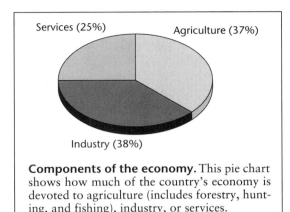

Components of the economy. This pie chart shows how much of the country's economy is devoted to agriculture (includes forestry, hunting, and fishing), industry, or services.

20 LABOR

The total labor force in Nigeria was 30.6 million in 1992, and civilian employment amounted to 8.4 million. The unemployment rate was officially estimated at 4.2%, but that amount is believed to be greatly underestimated. Of those employed, 71% are in agriculture, with about 15% in manufacturing and about 13% in services. As of 1992, the minimum wage was equivalent to approximately $26 per month.

The minimum age for employment in commerce and industry is 15. Children under that age may work at home-based agricultural or domestic work for no more than eight hours per day. In some cases, children aged 13 to 15 may be employed as apprentices. Although primary education is compulsory, the law is rarely enforced, and many children work instead of attending school. It is believed that child labor is on the increase in Nigeria, especially in the nonunionized, unregulated sector. The Nigerian government and the United Nations are working together to devise ways of solving this problem.

21 AGRICULTURE

In terms of employment, agriculture is by far the most important sector of Nigeria's economy. About 32 million hectares (79 million acres), or 36% of Nigeria's land area, were under cultivation in 1991. The agricultural products of Nigeria can be divided into two main groups: food crops, produced for home consumption, and export products. The most important food crops are yams and manioc (cassava) in the south and sorghum (Guinea corn) and millet in the north. In 1992, production of yams was 20 million tons; manioc, 20 million tons; sorghum, 4.1 million tons; and millet, 3.2 million tons. Other crops were cocoyams and sweet potatoes, 1.5 million tons; maize, 1.7 million tons; and bananas and plantains, 1.3 million tons. Rice, grown in several areas, yielded over 3.4 million tons. Production of peanuts (unshelled) was 1,214,000 tons (highest in Africa), and of raw sugar 75,000 tons.

Production of nonfood crops in 1992 included palm oil, 900,000 tons; palm kernels, 385,000 tons; cocoa beans, 130,000 tons; rubber, 110,000 tons; and cotton, 63,000 tons. Uneven rains and fertilizer shortages caused below average harvests of most staple and cash crops in 1992.

22 DOMESTICATED ANIMALS

In 1992 there were an estimated 15,700,000 head of cattle in Nigeria, over 90% of them in the north, owned mostly by nomadic Fulani. There were also an

Photo credit: Corel Corporation.

A young Nigerian farmer.

estimated 24 million goats, 13,500,000 sheep, 1,205,000 horses and donkeys, 5,328,000 pigs, and 160 million chickens. In 1992, 837,000 tons of meat and 370,000 tons of cow's milk were produced. An estimated 13.8 million sheep and goats and 2.57 million head of cattle were slaughtered in 1992.

23 FISHING

Fishing is carried on in Nigeria's many rivers, creeks, and lagoons, and in Lake Chad. Fishing boats also operate along the coast. The total fishing catch was 266,552 tons in 1991, not enough to meet national requirements. Fish ponds have been established in the southern part of the country.

24 FORESTRY

About 13% of Nigeria, or roughly 11,600 hectares (28,664,000 acres) is classified as forest or woodland. In 1991, 111,059,000 cubic meters of roundwood were produced, over 92% for fuel. However, the country suffers from weak reforestation efforts and high levels of wood consumption. Increasing amounts of land are turning to desert, in a process known as desertification.

25 MINING

Nigeria produced more than 246 tons of tin concentrates in 1991. In that year, production of columbite totaled 36 tons. Nigeria is the only West African producer of coal. Output in 1991 was 138,000 tons. Total reserves were estimated at 1.5 billion tons in 1991. Nigeria has plentiful supplies of limestone, and its production totaled 1,436,000 tons in 1991. Extensive iron deposits include reserves of 2.5 billion tons with an average content of 37%.

26 FOREIGN TRADE

In 1992, petroleum accounted for 97.9% of export income. Cocoa was the largest agricultural export. Primary imports (1987) are machinery and manufactured goods (38.2%), basic manufactures (25.1%), chemicals (16.9%), and food (10.5%).

In 1987, the United States (47%) was Nigeria's largest export market (principally for petroleum), followed by the Netherlands (11.3%), Spain (7.9%), and

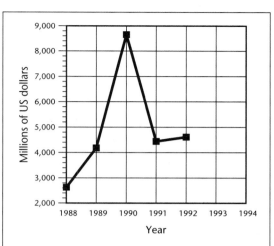

Yearly balance of trade measured in millions of US dollars. The balance of trade is the difference between what a country sells to other countries (its exports) and what it buys (its imports). If a country imports more than it exports, it has a negative balance of trade (a trade deficit). If exports exceed imports, there is a positive balance of trade (a trade surplus).

France (7.2%). The United Kingdom remained Nigeria's largest supplier of imports (16.8%), followed by Germany (13.4%), France (10.0%), Japan (9.0%), and the United States (8.3%).

27 ENERGY AND POWER

Coal has been replaced as the chief source of Nigeria's electric power by oil, natural gas, and newly developed hydroelectric facilities. Hydroelectric production accounted for 22% of total power generation during 1991, thermal for the rest, almost entirely with oil or gas for fuel. Electricity produced totaled an estimated 9,955 million kilowatt hours. Oil has become important in the Nigerian economy, with Nigeria the largest producer in Africa. Production in 1992 was 91.6 million tons, or an average of 1,850,000 barrels per day, down 2.1% from 1991. In 1992, Nigeria produced 4.9 billion cubic meters of natural gas. Gas reserves were estimated at 3.4 trillion cubic meters.

28 SOCIAL DEVELOPMENT

There are two kinds of welfare services in Nigeria—those provided by voluntary agencies and those provided by the government. Workers are protected under the Labor Code Act (1958) and the Workmen's Compensation Act, which provides protection for workers in case of industrial accidents. Most companies also provide pension plans for their employees. Despite recent gains in the workplace, women have only a minor role in politics.

29 HEALTH

According to 1992 data, primary care is largely provided through approximately 4,000 health clinics scattered throughout the country. There are 12 university teaching hospitals with about 6,500 beds. There is one doctor for every 5,191 people. Two-thirds of the population had access to health care services.

Malaria and tuberculosis are the most common diseases, but serious outbreaks of cerebrospinal meningitis still occur in the north. Just under half of all deaths are thought to be among children, who are especially vulnerable to malaria and account for 75% of registered malaria deaths. Schistosomiasis, Guinea worm, trachoma, river blindness, and yaws are also widespread. Progress, however, has

Selected Social Indicators

These statistics are estimates for the period 1988 to 1993. For comparison purposes, data for the United States and averages for low-income countries and high-income countries are also given.

Indicator	Nigeria	Low-income countries	High-income countries	United States
Per capita gross national product†	$300	$380	$23,680	$24,740
Population growth rate	3.1%	1.9%	0.6%	1.0%
Population growth rate in urban areas	5.3%	3.9%	0.8%	1.3%
Population per square kilometer of land	110	78	25	26
Life expectancy in years	51	62	77	76
Number of people per physician	5,191	>3,300	453	419
Number of pupils per teacher (primary school)	39	39	<18	20
Illiteracy rate (15 years and older)	49%	41%	<5%	<3%
Energy consumed per capita (kg of oil equivalent)	141	364	5,203	7,918

† The gross national product (GNP) is the total dollar value of all goods and services produced by a country in a year. The per capita GNP is calculated by dividing a country's GNP by its population. The World Bank defines low-income countries as those with a per capita GNP of $695 or less. High-income countries have a per capita GNP of $8,626 or more. Less than 14% of the world's 5.5 billion people live in high-income countries, while almost 60% live in low-income countries.

> = greater than   < = less than

Sources: World Bank, *Social Indicators of Development 1995,* Baltimore: Johns Hopkins University Press, 1995. Central Intelligence Agency, *World Fact Book,* Washington, D.C.: Government Printing Office, 1994.

been made in the treatment of sleeping sickness (trypanosomiasis) and leprosy.

30 HOUSING

Housing generally has not ranked high on the scale of priorities for social spending, and state governments have tended to rely upon local authorities to meet the problem. Efforts at providing low-cost rural housing have been slight, despite the creation of the Federal Mortgage Bank of Nigeria in 1977, and shantytowns and slums are common in urban areas. The total number of housing units in 1992 was 25,661,000.

31 EDUCATION

The first six years of primary education were made compulsory in 1976. Recent years have seen a marked growth in educational facilities, but the overall adult literacy rate for the country was only about 49% (males, 62.3% and females, 39.5%) in 1990.

Primary education begins in the local language but introduces English in the third year. In 1991 there were 13,776,854 students in 35,446 primary schools, with about 39 students per teacher. Secondary schools had 3,123,277 students and 141,491 teachers. Technical education is provided by technical institutes, trade centers, and handicraft centers.

There are also 13 polytechnic colleges and four colleges of technology. In 1989, all higher level institutions combined had 19,601 teaching staff and 335,824 pupils.

32 MEDIA

In 1991 there were 31 daily newspapers in Nigeria, some of them published by the federal or state governments. Leading Nigerian daily newspapers (with their 1991 estimated circulations) are the *Daily Times* (300,000), the *Concord* (200,000), and the *Guardian* (150,000), all published in Lagos.

In 1991 there were 259,626 telephones in service. There are post offices in all 305 local-government headquarters and other major towns. Operating under the Federal Radio Corp. of Nigeria, created in 1978, state radio stations broadcast in English and local languages. Television, introduced in 1959, now operates throughout the country. There is no private radio or television service. In 1991, the country had 19,350,000 radios and 3,650,000 television sets.

33 TOURISM AND RECREATION

There are five-star hotels in Lagos, Abuja, and Kaduna, and first-class hotels in all the state capitals, with occupancy rates in quality hotels at 80%. Sports and social clubs offer facilities for swimming, sailing, tennis, squash, golf, and polo. In 1990, 190,000 foreign tourists visited Nigeria.

34 FAMOUS NIGERIANS

Famous Nigerians of the nineteenth century include 'Uthman dan Fodio (d.1817), who founded the Fulani empire at the beginning of the century, and Samuel Ajayi Crowther (1809–92), a Yoruba missionary of the Church of England who was consecrated first bishop of the Niger Territories in 1864.

The Palm Wine Drinkard and other stories by Amos Tutuola (b.1920) exploit the rich resources of traditional Nigerian folk tales. Benedict Chuka Enwonu (b.1921), Nigeria's leading painter and sculptor, has gained international fame, as has Wole Soyinka (b.1934), a prominent playwright who was awarded the 1986 Nobel Prize for Literature, the first African so honored. Novelists of note include Chinua Achebe (b.1930) and Cyprian Ekwensi (b.1921). Sports figures include Dick Tiger (1929–71), twice world middleweight champion and once light-heavyweight champion.

Herbert Macaulay (1864–1946) is regarded as the father of Nigerian nationalism. Among contemporary political figures, Dr. (Benjamin) Nnamdi Azikiwe (b.1904) was a founder of the NCNC and first governor-general and president of independent Nigeria. Major General Yakubu Gowon (b.1934) headed the Federal Military Government from July 1966 to July 1975, when he was deposed in a bloodless takeover. Alhaji Shehu Shagari (b.1925) was elected president in 1979. Reelected in 1983, he was deposed in a military takeover from which Major General Muhammadu Buhari (b.1942) emerged as head of state, but was removed from office in 1985 by Major General Ibrahim Badamasi Babangida (b.1940 or 1941), who took over the presidency.

35 BIBLIOGRAPHY

Forrest, Tom. *Politics and Economic Development in Nigeria*. Boulder, Colo.: Westview Press, 1993.

Metz, Helen Chapin, ed. *Nigeria, a Country Study*. 5th ed. Washington, D.C.: Library of Congress, 1992.

Myers, Robert A. *Nigeria*. Santa Barbara, Calif.: Clio Press, 1989.

Nigeria in Pictures. Minneapolis: Lerner Publications Co., 1988.

Oyewole, A. *Historical Dictionary of Nigeria*. Metuchen, N.J.: Scarecrow Press, 1987.

Sutherland, D. *Nigeria*. Chicago: Children's Press, 1995.

NORWAY

Kingdom of Norway

Kongeriket Norge

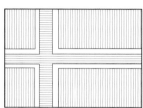

CAPITAL: Oslo.

FLAG: The national flag has a red field on which appears a blue cross outlined in white.

ANTHEM: *Ja, vi elsker dette landet (Yes, We Love This Country).*

MONETARY UNIT: The krone (Kr) of 100 øre is the national currency. There are coins of 50 øre and 1, 5, and 10 kroner, and notes of 20, 50, 100, 200, 500, and 1,000 kroner. Kr1 = $0.1370 (or $1 = Kr7.3005).

WEIGHTS AND MEASURES: The metric system is the legal standard.

HOLIDAYS: New Year's Day, 1 January; Labor Day, 1 May; National Independence Day, 17 May; Christmas, 25 December; Boxing Day, 26 December. Movable religious holidays include Holy Thursday, Good Friday, Easter Monday, Ascension, and Whitmonday.

TIME: 1 PM = noon GMT.

1 LOCATION AND SIZE

Norway occupies the western part of the Scandinavian peninsula in northern Europe, with almost one-third of the country situated north of the Arctic Circle. It has an area of 324,220 square kilometers (125,182 square miles), slightly larger than the state of New Mexico. Extending 1,752 kilometers (1,089 miles) north-northeast to south-southwest, Norway has the greatest length of any European country. It has a boundary length of 24,440 kilometers (15,273 miles).

Norway's capital city, Oslo, is in the southern part of the country.

2 TOPOGRAPHY

Norway is formed of some of the oldest rocks in the world. It is dominated by mountain masses, with only one-fifth of its total area less than 150 meters (500 feet) above sea level. The Galdhøpiggen (2,469 meters/8,100 feet) mountain peak is one of the highest points in Norway. The principal river is the Glåma. There are 1,700 glaciers totaling some 3,400 square kilometers (1,310 square miles). Excellent harbors are provided by the almost numberless fjords (deeply indented bays). Along many coastal stretches is a chain of islands known as the skjærgård.

3 CLIMATE

Because of the North Atlantic Drift, Norway has a mild climate for a country so far north. The north is considerably cooler than the south, while the interior is cooler than the west coast. Oslo's mean yearly temperature is 6°C (43°F) and ranges from a mean of –5°C (23°F) in January to 17°C (63°F) in July. The eastern valleys have

Photo credit: Susan D. Rock

Ships at anchor in a fjord.

elm, and maple are also common, especially at lower elevations. Above the conifer zone extends a zone of birch trees. Above that, a zone of dwarf willow and dwarf birch, and a zone of lichens and arctic plants.

Of the larger wild animals, elk, roe deer, red deer, and badger survive, as do fox, lynx, and otter. Bird life is plentiful and includes game birds such as capercaillie (cock of the woods) and black grouse. Trout, salmon, and char are found in the rivers.

5 ENVIRONMENT

Industry, mining, and agriculture have polluted 16% of Norway's lake water. Acid rain has affected the nation's water supply over an area of nearly 18,000 square kilometers (7,000 square miles). In the early 1980s, the government enacted strong regulations to prevent oil spills from wells and tankers.

Norway contributes 0.2% of the world's total gas emissions. Transportation vehicles account for 38% of the emissions.

Between 1962 and 1985, 15 national parks, with a total area of more than 5,000 square kilometers (2,000 square miles), and more than 150 nature reserves were established. In 1994, 3 of Norway's mammal species and 8 of its bird species were endangered, and 13 plant species were also threatened.

less than 30 centimeters (12 inches) of rain yearly, whereas along the west coast the average rainfall is 330 centimeters (130 inches).

The North Cape area of Norway is the land of the midnight sun, with "white nights" from the middle of May to the end of July, during which the sun does not set.

4 PLANTS AND ANIMALS

The richest vegetation is found in the southeast around the Oslofjord, which is dominated by conifers (spruce, fir, and pine). Deciduous trees such as oak, ash,

6 POPULATION

The population in 1990 was 4,274,553. The projection for the year 2000 is

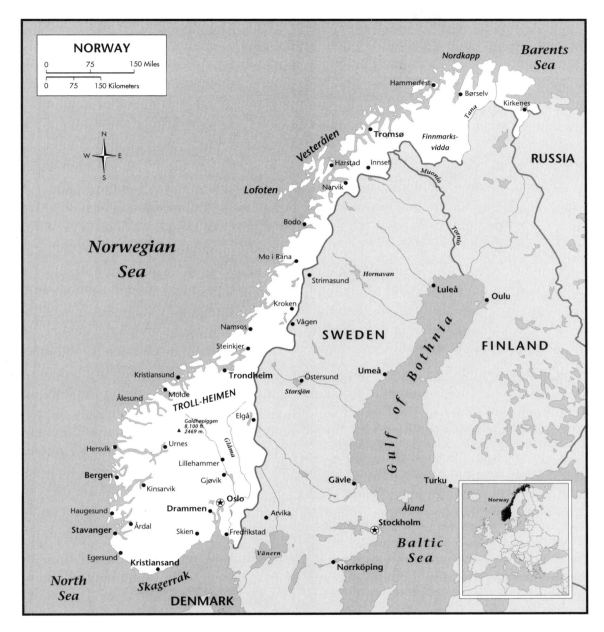

NORWAY

0   75   150 Miles
0   75   150 Kilometers

LOCATION: 57°57′31″ to 71°11′8″N; 4°30′13″ to 31°10′4″E. **BOUNDARY LENGTHS:** Finland, 729 kilometers (455 miles); Russia, 167 kilometers (104 miles); Sweden, 1,619 kilometers (1,011 miles); total coastline, 21,925 kilometers (13,703 miles). **TERRITORIAL SEA LIMIT:** 4 miles.

Photo credit: Susan D. Rock

A Lapp boy in traditional dress with a reindeer.

4,485,000. Average density in 1990, not including the islands of Svalbard (in the Arctic Ocean) and Jan Mayen (near Iceland), was 13 per square kilometer (34 per square mile). Oslo, the capital and principal city, had 467,090 inhabitants as of 31 December 1991.

7 MIGRATION

Emigration in recent years has not been significant. Norwegians moving abroad numbered 23,784 in 1990. Immigrants totaled 25,494. Most emigrants went to Sweden (7,631), Denmark (2,756), the United States (2,203), and the United Kingdom (1,980). Immigration was principally from the United States (1,908), the United Kingdom (1,250), Denmark (2,356), and Sweden (5,053). There were about 143,304 foreigners residing in Norway at the end of 1990. At the end of 1992, Norway had 35,700 refugees.

8 ETHNIC GROUPS

The Norwegians have for centuries been a population with only one ethnic heritage. The population is nearly all of Nordic stock, generally tall and fair-skinned, with blue eyes. Small minority communities include some 20,000 Lapps and 7,000 descendants of Finnish immigrants.

9 LANGUAGES

Norwegian, closely related to Danish and Swedish, is part of the Germanic language group. Many dialects are spoken. There are two language forms, Bokmål and Nynorsk. The former (spoken by a large majority of Norwegians) is based on the written language used in towns, and the latter on country dialects. Both forms of Norwegian have absorbed many modern international words, particularly from British and American English, despite attempts to provide native substitutes.

English is spoken widely in Norway, especially in the urban areas. The Lapps in northern Norway have retained their own language, which is different in origin from Norwegian.

10 RELIGIONS

The state church is the Evangelical Lutheran Church of Norway, with about 1,126 congregations grouped in 11 bishoprics (districts). The king nominates the bishops, and the church receives financial support from the state. About 89% of the population was registered as belonging to the state church in 1992.

Some 44,000 Norwegians belong to the Pentecostal movement, and a lesser number belong to the Evangelical Lutheran Free Church. There are small numbers of Roman Catholics, Greek Orthodox, Methodists, Baptists, Anglicans, Muslims, and Jews, as well as followers of the Salvation Army and the Mission Covenant Church. About 3% of Norwegians have no religious affiliation.

11 TRANSPORTATION

In spite of Norway's difficult terrain, the road system has been well engineered, but there are problems of maintenance because of heavy rain in the west and freezing in the east. Road transport accounts for nearly 90% of inland passenger transport. At the end of 1991, the total length of highway was 79,540 kilometers (49,394 miles). At the end of 1991 there were 1,614,623 passenger cars, 311,063 trucks, and 23,288 buses. At the end of 1991, 4,223 kilometers (2,624 miles) of rail line was operational. In 1991, the Norwegian National Railroad carried 35 million passengers and 22 million tons of freight.

With a merchant fleet of 830 vessels (21,699,000 gross registered tons) at the end of 1991, Norway possessed the world's seventh-largest fleet. Oslo and Bergen have excellent harbor facilities, but several other ports are almost as fully equipped.

Fornebu Airport (Oslo), Flesland (Bergen), and Sola (Stavanger) are the main centers of air traffic. External services are operated by the Scandinavian Airlines System (SAS). Braathens Air Transport operates most of the domestic scheduled flights. In 1991, Norway's four largest airports handled 10,559,000 passenger arrivals and departures.

12 HISTORY

Humans have lived in Norway for about 10,000 years. In the early centuries of the Christian era small kingdoms were formed. The name Norge ("Northern Way") was in use for parts of the coastal district before AD 900. The Vikings were seagoing adventurers who lived from the eighth to tenth centuries. The Viking period (800–1050) was one of vigorous expansion under Olav Haraldsson. Vikings took territory by force for Norway. From the death of Olav in 1030, the nation was officially Christian.

The next two centuries were marked by dynastic conflicts and civil wars. A landed aristocracy emerged, displacing peasant farmers. A common legal code was adopted in 1274–76, and the right of succession to the crown was established. Iceland came under Norwegian rule in 1261 and Greenland between 1261 and 1264. However, the Hebrides (Western Isles) near Scotland were lost in 1266.

Norway lost its independence at the death of Haakon V in 1319, when Magnus VII became ruler of both Norway and Sweden. The Bubonic Plague, known as the Black Death, swept the country in the middle of the fourteenth century.

Photo credit: Susan D. Rock

Typical regional architecture, Trondheim.

In 1397, three Scandinavian countries, Norway, Sweden, and Denmark, were united under Queen Margrethe of Denmark. Sweden left the union in 1523, but for nearly 300 more years Norway was ruled by Danish governors.

Denmark's support of France during the Napoleonic Wars (1803–15) resulted in the breakup of the union. With the Peace of Kiel (1814), Norway was turned over to Sweden, but the Faroe Islands, Iceland, and Greenland were kept by Denmark. However, Norwegians resisted Swedish rule. They adopted a new constitution on 17 May 1814, and elected the Danish prince Christian Frederick king of Norway. Sweden then invaded Norway, but agreed to let Norway keep its constitution in return for accepting union with Sweden under the rule of the Swedish king.

Independence From Sweden

During the second half of the nineteenth century, the Storting (parliament) became more powerful. An upsurge of nationalist feeling, both within the Storting and among Norway's cultural leaders, paved the way for the election that in 1905 gave independence to Norway. Feelings ran high on both sides, but once the results were announced, Norway and Sweden settled down to friendly relations. The Danish prince Carl was elected king of Norway, assuming the name Haakon VII.

World War II and the End of Neutrality

Although Norway remained neutral during World War I (1939–45), its merchant marine suffered losses. Norway proclaimed its neutrality during the early days of World War II (1939–45), but Norwegian waters were strategically too important for Norway to remain outside the war. On 9 April 1940, Germany invaded. The national resistance was led by King Haakon. In June 1940, Haakon escaped, taking the government with him. Then he established Norway's government-in-exile in England.

The government that remained in Oslo fell to Vidkun Quisling, a former Norwegian defense minister who had aided the German invasion. His name afterwards became a term in the Norwegian language for one who collaborates with the enemy. After the German surrender, he was arrested, convicted of treason, and shot. During the late 1940s, Norway abandoned its former neutrality, accepted aid from the United States, and joined the North Atlantic Treaty Organization (NATO). King Haakon died in 1957 and was succeeded by Olav V.

Norway After World War II

The direction of economic policy has been the major issue in Norway since World War II. Especially controversial have been the issue of taxation and the degree of government involvement in private industry. Economic planning has been introduced, and several state-owned enterprises established. Prior to the mid-1970s, Labor Party-dominated governments enjoyed a broad public consensus for their foreign and military policies.

In November 1972, about 54% of Norwegians voting rejected Norway's entry into what was then the European Economic Community (EEC). The EEC, now the European Union (EU), is intended to make trade between European countries as easy as it is between Michigan and New York.

After the 1973 general elections, the Labor Party, which had been in favor of joining the EEC, found its control over the government had begun to weaken. The Labor Party, under the leadership of Gro Harlem Brundtland, lost control of the government to the Conservatives in the 1981 elections. Brundtland (b. 1939), at age 41, was the youngest woman ever to run a modern government. The Labor Party regained control in 1986, and Brundtland resumed her role as prime minister.

On 17 January 1991, King Harald took over the throne when his father died. The heir-apparent (next king) is Haakon Magnus (b. 1973), Harald's son.

The EU issue has remained controversial. In late November 1994, Norwegians again voted to reject membership in the EU, despite the fact that its neighbors, Sweden and Finland, would become members in January 1995. Those in favor of membership are primarily from urban areas, and are engaged in business or the professions. Those opposed, from coastal areas to the north and the western rural areas, feel that Norway is strong enough and rich enough in natural resources to remain independent. Of special concern is protection of the rich fishing grounds in Norway's territorial waters.

13 GOVERNMENT

Norway is a constitutional monarchy. The constitution of 17 May 1814, as amended, places executive power in the king and legislative power in the Storting. The sovereign (king or queen) must be a member of the Evangelical Lutheran Church of Norway, which he heads. A constitutional amendment in May 1990 allows females to take the throne. Royal power is exercised through a cabinet (the Council of State), consisting of a prime minister and at least seven other ministers of state. The prime minister since 1986 has been Gro Harlem Brundtland of the Labor Party. She is the youngest woman ever to head the government of a major country.

Since the introduction of parliamentary rule in 1884, the Storting (parliament) has become the supreme authority, with complete control over finances and with power to override the king's (or queen's) veto under a specified procedure. The monarch is theoretically free to choose his or her own cabinet. In practice the Storting selects the ministers, who must resign if the Storting votes no confidence (in their abilities).

The Storting is made up of 165 representatives from 18 counties. Election for a four-year term is by direct voting. After election, the Storting divides into two sections by choosing one-fourth of its members to form the upper chamber Lagting, with the rest constituting the lower chamber Odelsting. The Odelsting deals with certain types of bills (chiefly proposed new laws) after the committee stage and forwards them to the Lagting. After approving bills, the Lagting sends them to the king for the royal assent (agreement).

Norway had 47 urban municipalities (*bykommuner*) and 407 rural municipalities (*herredskommuner*) in 1986. They are grouped into 18 counties (*fylker*), each governed by an elected county council.

14 POLITICAL PARTIES

The present-day Conservative Party (Høyre) was established in 1885. The Liberal Party (Venstre), founded in 1885, stresses social reform. Industrial workers founded the Labor Party (Arbeiderparti) in 1887 and, with the assistance of the Liberals, obtained the universal vote for men in 1898, and for women in 1913. The Social Democrats broke away from the Labor Party in 1921–22, and the Communist Party (Kommunistparti), made up of former Laborites, was established in 1923.

The Agrarian (Farmers) Party was formed in 1920. It changed its name to the Center Party (Senterparti) in 1958. The Christian People's Party (Kristelig Folkeparti), founded in 1933, and also known as the Christian Democratic Party, supports the principles of Christianity in public life.

Labor increased its support in the 1993 election, winning 67 seats. The Center Party became the second largest party while the Conservatives and other right-wing parties suffered a decline. The results were as follows: Labour Party (67), Center Party (32), Conservative Party (28), Christian People's Party (13), Socialist Left Party (13), Progress Party (10), and others (2).

15 JUDICIAL SYSTEM

Each municipality has a conciliation council, elected by the municipal council, to mediate in lesser civil cases so as to settle them, if possible, before they go to court. Cases receive their first hearing in town courts (byrett) and rural courts (herredsrett), which try both civil and criminal cases. Their decisions may be brought before a court of appeals (lagmannsrett); there are five such courts, at Oslo, Skien, Bergen, Trondheim, and Tromsø.

Appeals may be taken to the Supreme Court (Høyesterett) at Oslo, which consists of a chief justice and 17 judges, of whom 5 sit in a single case. Special courts include a Social Insurance Court and a Labor Disputes Court which handles industrial relations disputes.

16 ARMED FORCES

The king (or queen) is supreme commander of the armed forces. About 22,800 draftees served in the armed forces of 32,700 officers and enlisted men in 1993. National service is required and universal, but exceptions may be made for religious reasons. Those exempted must serve for two years in the civil labor corps.

The army's total strength is 15,900 officers and men. The navy has a total of 7,300 men, including 2,000 men in the coastal artillery. The air force consists of

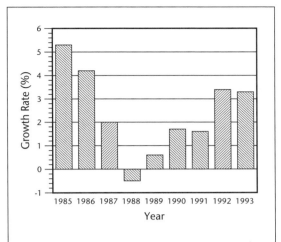

Yearly growth rate of the economy. This economic indicator tells by what percent the economy has increased or decreased when compared with the previous year.

9,500 officers and men, with 85 combat aircraft. Reservists of all services number approximately 285,000, and the home guards has 85,000 men.

Norway is the host nation for the North Atlantic Treaty Organization (NATO) Allied Forces North, and provides troops for six peacekeeping operations. The nation spent $3.8 billion on defense in 1991.

17 ECONOMY

Norway, with its long coastline and vast forests, was traditionally a fishing and lumbering country. Since the end of World War I it has greatly increased its transport and manufacturing activities. The discovery since the late 1970s of major new oil reserves in the North Sea has had considerable impact on the Norwegian economy.

Foreign trade is a critical economic factor. Norway was especially sensitive to the effects of the worldwide recession of the early 1980s and is affected by variations in world prices, particularly those of oil, gas, and shipping. Since the early 1980s, Norway's exports have been dominated by petroleum and natural gas.

The drastic decline of oil prices in 1986 caused the value of Norway's exports to fall by about 20%. Since 1989, the economy has grown each year—by over 3% in 1992 and 1993. Unemployment, however, rose to a post-World War II high of 6% in 1993. Inflation fell from 8.7% in 1987 to 2.2% in 1993.

18 INCOME

In 1992, Norway's gross national product (GNP) was $110,465 million at current prices, or about $25,970 per person. For the period 1985–92 the average inflation rate was 4.5%, resulting in a real growth rate in GNP of 0.2% per person.

19 INDUSTRY

The most important export industries are oil and gas production, metalworking, pulp and paper, chemical products, and processed fish. Products traditionally classified as home market industries (electrical and nonelectrical machinery, casting and foundry products, textiles, paints, varnishes, rubber goods, and furniture) also make an important contribution.

Electrochemical and electrometallurgical products—aluminum, ferroalloys, steel, nickel, copper, magnesium, and fertilizers—are based mainly on Norway's

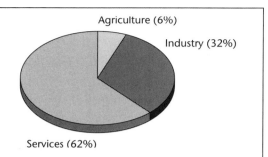

Components of the economy. This pie chart shows how much of the country's economy is devoted to agriculture (includes forestry, hunting, and fishing), industry, or services.

low-cost electric power. Without any bauxite reserves of its own, Norway has thus been able to become a leading producer of aluminum (813,000 tons in 1992). Industrial output is being increasingly diversified.

About half of Norway's industries are situated in the area of Oslo's fjord. In 1991, 11,532 establishments in this area employed 298,982 persons.

20 LABOR

Employed workers in 1992 totaled 2,004,000, of whom 38.1% were engaged in community, social, and government services; 16% in industry; 17.6% in wholesale and retail trade; 7.8% in transportation, storage, and communications; 6.1% in construction; 5.5% in agriculture, forestry, fishing, and hunting; 7.6% in banking and financial services; and 1.3% in other sectors. Unemployment gradually increased during the 1970s, and jumped from 2.1% in 1987 to 6% in 1993.

In 1991, Norway's 29 unions represented some 776,773 workers, or 38.6% of the employed labor force. In 1992, employees averaged only 34.9 hours of actual work per week. Norwegian workers receive four weeks plus one day of annual vacation time with pay. Generally, employee representatives make up one-third of a company board of directors.

Children aged 13 to 18 may work part-time in light work that will not have a negative effect on their health, development, or schooling.

21 AGRICULTURE

Agricultural land in 1991 comprised 892,000 hectares (2,204,170 acres), or about 3% of the country's total land. Although the proportion of larger farms has been increasing, most farms in 1990 were still small, with about 99% of the 84,635 farms consisting of less than 50 hectares (124 acres) of fertile land.

Crop production in 1991 included 1,482,000 tons of grain, 415,000 tons of potatoes, 101,000 tons of fodder roots, and 3,420,000 tons of hay. Norway imports most of its grain and large quantities of its fruits and vegetables. Mechanization of agriculture is developing rapidly. In 1992, farmers owned 156,000 tractors and 16,300 combines.

Since 1928, the government has supported Norwegian grain production.

22 DOMESTICATED ANIMALS

Norway provides all its own farm animals and livestock products. In 1992, there were 2,211,000 sheep, 1,011,000 head of cattle, 749,000 hogs, 20,000 horses, and 4,000,000 fowl. Norway is well known for its working horses. By careful breeding, Norway has developed dairy cows with very good milk qualities. In 1992, production included 83,000 tons of beef and veal, 90,000 tons of pork, 25,000 tons of mutton and lamb, and 55,000 tons of eggs. Norwegian production of milk, cheese, and meat satisfies local demand.

23 FISHING

Fishing is of modest importance, with 2,095,912 tons caught in 1991 by 26,000 fishermen. Cod, herring, haddock, mackerel, and sardines are the main commercial species. The value of fish and fishery products exported in 1992 was $2.43 billion.

In 1991, sealing expeditions hunting in the Arctic Ocean caught 14,719 seals. Norway was one of four countries that did not agree to phase out whaling by 1986, having opposed a 1982 resolution of the International Whaling Commission to that effect. In 1991, only two whales were reportedly caught by Norwegian whalers.

24 FORESTRY

Norway's forestland totals 8,330,000 hectares (20,583,000 acres). In 1991, timber shipments amounted to 11 million cubic meters, of which 90% was coniferous timber, 19% pulpwood, and 8% fuel wood. The value of roundwood exported was $44.7 million in 1991.

25 MINING

Mining is Norway's oldest major export industry, and for a time silver, iron, and copper were important exports. Some of the mines now being worked were established more than 300 years ago. Copper, iron pyrites, and iron ore are still mined in considerable quantities.

Known deposits of other minerals are small. They include limestone, quartz, dolomite, feldspar, and slate. In 1991, production of iron ore was 2,209,000 tons; titanium, 800,000 tons; copper, 17,393 tons; and zinc and lead, 22,403 tons. The largest titanium deposit in Europe is located in southwest Norway. Norway's only coal mines, at Spitsbergen on the Svalbard islands in the Arctic Ocean, produced 389,000 tons in 1991.

26 FOREIGN TRADE

Foreign trade plays an exceptionally important role in the Norwegian economy. Exports are largely based on oil, natural gas, shipbuilding, metals, forestry (including pulp and paper), fishing, and electrochemical and electrometallurgical products. The manufacture of oil rigs, drilling platforms, and associated equipment has developed into a sizable export industry. Norway imports large quantities of motor vehicles and other transport equipment, raw materials, and industrial equipment.

In 1992, the United Kingdom was Norway's most important customer, followed by Germany, Sweden, the United States, and Denmark. Sweden and Germany were the main suppliers of imports.

27 ENERGY AND POWER

Norway, always well supplied with water-power, also has the advantage of vast

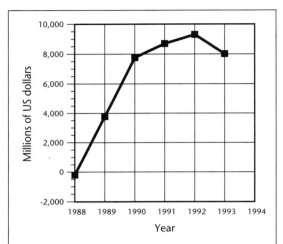

Yearly balance of trade measured in millions of US dollars. The balance of trade is the difference between what a country sells to other countries (its exports) and what it buys (its imports). If a country imports more than it exports, it has a negative balance of trade (a trade deficit). If exports exceed imports, there is a positive balance of trade (a trade surplus).

petroleum and natural gas deposits in the North Sea. Altogether, the nation's remaining reserves of oil totaled 8.8 billion barrels as of 1 January 1993. Natural gas reserves totaled 200 billion cubic meters. In 1992, Norwegian production of crude petroleum totaled an estimated 106,600,000 tons, or 3.4% of the world supply, and natural gas 28.1 billion cubic meters (1.4% of world supply).

Electric power production in 1991 totaled 110,950 million kilowatt hours, which was almost entirely hydroelectric. The first gas-fired power plant is expected to open in the late 1990s. The importance of coal and other solid fuels has steadily declined in recent years.

Selected Social Indicators

These statistics are estimates for the period 1988 to 1993. For comparison purposes, data for the United States and averages for low-income countries and high-income countries are also given.

Indicator	Norway	Low-income countries	High-income countries	United States
Per capita gross national product†	**$25,970**	$380	$23,680	$24,740
Population growth rate	**0.5%**	1.9%	0.6%	1.0%
Population growth rate in urban areas	**0.7%**	3.9%	0.8%	1.3%
Population per square kilometer of land	**13**	78	25	26
Life expectancy in years	**77**	62	77	76
Number of people per physician	**411**	>3,300	453	419
Number of pupils per teacher (primary school)	**6**	39	<18	20
Illiteracy rate (15 years and older)	**<1%**	41%	<5%	<3%
Energy consumed per capita (kg of oil equivalent)	**5,096**	364	5,203	7,918

† The gross national product (GNP) is the total dollar value of all goods and services produced by a country in a year. The per capita GNP is calculated by dividing a country's GNP by its population. The World Bank defines low-income countries as those with a per capita GNP of $695 or less. High-income countries have a per capita GNP of $8,626 or more. Less than 14% of the world's 5.5 billion people live in high-income countries, while almost 60% live in low-income countries.

> = greater than   < = less than

Sources: World Bank, *Social Indicators of Development 1995,* Baltimore: Johns Hopkins University Press, 1995. Central Intelligence Agency, *World Fact Book,* Washington, D.C.: Government Printing Office, 1994.

28 SOCIAL DEVELOPMENT

Norway has been a pioneer in the field of social welfare and is often called a welfare state. Accident insurance for factory workers was introduced in 1894 and compulsory health insurance in 1909. Sickness benefits, family allowances during hospitalization, and grants for funeral expenses are paid. Public assistance, available in Norway since 1845, supplements the foregoing programs. Social welfare has long included maternity benefits with free prenatal clinics.

The National Insurance Act, which came into effect in 1967, provides old-age pensions, rehabilitation allowances, disability pensions, widow and widower pensions, and survivor benefits to children. Workers' compensation covers both accidents and occupational diseases. Family allowance coverage, in force since 1946, is provided for children under the age of 16.

In spite of a 1978 law mandating equal wages for equal work by men and women, economic discrimination continues, and the average pay for women in industry is lower than that for men.

29 HEALTH

Since 1971, there has been a National Insurance Scheme. Hospital care is free of charge, but a minor sum is charged for medicine and primary health care.

In 1988, there were 1,200 health institutions, including 92 hospitals. In 1991, there were 15,533 hospital beds. In the same year, there were 13,826 doctors and 58,561 nurses.

Average life expectancy, among the highest in the world, is 77 years. Major causes of death in 1990 were: communicable diseases and maternal/perinatal causes; noncommunicable diseases; and injuries. In 1991, there were 60 cases of AIDS.

30 HOUSING

Housing problems were complicated by the destruction caused by World War II and postwar increases in the birthrate. Norway built more dwellings per 1,000 inhabitants than any other European country, completing between 31,000 and 42,000 units annually from 1967 through 1981. Construction of new dwellings has slowed in recent years, however; only 21,689 units were completed in 1991. As of 1990, Norway had a total of 1,751,358 dwelling units. Since 1988, housing demand has fallen more than 50%.

31 EDUCATION

There is practically no adult illiteracy in Norway. The Basic Education Act of 1969 introduced a nine-year system of compulsory education for all children between the ages of 7 and 16. Local authorities generally provide school buildings and equipment and the central government contributes funds towards teachers' sala-

ries and covers a considerable portion of the cost of running the schools.

Secondary school for students from 16 to 19 may involve theoretical studies, practical training, or a combination of both. Three-year general secondary schools (gymnasiums) prepare students to go on to a university. In the 1991 academic year, 386,238 students were enrolled in the gymnasiums and other secondary schools. In the 1990s, it is possible for students to enter a university without having passed through a gymnasium.

Since 1976, the upper secondary school system has included vocational schools. These may be operated by the state, by local authorities, or by the industrial sector.

Norway's institutions of higher education include 215 colleges and 14 universities, with a total enrollment of 154,180 in 1991. The largest universities include the University of Oslo, the University of Bergen, the University of Trondheim, and the University of Troms. There are also specialized institutions such as the Agricultural University of Norway (near Oslo); the Norwegian School of Economics and Business Administration (Bergen); and the Norwegian College of Veterinary Medicine (Oslo) representing fields not covered by the universities.

32 MEDIA

Norway has over 300 radio broadcasting stations. Educational broadcasts supplement school facilities in remote districts. Full-scale television transmission began in July 1960. Most households have at least one television set. In 1991 there were 3,390,000 radios and 1,805,000 television sets. Telephones in 1991 numbered 2,579,000, or 62 for every 100 persons.

The Norwegian press is characterized by a large number of small newspapers. The 83 dailies appear six times a week. Publishing newspapers on Sundays and holidays is prohibited by law. Total circulation of all daily newspapers in 1991 was 2,309,000. The following are some of the largest dailies with their circulations in 1991: *VG-Verdens Gang* (360,300); *Aftenposten* (267,000); *Dagbladet* (214,600); *Bergens Tidende* (99,400); *Adresseavisen* (88,700); and *Arbeiderbladet* (57,000).

33 TOURISM AND RECREATION

Norway's main tourist attractions are the cities of Oslo, Bergen, and Trondheim, which are connected by road, rail, and daily flights; the marvelous scenery of the fjord country in the west; and the arctic coast with the North Cape and "midnight sun." In 1991, foreign tourists numbered 2.1 million. There were 55,887 hotel rooms with a 36% occupancy rate.

A favorite method of tourist travel is by coastal steamer, sailing from Bergen northward to Kirkenes, near the Russian frontier. Many cruise ships sail the Norwegian fjords and coastal towns. Notable outdoor recreational facilities include the Oslomarka, a 100,000-hectare (247,000-acre) area located near Oslo, with ski trails and walking paths. To compensate for the shortness of winter days, several trails are illuminated for evening skiing.

Other popular sports include ice skating, freshwater fishing, mountaineering, hunting (grouse, reindeer, and elk), and soccer. There are major theaters in Oslo and Bergen, as well as six regional theaters; Den Norske Opera in Oslo; and four symphony orchestras. International musical events include the Bergen Festival, held annually in late May or early June; and several jazz festivals in July. In 1994, Norway hosted the XVII Olympic Winter Games in Lillehammer.

34 FAMOUS NORWEGIANS

Ludvig Holberg (1684–1745), the father of Danish and Norwegian literature, was a leading dramatist whose comedies are still performed. Henrik Wergeland (1808–45), Norway's greatest poet, was also a patriot and social reformer; his sister Camilla Collett (1813–95), author of the first Norwegian realistic novel, was a pioneer in the movement for women's rights. Henrik Ibsen (1827–1906), founder of modern dramas, placed Norway in the forefront of world literature. Bjørnstjerne Bjørnson (1832–1910), poet, playwright, and novelist, received the Nobel Prize for Literature in 1903. Other noted novelists are Knut Hamsun (1859–1952), Nobel Prize winner in 1920, and Sigrid Undset (1882–1949), awarded the Nobel Prize in 1928.

Ole Bull (1810–80) was a world-famous violinist. Edvard Grieg (1843–1907) was the first Norwegian composer to win broad popularity. Kirsten Flagstad (1895–1962), world-renowned soprano, served for a time as director of the Norwegian State Opera. Edvard Munch (1863–1944) was an outstanding expressionist painter. Norway's foremost sculptor is Gustav Vigeland (1869–1943).

Outstanding scientists are Armauer (Gerhard Henrik) Hansen (1841–1912), discoverer of the leprosy bacillus; Fridtjof Nansen (1861–1930), an oceanographer and Arctic explorer who won the Nobel Peace Prize in 1922 for organizing famine relief in Russia; Roald Amundsen (1872–1928), polar explorer; Regnar Frisch (1895–1978), who shared the first Nobel Prize in Economic Science in 1969 for developing econometrics; and Thor Heyerdahl (b.1914), explorer and anthropologist.

The first secretary-general of the United Nations was a Norwegian, Trygve (Halvdan) Lie (1896–1968), who served from 1946 to 1953. The historian Christian Louis Lange (1869–1938) was co-winner of the Nobel Peace Prize in 1921.

Sonja Henie (1913–69) was the leading woman figure skater of her time, and Liv Ullmann (b.1939) is an internationally known actress. Grete Waitz (b.1953) is a champion long-distance runner.

35 BIBLIOGRAPHY

Charbonneau, Claudette. *The Land and People of Norway*. New York: HarperCollins, 1992.

Derry, Thomas K. *A Short History of Norway*. Westport, Conn.: Greenwood, 1979.

Hintz, M. *Norway*. Chicago: Children's Press, 1982.

Hølaas, Odd. *The World of the Norsemen*. London: Bond, 1949.

Vanberg, B. *Of Norwegian Ways*. New York: Harper & Row, 1984.

OMAN

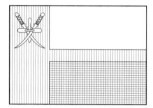

Sultanate of Oman

Saltanat 'Uman

CAPITAL: Muscat (Masqat).

FLAG: The flag is red with a broad stripe of white at the upper fly and green at the lower fly. In the upper left corner, white crossed swords overlay a ceremonial dagger.

ANTHEM: *Nashid as-Salaam as-Sutani (Sultan's National Anthem).*

MONETARY UNIT: The Omani riyal (RO), established in November 1972, is a paper currency of 1,000 baizas. There are coins of 2, 5, 10, 25, 50, 100, 250, and 500 baizas, and notes of 100, 250, and 500 baizas (the last two being replaced by coins) and 1, 5, 10, 20, and 50 riyals. RO1 = $2.6008 (or $1 = RO0.3845).

WEIGHTS AND MEASURES: The metric system was adopted on 15 November 1974. The imperial and local system are also used.

HOLIDAYS: Accession of the Sultan, 23 July; National Day, 18 November; Sultan's Birthday, 19 November. Movable Muslim religious holidays include 'Id al-Fitr, 'Id al-'Adha', and Milad an-Nabi.

TIME: 4 PM = noon GMT. Solar time is also observed.

1 LOCATION AND SIZE

The Sultanate of Oman is the second-largest country on the Arabian Peninsula after Sa'udi Arabia, with an area officially estimated at 212,460 square kilometers (82,031 square miles), slightly smaller than the state of Kansas. The northernmost part of Oman, separated from the rest of the country by the United Arab Emirates, juts into the Strait of Hormuz. The total estimated boundary length is 3,466 kilometers (2,154 miles). The capital, Muscat, is in the northeastern part of the country.

2 TOPOGRAPHY

Oman, except for barren coastline southward to Zufar, consists of three regions: a coastal plain, a mountain range at Al Jabal, and a plateau.

3 CLIMATE

Annual rainfall varies from 10 centimeters (4 inches) in Muscat to up to 64 centimeters (25 inches) in Zufar. The climate generally is very hot, with temperatures reaching 54°C (129°F) in the hot season.

4 PLANTS AND ANIMALS

Coconut palms grow in Zufar, and frankincense grows in the hills. Oleander and varieties of acacia are plentiful. Native mammals include the cheetah, hyena, fox, wolf, and hare. Birds include the Arabian see-see partridge, and Muscat bee eater.

5 ENVIRONMENT

Maintaining an adequate water supply is Oman's most pressing environmental problem. The nation has only 0.5 cubic miles of water. In 1994, the nation had six

Photo credit: AP/Wide World Photos

Omani tribesmen with their camels at the remote southern province of Dhofar in Oman where they pray for rain.

endangered species of mammals and one endangered type of bird. Two plant species are threatened with extinction.

6 POPULATION

The United Nations, which estimated the population at 1,637,000 in mid-1992, projected a population of 2,168,000 for the year 2000. Muscat had an estimated population of 53,000 in 1990.

7 MIGRATION

There is frequent movement of workers between Oman and neighboring states. In 1992, about 350,000 foreigners were working in Oman, most of them Indian, Pakistani, or Bangladeshi.

8 ETHNIC GROUPS

The native population is mostly Arab except on the northern coast, where there is significant Baluchi, Iranian, and African representation, and in Muscat and Matrah, where there are Khojas and other Indians, Baluchis, and Pakistanis. Tribal groups are estimated to number over 200.

9 LANGUAGES

The official language is Arabic. Urdu, Farsi, and several Indian dialects are also spoken. English is taught as a second language.

10 RELIGIONS

Three-quarters of the population belongs to the Ibadhi Islamic sect. Tribes in the north are mainly Sunni Muslims of the Hanbali, Shafai, and Wahhabi rites. The remainder of the population is Hindu. In 1993 there were about 75,000 Roman Catholics.

11 TRANSPORTATION

At the end of 1991 there were 22,800 kilometers (14,170 miles) of roads. In 1991, vehicle registrations totaled 220,000. In 1992, Gulf Air provided airline service to Oman.

12 HISTORY

Present-day Oman was already a commercial and seafaring center in ancient Sumerian times, and Phoenicians (from the region that is present-day Syria and Lebanon) probably visited the coastal region. The entire population was converted to Islam during the lifetime of Mohammad (570–632), but Oman soon became—and remains today—the center of the Ibadhi sect.

In 1507–08, the Portuguese overran Muscat and maintained control until they were driven out with Persian aid in 1649. The first sultanate (kingdom) was established in Muscat about 1775 and concluded its first treaty with the British in 1798. Weakened by political division, Muscat lost control of the interior in the second half of the nineteenth century. In 1920, the Treaty of Seeb was signed

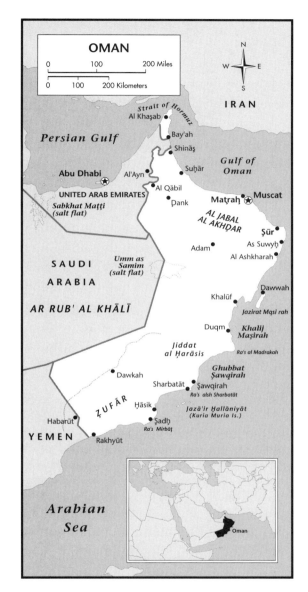

LOCATION: 51°50′ to 59°40′E; 16°40′ to 26°20′N.
BOUNDARY LENGTHS: Total coastline, 2,092 kilometers (1,301 miles); Yemen, 288 kilometers (179 miles); Sa'udi Arabia, 676 kilometers (420 miles); UAE, 410 kilometers (255 miles). **TERRITORIAL SEA LIMIT:** 12 miles.

between the sultan (king of a Muslim state) of Muscat and the imam (Muslim leader) of Oman, placing Oman under the rule of the Sultan as an independent area. From 1920 to 1954 there was comparative peace.

In that year, Petroleum Development (Oman) Ltd., a British-managed oil company, won permission to maintain a small army, the Muscat and Oman Field Force (MOFF). In early 1955, MOFF, together with British troops, occupied all of Oman and expelled the imam. In 1962 the sultanate of Muscat was proclaimed an independent state. Oman joined the United Nations late in 1971.

The present sultan, Qabus bin Sa'id changed the name of the country from Muscat and Oman to the Sultanate of Oman in 1970. He has presided over a broad modernization program, opening the country to the outside world while preserving political and military ties with the British. Oman dominates the Strait of Hormuz, which links the Gulf of Oman with the Persian Gulf. Its strategic importance drew Oman and the United States closer together when the Iran–Iraq war started in 1979.

In 1992, Oman and Yemen ratified a treaty to settle disputes about their boundary.

13 GOVERNMENT

Oman's sultan is an absolute monarch. The country has no constitution, legislature, or voting. The Majlis Ash-Shura, or Consultative Council, established in 1991, is seen as a first step toward popular participation in government. It has no legislative function, but can question cabinet members on their policies and plans.

Oman is divided into three governates and 41 wilayats (districts).

14 POLITICAL PARTIES

There are no legal political parties nor, at present, is there any active opposition movement.

15 JUDICIAL SYSTEM

Shari'a courts based on Islamic law administer justice, with the Chief Court at Muscat. Appeals from the Chief Court are made to the sultan, who exercises powers of clemency (mercy or leniency in setting punishment). The magistrate court, a criminal court, rules on violations of the criminal code.

16 ARMED FORCES

Oman's armed forces, including some 3,700 foreign members and British advisors numbered 35,700 in 1993. The army had 20,000 members, the air force 3,500, and the navy 3,000. In 1992 Oman spent $1.7 billion on defense.

17 ECONOMY

Since the mid-1970s most of the economy has revolved around oil. Based on current oil production, reserves should last some 16 years. In recent years, the production of natural gas has become a significant factor in the economy.

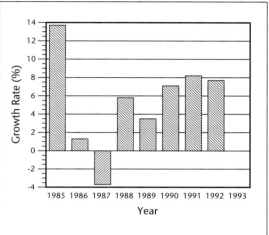

Yearly growth rate of the economy. This economic indicator tells by what percent the economy has increased or decreased when compared with the previous year.

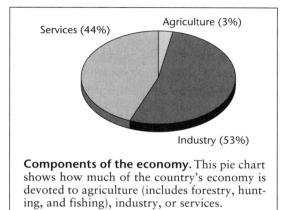

Components of the economy. This pie chart shows how much of the country's economy is devoted to agriculture (includes forestry, hunting, and fishing), industry, or services.

18 INCOME

In 1992, Oman's gross national product (GNP) was $10,683 million at current prices. The national product averages about $4,850 per person. For the period 1985–92 the average inflation rate was 1.1%, resulting in a real growth rate in GNP of 1.0% per person.

19 INDUSTRY

From 1981 to 1987, 2,587 new industrial establishments were registered, bringing the total to 2,990.

20 LABOR

Of an estimated Omani work force of 430,000 in 1992, approximately 258,000 were still engaged in agriculture or fishing. Many of the larger industries depend on foreign workers, who made up 58% of the work force in 1992.

Children under the age of 13 may not work. Young people between the ages of 13 and 16 may not work during evenings or at night, or perform strenuous labor. They are also prohibited from working overtime, or on weekends or holidays without special permission. Some children are employed as riders in camel races, but they almost always have parental consent. There is no recorded case of a child camel jockey suffering a serious injury.

21 AGRICULTURE

The principal agricultural product is the date. Bananas, mangoes, coconuts, citrus fruits (notably limes), nuts, melons, bananas, coconuts, alfalfa, and tobacco are also grown.

22 DOMESTICATED ANIMALS

Goats, sheep, cattle, donkeys, and camels are widely raised.

23 FISHING

The waters of the Gulf of Oman are rich in sardines, mackerel, shrimp, lobster, crayfish, tuna, barracuda, grouper, and shark. The annual catch in 1991 was 117,780 tons, mainly sardines.

24 FORESTRY

The use of wood as the sole fuel and over-grazing by goats have depleted the forests of Oman, but the interior of the country is fairly well wooded.

25 MINING

As of 1991, more than half of Oman's copper production was taken from the Lasail Mine. Oman also has large deposits of limestone, gypsum, asbestos, and marble, along with chromite and manganese.

26 FOREIGN TRADE

Since 1967, oil has been the chief export. The main imports are food, live animals, machinery, textiles, chemicals, petroleum products, and motor vehicles. In 1992, exports totaled $5.4 billion, over 80% of which was from oil. Imports were worth $3.5 billion. Most of the non-oil exports go to the United Arab Emirates (UAE). Japan is now the principal source of imports, followed by the United Kingdom, Germany, United States, and France.

27 ENERGY AND POWER

Annual crude oil output during 1992 averaged 720,000 barrels per day. Petroleum reserves are estimated at 4.5 billion barrels (600 million tons). In 1991, electric power production totaled 5,548 million kilowatt hours.

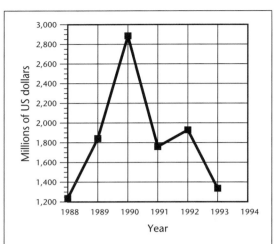

Yearly balance of trade measured in millions of US dollars. The balance of trade is the difference between what a country sells to other countries (its exports) and what it buys (its imports). If a country imports more than it exports, it has a negative balance of trade (a trade deficit). If exports exceed imports, there is a positive balance of trade (a trade surplus).

28 SOCIAL DEVELOPMENT

Oman maintains a welfare program that, in 1985, gave direct monetary aid to 27,973 families. Women have begun to enter professional areas such as medicine and communications in greater numbers in recent years.

29 HEALTH

In 1985 there were 40 hospitals. In 1990, the population per physician was about 1,202. Average life expectancy in 1992 was 70 years. In 1992, 97% of the population had access to health care services.

Selected Social Indicators

These statistics are estimates for the period 1988 to 1993. For comparison purposes, data for the United States and averages for low-income countries and high-income countries are also given.

Indicator	Oman	Low-income countries	High-income countries	United States
Per capita gross national product†	**$4,850**	$380	$23,680	$24,740
Population growth rate	**4.2%**	1.9%	0.6%	1.0%
Population growth rate in urban areas	**7.9%**	3.9%	0.8%	1.3%
Population per square kilometer of land	**9**	78	25	26
Life expectancy in years	**70**	62	77	76
Number of people per physician	**1,202**	>3,300	453	419
Number of pupils per teacher (primary school)	**27**	39	<18	20
Illiteracy rate (15 years and older)	**<50%**	41%	<5%	<3%
Energy consumed per capita (kg of oil equivalent)	**2,408**	364	5,203	7,918

† The gross national product (GNP) is the total dollar value of all goods and services produced by a country in a year. The per capita GNP is calculated by dividing a country's GNP by its population. The World Bank defines low-income countries as those with a per capita GNP of $695 or less. High-income countries have a per capita GNP of $8,626 or more. Less than 14% of the world's 5.5 billion people live in high-income countries, while almost 60% live in low-income countries.

> = greater than   < = less than

Sources: World Bank, *Social Indicators of Development 1995,* Baltimore: Johns Hopkins University Press, 1995. Central Intelligence Agency, *World Fact Book,* Washington, D.C.: Government Printing Office, 1994.

30 HOUSING

In 1989, 34% of all housing units were traditional Arabic houses, 30% were modern apartments, and 27% were detached houses.

31 EDUCATION

The adult literacy rate was estimated to be below 50% in 1985. In 1991, there were 436 primary schools with 277,370 students and 10,184 teachers, of whom 48% were women. There are about 27 students per teacher at the primary level. In secondary schools, there were 7,264 teachers and 119,497 students. Sultan Qabus University

opened in 1986. In 1991, all higher level institutions had 7,322 students.

32 MEDIA

By the end of 1991, the entire country was connected to a 79,000-line telephone network. Color television was introduced in 1974. There were 1,150,000 television sets and 1,006,000 radios in use in 1991.

Newspapers and journals in Arabic include the daily *Al-Wattan* (1991 circulation 23,500) and *Oman* (20,000) and weekly periodicals such as *Al-Aquida* and *Al-Usra.*

[33] TOURISM AND RECREATION

In 1991, 161,000 foreign tourists visited Oman, spending an estimated $63 million. There were 2,204 hotel rooms with a 45.2% occupancy rate. Water sports are popular.

[34] FAMOUS OMANIS

Oman's great Islamic religious leader, was 'Abdallah bin Ibad (fl.8th century). Ahmad ibn Sa'id (r.1741–83) was the founder of the present dynasty. Sultan Qabus bin Sa'id (b.1940) has ruled Oman since 1970.

[35] BIBLIOGRAPHY

Range, Peter Ross. "Oman." *National Geographic,* May 1995, 112–138.

Townsend, John. *Oman: The Making of the Modern State.* London: Croom Helm, 1977.

Wilkinson, John Craven. *The Imamate Tradition of Oman.* New York: Cambridge University Press, 1987.

PAKISTAN

Islamic Republic of Pakistan
Islami Jamhooria Pakistan

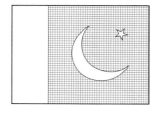

CAPITAL: Islāmābād.

FLAG: The national flag is dark green, with a white vertical stripe at the hoist and a white crescent and five-pointed star in the center.

ANTHEM: The opening lines of the national anthem, sung in Urdu, are "Blessed be the sacred land, Happy be the bounteous realm, Symbol of high resolve, land of Pakistan, Blessed be thou citadel of faith."

MONETARY UNIT: The rupee (R) is a paper currency of 100 paisa. There are coins of 1, 2, 5, 10, 25, and 50 paisa and of 1 rupee, and notes of 1, 2, 5, 10, 50, 100, 500, and 1,000 rupees. R1 = $0.0328 (or $1 = R30.500).

WEIGHTS AND MEASURES: The metric system was introduced in 1966 and made mandatory as of 1 January 1979.

HOLIDAYS: Pakistan Day, 23 March; May Day, 1 May; Independence Day, 14 August; Defense of Pakistan Day, 6 September; Anniversary of Death of the Quaid-e-Azam, Mohammad Ali Jinnah, 11 September; Christmas and Birthday of the Quaid-e-Azam, 25 December. Religious holidays include 'Id al-Fitr, Id al-'Adha', 1st of Muharram, and Milad an-Nabi.

TIME: 5 PM = noon GMT.

1 LOCATION AND SIZE

Situated in southern Asia, Pakistan has an area of 803,940 square kilometers (310,403 square miles), slightly less than twice the size of the state of California. The total boundary length is 7,820 kilometers (4,870 miles). Pakistan's capital city, Islāmābād, is located in the northern part of the country.

2 TOPOGRAPHY

More than two-thirds of Pakistan is desert area. The west is dominated by a plateau, consisting of dry plains and ridges. Another plateau surrounds Rawalpindi in the northeast. Southward, the extensive plains along the border with India support about 60% of the country's population.

In the northern areas of Pakistan, forest-clad hills give way to lofty mountain ranges. K-2 (Godwin Austen), at 8,611 meters (28,250 feet), is the second-highest mountain in the world. The Indus is the principal river of Pakistan.

3 CLIMATE

Pakistan's climate is dry and hot near the coast, becoming progressively cooler toward the northeastern uplands. The winter season is generally cold and dry. By the end of June the temperature may reach 49°C (120°F). Between July and September, the monsoon (very heavy rainfall)

121

provides an average rainfall of about 38 centimeters (15 inches) in the river basins and up to about 150 centimeters (60 inches) in the northern areas.

4 PLANTS AND ANIMALS

The mangrove (trees that send out many dense roots) forests of the coastal region give way to the mulberry, acacia, and date palms of the sparsely vegetated south. The foothills support phulai, kao, chinar, and wild olive, and the northern forests have stands of oak, chestnut, walnut, pine, ash, spruce, yew, and fir. Birch, dwarf willow, and juniper are also found.

Pakistan's wide range of animal life includes the Siberian ibex, wild sheep, buffalo, bear, wolf, jackal, fox, wildcat, musk cat, hyena, porcupine, gazelle, peacock, python, and boar.

5 ENVIRONMENT

Relatively high population growth contributed to the depletion of forestland from 9.8% of Pakistan's total area in 1947 to 4.5% by 1986. The loss of forests has contributed to increased soil erosion, decreasing soil fertility, and severe flooding. The nation's water supply is at risk due to untreated sewage along with agricultural and industrial pollutants. Some 18% of the people living in cities and 58% of rural dwellers do not have pure water.

In 1994, 15 mammal species were endangered, as well as 25 bird species and 14 plant species.

6 POPULATION

The estimated population in 1993 was 125,213,732. The population density was estimated at 150 persons per square kilometer (388 per square mile) in 1992. The national capital, Islāmābād, had about 558,000 inhabitants in 1990. Karāchi (the former national capital) had 7,943,000, and Lahore, 4,179,000.

7 MIGRATION

Some 6,000,000 Muslims migrated to Pakistan from India at the time of independence in 1947. Muslims have continued to arrive from India in much lesser numbers since then.

The Soviet military action in Afghanistan in December 1979 led to an inflow of Afghan refugees. As of the end of 1991, Pakistan was officially harboring 3,098,000 Afghan refugees. The number is believed to be higher, since many Afghan refugees were uncounted.

As of 1986, at least 2,500,000 Pakistanis were working abroad, chiefly in Middle Eastern countries and the United Kingdom.

8 ETHNIC GROUPS

The majority (an estimated two-thirds) of the population is Punjabi (native of northwest India). Other major ethnic groups include the Sindhi (13%), Pathan (8.5%), and Urdu speakers or Muhajirs, (7.6%). The Baluchi (2.5%) are divided into 12 major tribes. In the area of the Indus River are Sindhi peasant tribesmen.

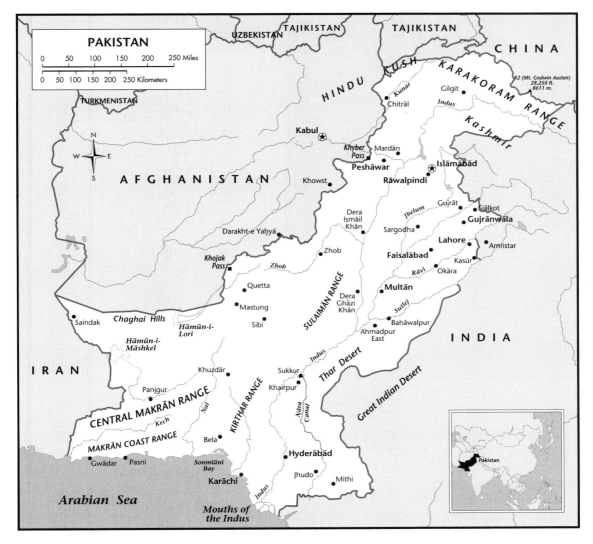

LOCATION: 23°41′ to 37°5′N; 60°52′ to 77°49′E. **BOUNDARY LENGTHS:** China, 523 kilometers (325 miles), including boundary of Jammu and Kashmir to the Karakoram Pass; India, 2,912 kilometers (1,812 miles); Arabian Sea coastline, 1,046 kilometers (655 miles); Iran, 909 kilometers (568 miles); Afghanistan, 2,430 kilometers (1,510 miles). **TERRITORIAL SEA LIMIT:** 12 miles.

The Rajputs and the Jats are the most numerous of the Punjabi castes. In the north and northwest are the nomadic Pathans. Native speakers of Urdu, the Muhajirs, refugees from pre-partition India, are well represented in the cities.

Photo credit: Corel Corporation.

Moslem mystic at a shrine in Pakistan.

9 LANGUAGES

Although regional languages and dialects persist, Urdu is the official language of Pakistan. While it is spoken by only about half the population, it is understood almost everywhere and is becoming the language of higher education. Punjabi, Pushtu, Baluchi, Gujarati, and Sindhi are important regional languages.

Many other languages, including representatives of the Austroasiatic, Dravidian, Indo-European, Central Asian, and Tibeto-Chinese families, are spoken by small groups. English, which formerly had official status, is still used extensively in business, government, and higher education.

10 RELIGIONS

In 1993 some 118,952,000 people, or 95% of the population, were Muslim, giving Pakistan one of the largest Islamic communities in the world. Most of the Muslims are of the Sunni sect, although there are a substantial number of Shi'ites and a few members of the Isma'ili sect, concentrated at Karāchi. Ahmadis, who consider themselves Muslims but who are not accepted by other Muslim groups, numbered perhaps 2,500,000.

Christians constituted an estimated 2% of the population in 1993, and Hindus about 1.8%. About 5,000 Parsis, believers in Zoroastrianism, live in Karāchi.

11 TRANSPORTATION

In 1991, Pakistan Railways operated 8,775 kilometers (5,453 miles) of track and owned 714 locomotives, more than 3,000 coaching vehicles, and about 36,000 freight cars.

In 1991, Pakistan's road system included 120,000 kilometers (74,600 miles) of all-weather roads. There were 690,850 passenger cars, 84,814 buses, 30,300 taxis, and 115, 346 trucks in use in 1991. The road network carries 85% of all goods and passengers moving within the country.

The harbor of Karāchi, which provides Pakistan with its major port, handles over 10.5 million tons annually.

The government-run Pakistan International Airlines (PIA) maintains all domestic services as well as flights to Europe, the United States, and the Far East. In 1992, PIA carried 5,680,600 passengers. Karāchi Airport is the main international terminus.

12 HISTORY

The ruins of ancient civilizations at Mohenjodaro (near Khairpur) and at Harappa (near Okāra) testify to the existence of an advanced urban civilization that flourished in what is now Pakistan in the second half of the third millennium BC. It was overwhelmed from 1500 BC onward by large migrations of nomadic Indo-European-speaking people from the Caucasus region between the Black and Caspian Seas. The invaders included Persians in 500 BC; Greeks under Alexander the Great in 326 BC; Arabs, Afghans, Turks, Persians, and Mughals (Mongols) after AD 800; and Europeans, who first arrived by sea beginning in AD 1601.

Islam, the dominant cultural influence in Pakistan, arrived with Arab traders in the eighth century AD. Waves of Muslims followed, leading to control by the Mughals (Mongols) over most of the subcontinent. The Mughal empire flourished in the sixteenth and seventeenth centuries and remained officially in control until well after the British East India Company came to dominate the region in the early eighteenth century. Effective British governance of the areas that now make up Pakistan was not achieved until well into the second half of the nineteenth century.

In the early twentieth century, British power was increasingly challenged by the rise of nationalist mass movements. The Indian National Congress began to attract wide support in this century with its advocacy of non-violent struggle. But because its leadership style appeared, to many Muslims, to be uniquely Hindu, Muslims formed the All-India Muslim League to look after their interests.

Independence

On 14 August 1947, British India was divided into the two self-governing dominions of India and Pakistan. This division, known as partition, resulted in a mass movement of Hindus, Muslims, and Sikhs who found themselves on the "wrong" side of new international boundaries. More than 20 million people moved, and up to 3 million of these were killed.

The new Pakistan was a state divided into two wings: East Pakistan (with 42 million people crowded mainly into what had been the eastern half of India's Bengal province) and West Pakistan (with 34 million in a much larger territory that included the former Indian provinces of Baluchistan, Sind, the Northwest Frontier, and western Punjab). In between, the wings were separated by 1600 kilometers (1000 miles) of an independent, mainly Hindu, India.

From the capital in Karāchi, in West Pakistan, the leaders of the new state worked hard to establish a workable parliamentary government with broad acceptance in both East and West. Political stability proved hard to achieve, with frequent declarations of martial law and states of emergency in the years following 1954.

In the years leading up to 1971, domestic politics in Pakistan were dominated by efforts to bridge the political and ethnic gap that—more than geography—separated East and West. The gap persisted despite their common feelings of anxiety about India and shared commitment to Islam. Economically more important, East Pakistan, governed as a single province, disliked national policies laid down in West Pakistan, dominated by Punjabis and recent refugees from northern and western India.

In 1958, the Army chief, General Mohammad Ayub Khan, seized control of Pakistan, imposing martial law and banning all political activity for several years. He later began policies designed to reduce the political influence of East Pakistan in the government. Amid rising political tension in both East and West in 1968, Ayub was forced from office, and General Mohammad Yahya Khan, also opposed to greater independence for East Pakistan, assumed the presidency in 1969.

Yahya's attempt to restore popular government in the general elections of 1970 failed when the popular verdict supported greater independence for East Pakistan. The election results were ignored, and civil unrest in East Pakistan rapidly spread to become civil war. India, with more than a million refugees pouring into its West Bengal state, joined in the conflict in support of the rebellion in November 1971, tipping the balance in favor of East Pakistan. In early 1972, the country of Bangladesh was created from the ruins of East Pakistan.

Bhutto and his successors

The outcome of the civil war led to the resignation on 20 December 1971 of Yahya Khan and brought to the presidency Zulfikar Ali Bhutto, whose populist Pakistan Peoples Party (PPP) had won a majority of seats in West Pakistan. Bhutto quickly charted an independent course for West Pakistan, which became the Islamic Republic of Pakistan. He distanced Pakistan from former close ties with the United States and Europe, seeking a much more active role in the Third World, especially in the growing international Islamic movement. Bhutto began limited land reform, nationalized banks and industries, and obtained support among all parties for a new constitution adopted in 1973, restoring a strong prime ministership, which he then assumed.

In the following years, Bhutto grew more and more dictatorial, until he was finally removed from office by the army on 5 July 1977. General Mohammad Zia-ul-Haq partially suspended the 1973 constitution and imposed martial law, which was extended despite repeated broken promises to hold popular elections.

Zia expanded the role of Islamic values and institutions in society. When the Soviet Union invaded Afghanistan in 1979, he assumed a strong anti-communist leadership role and renewed close ties with the United States to enhance Pakistan's security. He also improved relations with

India, including normalization of trade, transport, and other nonsensitive areas.

In the late 1980s, India cancelled election results and dismissed the state government. This led to the beginning of an armed rebellion against Indian rule by Muslim militants in Kashmir, an Indian province which had been split uneasily between Indian and Pakistani influence since 1949. Indian repression and Pakistan's support of the militants continues to threaten to spark new Indo-Pakistan conflict.

Zia was among 18 officials (including the American ambassador) killed in the crash of a Pakistan Air Force plane in 1988. In November of that year, Benazir Bhutto, Zulfikar's daughter, became prime minister but was removed from office two years later by president Ghulam Ishaq amid growing power struggles within the government.

In 1993, under interim prime minister Moeen Qureshi, widespread corruption was exposed, corrupt officials dismissed, and political reforms undertaken. Qureshi held elections on 19 October, and the PPP, leading a coalition called the People's Democratic Alliance (PDA), was returned to power, with Benazir Bhutto again Prime Minister. On 13 November, with her support, Farooq Leghari was elected president.

13 GOVERNMENT

Pakistan is governed under the constitution of 14 August 1973 (as amended) which declared Islam the state religion and provided for a president as official head of state and a prime minister as executive head of government. The parliament consists of a National Assembly of 217 members elected for five-year terms, plus 20 seats to be filled by vote of the elected members. The Senate has 84 members elected for six-year terms by the provincial assemblies and tribal councils, plus 3 seats reserved for the federal capital area.

Pakistan is divided into 4 provinces. Outside the provinces, there are 11 federally administered tribal land areas.

14 POLITICAL PARTIES

The populist Pakistan Peoples Party (PPP) is now led by Benazir Bhutto, daughter of the late Prime Minister Zulfikar Bhutto. Opposition parties include the Pakistan Muslim League (PML), and the Jamaat-i-Islami (JI). In the 1990s, party politics in Pakistan became increasingly regional, with much shifting of supporters into and out of the PPP and the PML. Each of these parties drew nearly 40% of the popular vote, and they have emerged as the only parties with national scope.

Both the PPP and the PML have competed successfully in forming governments in provincial assemblies only when they have recruited (or neutralized) strong regional parties, like the Awami National Party (ANP) in the Northwest Frontier Province and the Muhajir Quami Movement (MQM) in Sindh.

15 JUDICIAL SYSTEM

The Supreme Court has original, appeals, and advisory jurisdictions. Each province has a high court. Below the high courts are

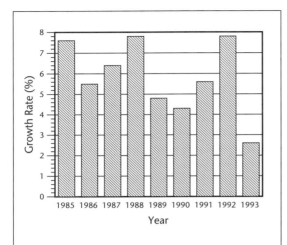

Yearly growth rate of the economy. This economic indicator tells by what percent the economy has increased or decreased when compared with the previous year.

district and session courts, and below these are subordinate courts and village courts on the civil side and magistrates on the criminal side.

16 ARMED FORCES

In 1993, Pakistan's armed forces totaled 580,600. Its army of 515,000 was the world's ninth largest, comprising 2 armored divisions, 19 infantry divisions, and 40 brigades of specialized troops and supporting arms. The navy (20,000) had 6 submarines, 3 destroyers, and 25 patrol and coastal combatants with a small naval air arm. The air force, with a total strength of 45,000, had 352 combat aircraft. Paramilitary forces, including the Pakistan rangers, the frontier corps, a maritime security agency, a national guard and local defense units, totaled 260,000.

Military service is voluntary. Defense expenditures in 1992 were estimated at $2.9 billion.

17 ECONOMY

Despite steady expansion of industry during the 1980s, Pakistan's economy remains dominated by agriculture. At $430, per person income has improved slightly since the mid-1980s when it was $400. Pakistan is generally poor in natural resources, although extensive reserves of natural gas and petroleum are being exploited. Iron ore, chromite, and low-quality coal are mined.

A growing debt, large government expenditures on public enterprises, low tax revenues, and high levels of defense spending contributed to serious financial deficits during the late 1980s. In response, in 1988 the government began a major economic reform program with World Bank and International Monetary Fund (IMF) support.

Rising inflation became a serious problem in the early 1990s, reaching 11.8% in 1990/91 and declining only somewhat to 9.2% in 1991/92. Severe floods in late 1992 weakened exports during 1992/93. Performance is expected to improve again with continued policy reform, although the country's dependence on a narrow range of exports with uncertain price prospects on the international market may prove a serious constraint.

18 INCOME

In 1992, Pakistan's gross national product was $49,477 million at current prices, or

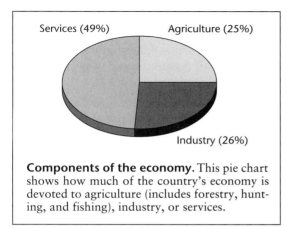

Services (49%) Agriculture (25%)

Industry (26%)

Components of the economy. This pie chart shows how much of the country's economy is devoted to agriculture (includes forestry, hunting, and fishing), industry, or services.

Other important industries include food processing, chemicals manufacture, and the iron and steel industries.

20 LABOR

In 1991–92, the total labor force was estimated at 33,800,000. In 1991–92, agriculture accounted for 51% of the total work force, and industry for 19%. Some 70% of rural residents engage in agriculture. While unemployment is officially 3.1%, underemployment has frequently gone as high as 25%, and ranged from 10–15% in 1991–92.

Workers' compensation and child labor provisions are in force, even though the practice of child labor is widespread, with some 2 to 8 million persons under 14 years of age working. Unofficial estimates indicate that as many as one-third of Pakistan's total labor force may be made up of children under age 18. Working children in Pakistan often suffer from work-related health problems and are beaten and abused. They also miss out on their education: an estimated 42% of Pakistan's children have never attended school.

Employment abroad is an important source of domestic income, with some 1.6 to 2 million Pakistanis working abroad, mostly in 13 European and Persian Gulf countries. There are also several million refugees from Afghanistan that have, in part, become part of the Pakistan labor force in those regions and in Karāchi.

21 AGRICULTURE

The development of a huge irrigation network covering two-thirds of the total cul-

$430 per person. For the period 1985–92 the average inflation rate was 8.6%, resulting in a real growth rate in gross national product of 1.7% per person.

19 INDUSTRY

Despite steady overall industrial growth during the 1980s, manufacturing remains concentrated in cotton processing, textiles, food processing and petroleum refining. Small-scale and cottage industries employ about three-fourths of Pakistan's industrial workers and account for about one-fourth of its industrial production.

Cotton textile production is the most important of Pakistan's industries. Pakistan supplies its own cotton fabrics (307 million square meters/367 million square yards produced in 1992) and exports substantial quantities. Factories also produce synthetic fabrics, worsted yarn, and jute textiles. Cotton yarn production equalled 1,171,000 tons in 1992. Jute textile output amounted to over 100,000 tons.

tivated area has made possible the farming of vast areas of previously barren and unusable land. Grains constitute the most important food crops, with wheat, rice, and corn the major products. Citrus products are also important. Cotton, the most important cash crop, generates more foreign trade income than any other export item. Rice, sugarcane, tobacco, rapeseed, and mustard are also large export earners.

Improved government policies over the past decade have made Pakistan an overall exporter of guar products, tobacco, cotton, and rice. Main crops with 1992 output (in thousands of tons) were wheat, 15,684; rice, 2,509; and sugarcane, 1,291. Seed cotton production for the year totaled 4,782,000 (9% of the world's total).

Other crops include millet, barley, sesame, flax, groundnuts, mangoes, citrus fruits, and vegetables. Opium poppies are grown in the North-West Frontier Province, despite government efforts to stamp out the opium and heroin trade, which grew rapidly during the 1980s.

22 DOMESTICATED ANIMALS

About 30 million people are engaged in the livestock industry. Camels are used for transport throughout the more barren south and west, and bullocks and donkeys elsewhere. Sheep range widely over the grazing lands of middle and northern Pakistan. The bulk of their wool is exported.

In 1992 there were 17.7 million head of cattle, 26.9 million sheep, 18.2 million buffalo, 38.5 million goats, 1 million camels, and 164 million poultry. In 1991/92, leather exports represented 3.5% of total export value. Cattle dung is an important cooking fuel and fertilizer.

23 FISHING

Almost the entire population of the coastal areas depends on fisheries for its livelihood. In all, fishing engages some 220,000 persons. The fish catch in 1991 was estimated at 515,497 tons, 78% of it landed off coastal waters. Species include salmon, mullet, pomfret, mackerel, shrimp, and local varieties. About 10% of the annual catch is exported.

24 FORESTRY

Pakistan's depleted forest resources amount to about 4.8% of the nation's total area. Hill forests are the main source for constructional timber and supply great quantities of fuel, while providing groundcover to the fragile mountain ecosystems (thereby lessening floods and droughts in the plains). Irrigated plantation forests grow species for timber, furniture, and sporting goods production.

About 500,000 cubic meters of timber is produced annually by state forests. One-half of annual wood production is consumed as fuel. Since forest resources are limited, Pakistan must import wood and wood products in increasing volumes to satisfy rising demand.

25 MINING

Except for petroleum and natural gas, mineral reserves are slight and of poor quality. Local coal is of inferior grade, and the demand requires massive imports.

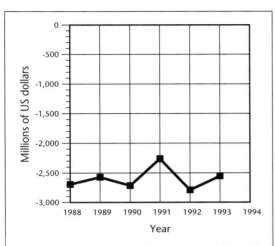

Yearly balance of trade measured in millions of US dollars. The balance of trade is the difference between what a country sells to other countries (its exports) and what it buys (its imports). If a country imports more than it exports, it has a negative balance of trade (a trade deficit). If exports exceed imports there is a positive balance of trade (a trade surplus).

Coal production stood at 3,040,000 tons in 1991. Chromite is one of the few valuable minerals available. Chromium content in mined ore rose from 1,090 tons in 1988 to 10,380 tons in 1991. Small quantities of antimony, fire clays, iron ore, uranium, gold, and silver are also produced.

26 FOREIGN TRADE

Pakistan has suffered a weak trade position since the early 1970s, as the cost of oil imports has risen while prices for the country's main exports have declined on the international market. Manufactured goods now dominate Pakistan's exports, though these are concentrated in textile and leather goods.

During the 1980s, the United Kingdom, traditionally Pakistan's most important trading partner, slipped behind the United States, Japan, and Germany. In 1992, the United States was the leading purchaser of Pakistan's export goods, and Hong Kong emerged as its third largest market, behind Japan.

Leading import suppliers were Japan, the United States, and Germany, with both China and Malaysia becoming important new sources as well.

27 ENERGY AND POWER

Pakistan is about 64% self-sufficient in energy, owing largely to crude oil reserves of an estimated 118 million barrels and large natural gas reserves of 736 billion cubic meters. Oil, about two-thirds of which is imported, meets about 40% of Pakistan's energy needs. Natural gas satisfies 35% of energy needs, while the remainder is met by hydroelectricity (18%) and coal (7%).

28 SOCIAL DEVELOPMENT

A social security scheme enacted in 1972 covers employees of firms with 10 or more workers. Social security coverage includes old age, disability, and survivor benefits, as well as sickness and maternity payments, workers' compensation, and unemployment benefits. Since 1973, cost-of-living allowances have been paid to workers earning less than minimum wage.

The government's Islamization program to promote social welfare in accordance with Islamic ideals was introduced in 1977. Islamic welfare taxes, the *zakat* and *ushr*, were levied to redistribute wealth. The ushr tax on landowners took effect in 1983. Islamic beliefs are taught in the public schools and reflected widely by the mass media. Laws against drinking alcoholic beverages, adultery, and bearing false witness have been strictly enforced.

The Women's Ministry, established in 1979, has sponsored some 7,000 centers in rural areas and urban slums to provide women with a basic education and to teach them such skills as livestock farming, midwifery, and secretarial work.

The government has taken steps to meet the threats of overpopulation. In 1991, 1,749,300 persons used family planning services.

29 HEALTH

Health facilities in Pakistan are inadequate, mainly due to a lack of resources and a high population growth rate. Despite notable advances in health care provision, 45% of the population was still without modern medical care in 1992. Total health care expenditures in 1990 were $1,394 million.

In 1992, there were 60,250 physicians and 20,000 registered homeopathic medical practitioners. Special attention has been given to the training of nurses, and several training centers are in operation. However, medical personnel ratios, though much improved, remain inadequate: 1 doctor per 2,078 persons and 1 nurse per 5,040 in 1990. The country's 652 hospitals had 55,000 beds in 1986, the vast majority located in urban areas.

Malaria, tuberculosis, intestinal diseases, venereal diseases, and skin diseases remain Pakistan's main public health problems. Drug addiction, especially among university students, is an increasing concern. Government detoxification centers helped about 30,000 addicts recover during 1981–85. Average life expectancy is estimated at 62 years.

30 HOUSING

The rapid increase in urbanization, coupled with the rising population, has added to the housing shortage in urban areas. About 25% of the people in large cities live in *katchi abadis* (shantytowns). The Public Works Department has built more than 8,000 units in Islāmābād, Lahore, and Peshāwar. In 1987, the National Housing Authority was created to coordinate the upgrading of the existing *katchi abadis* and prevent the growth of new ones. As of 1991, 171 *abadis* had been renovated, and 522 more were under development.

31 EDUCATION

In 1990, the literacy rate was 35% (male 47.3% and female 21.1%). As of 1989–90, there were 107,210 primary schools with some 9,236,000 pupils and 13,911 secondary schools with 3,647,000 students. Girls attend separate schools at both primary and secondary levels.

During the same year, 483,000 students were enrolled at 619 arts and sciences colleges, and an additional 83,482 attended 22 universities. An agricultural university was established in 1961 at Lyallpur (now Faisalābad). Two engineer-

Selected Social Indicators

These statistics are estimates for the period 1988 to 1993. For comparison purposes, data for the United States and averages for low-income countries and high-income countries are also given.

Indicator	Pakistan	Low-income countries	High-income countries	United States
Per capita gross national product†	$430	$380	$23,680	$24,740
Population growth rate	2.8%	1.9%	0.6%	1.0%
Population growth rate in urban areas	4.4%	3.9%	0.8%	1.3%
Population per square kilometer of land	150	78	25	26
Life expectancy in years	62	62	77	76
Number of people per physician	2,078	>3,300	453	419
Number of pupils per teacher (primary school)	41	39	<18	20
Illiteracy rate (15 years and older)	65%	41%	<5%	<3%
Energy consumed per capita (kg of oil equivalent)	226	364	5,203	7,918

† The gross national product (GNP) is the total dollar value of all goods and services produced by a country in a year. The per capita GNP is calculated by dividing a country's GNP by its population. The World Bank defines low-income countries as those with a per capita GNP of $695 or less. High-income countries have a per capita GNP of $8,626 or more. Less than 14% of the world's 5.5 billion people live in high-income countries, while almost 60% live in low-income countries.

> = greater than   < = less than

Sources: World Bank, *Social Indicators of Development 1995,* Baltimore: Johns Hopkins University Press, 1995. Central Intelligence Agency, *World Fact Book,* Washington, D.C.: Government Printing Office, 1994.

ing and technological universities have been founded at Lahore (1961) and Islāmābād (1966). Research institutions include the Institute of Islamic Studies at Lahore, the Iqbal Academy at Lahore, and the Pakistan Institute of International Affairs at Karāchi. Urdu and English are the languages of instruction.

Many adult literacy centers have been established in recent years. In addition, the People's Open University was established at Islāmābād (1974) to provide mass adult education through correspondence and the communications media.

32 MEDIA

As of 1991 there were 11,985 post offices. The number of telephones then in use totaled 740,340, or about 6 per 1,000 population. In 1991 there were 945,000 licensed radios and 1,558,000 licensed television receivers.

In 1991 there were 183 daily newspapers—most of them with very small circulations—printed in Urdu, English, and a few other languages. English-language newspapers are read by less than 1% of the population but are very influential, especially *Dawn* (1991 estimated circulation, 70,000) and *Pakistan Times* (75,000). Leading Urdu-language dailies (with 1991 circulations) are *Jang* (215,000) and *Jasarat Karāchi* (50,000), both in Karāchi; and *Mashriq* (4,100,000) and *Nawa-i-Waqt* (450,000), both in Lahore.

33 TOURISM AND RECREATION

In Karāchi are the National Museum and the Mausoleum of the Quaid-e-Azam. In Lahore, the "city of gardens" and Pakistan's foremost cultural and educational center, remnants of the Mughal Empire are beautifully preserved. Islāmābād, the wholly planned capital, offers notable examples of architecture in the modern style.

Popular recreations include mountain climbing in the Himalaya foothills, sailing, and deep-sea fishing off the Arabian Sea coast. Hockey and cricket are the leading sports, but golf is also popular, with courses in Lahore, Rawalpindi, Islāmābād, and other cities.

In 1991, 438,088 tourists visited the country, 212,887 from eastern Asia and 127,934 from Europe. There were 26,329 hotel rooms with a 60.5% occupancy rate.

34 FAMOUS PAKISTANIS

Several figures of monumental stature are associated with the creation and establishment of Pakistan. The poet and philosopher of a revitalized Islam, Mohammad Iqbal (1873–1938) first called for the establishment of a Muslim state on the subcontinent. Mohammad Ali Jinnah (1876–1948), the Quaid-e-Azam, or "Great Leader," became the first governor-general of the Commonwealth of Pakistan. His "right hand," Liaquat Ali Khan (1896–1951), was the first prime minister of the nation until his assassination.

Zulfikar Ali Bhutto (1928–79), who rose to prominence as founder and leader of the socialist-leaning Pakistan People's Party, was prime minister during 1973–77. After Bhutto's execution in 1979, his elder daughter, Benazir (b.1953), became official head of the Pakistan People's Party. She served as prime minister from 1988–1990 and was again chosen for the post in 1993.

In literature, the paramount position is still held by the great Urdu writers who lived before the establishment of Pakistan. Ghalib (1796–1869) and Iqbal are recognized as the two greatest Urdu poets. The Pakistani-born scientist Abdus Salam (b.1926) shared the 1979 Nobel Prize for Physics for his work in electromagnetism and the interaction of elementary particles.

35 BIBLIOGRAPHY

McCarry, John. "High Road to Hunza." *National Geographic*, March 1994, 114–134.

Mahmud, S. F. *A Concise History of Indo-Pakistan.* 2d ed. New York: Oxford University Press, 1988.

Noman, Omar. *Pakistan: A Political and Economic History Since 1947.* New York: Kegan Paul International, 1990.

Rowell, Galen. "Baltistan: The 20th Century Comes to Shangri-la." *National Geographic*, October 1987, 526–550.

Taylor, David D. *Pakistan.* Santa Barbara, Calif.: Clio Press, 1990.

PALAU

Republic of Palau
Belau

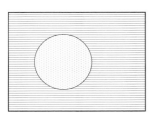

CAPITAL: Koror, Koror Island.

FLAG: The flag, adopted 1 January 1981, is light blue, with a yellow disc set slightly off center toward the hoist.

ANTHEM: *Belau er Kid.*

MONETARY UNIT: The US dollar is the official medium of exchange.

WEIGHTS AND MEASURES: British units are used, as modified by US usage.

HOLIDAYS: New Year's Day, 1 January; Youth Day, 15 March; Senior Citizens Day, 5 May; Constitution Day, 9 July; Labor Day, 1st Monday in September; United Nations Day, 24 October; Thanksgiving Day, 4th Thursday in November; Christmas, 25 December.

TIME: 8 PM = noon GMT.

1 LOCATION AND SIZE

Palau (also known as Belau) consists of the Palau group of Pacific islands, in the western Caroline Islands, and four remote islands to the southwest. The country consists of more than 200 islands, with a total land area of 441 square kilometers (170.4 square miles).

2 TOPOGRAPHY

The islands include four types of land formation: volcanic, high limestone, low platform, and coral atoll. The Palau barrier reef encircles the Palau group, except Angaur Island and the Kayangel atoll.

3 CLIMATE

The annual mean temperature is 28°C (82°F) in the coolest months. There is high precipitation throughout the year—up to 381 centimeters (150 inches)—and a relatively high humidity of 82%.

4 PLANTS AND ANIMALS

Plant life includes mangrove (trees that send out many dense roots) swamps, savanna land, and rain forest in upland areas. There are more than 1,500 species of tropical fish and 700 species of coral and anemones in the lagoons and reefs. Native animals include the sea turtle and the dugong, or sea cow.

5 ENVIRONMENT

While much of Palau is free of environmental damage, there are several areas of concern. These include illegal fishing with the use of dynamite, inadequate facilities for disposal of solid waste in the capital city of Koror, and extensive sand and coral dredging.

6 POPULATION

The 1990 census recorded a total population of 15,122. Overall population density in 1990 was 34 per square kilometer (89 per square mile).

7 MIGRATION

In 1990, persons not Palau-born numbered 2,801, or 18.5% of the total population. About one-fifth of all Palauans live abroad, many on Guam.

8 ETHNIC GROUPS

Most Palauans are Micronesians with some Melanesian genetic traits. In 1990, the largest non-Palauan ethnic groups included Filipinos (9.8%), other Micronesians (1.8%), Chinese (1.3%), and people of European descent (0.8%).

9 LANGUAGES

Palauan, a Malayo-Polynesian language related to Indonesian, is the most commonly spoken language. It is used, in addition to English, as an official language. It was the language spoken at home by 81% of the people five years of age or over in 1990.

10 RELIGIONS

Most Palauans are Roman Catholic Christians, but native religions are widespread.

11 TRANSPORTATION

The nation's roads in 1991 totaled 171.1 kilometers (106.3 miles). Palau's deepwater harbor at Koror offers international port facilities. There is one international airport. Air Micronesia/Continental, Air Nauru, and South Pacific Island Airways provide international service.

12 HISTORY

Until the end of the nineteenth century, the Carolinian island group was under Spanish colonial administration. In 1899, Spain sold the islands to Germany. At the outbreak of World War I in 1914, the islands were taken by the Japanese, who were given control of them in 1920, and Koror was developed as a Japanese administrative center in the north Pacific.

In 1947, Palau became part of the United Nations Trust Territory of the Pacific Islands, which was administered by the United States. Palau became a self-governing republic in 1981. Since 1982, the republic has been negotiating a Compact of Free Association (CPA) with the United States. Negotiations have stalled over American intentions to use the islands as a military site. In November 1993 the eighth attempt at establishing the CPA finally won approval of 68% of voters.

A new capital is under construction in eastern Babelthuap, about 20 kilometers northeast of Koror.

13 GOVERNMENT

The government is made up of executive, legislative, and judicial branches. The executive branch is headed by the president, who is elected by popular vote. The legislative branch, known as the Olbiil Era Kelulau, or National Congress, is a two-chamber legislature with 14 senators and 16 delegates. Each of Palau's 16 states has its own executive and legislative branches.

14 POLITICAL PARTIES

Palau does not have formal political parties.

15 JUDICIAL SYSTEM

The Supreme Court is the highest court in the land. Other courts include the National Court and the Court of Common Pleas.

16 ARMED FORCES

The United States is responsible for defense.

17 ECONOMY

Large gaps exist between what money the government takes in (revenues) and expenditures (what it spends). The country also imports more than it exports. These gaps are financed largely by grant aid from the United States.

18 INCOME

The gross domestic product (GDP) of Palau was estimated to be $36.1 million in 1986; or about $2,260 per person.

19 INDUSTRY

A plant to process copra (dried coconut meat) is located south of Koror. Concrete blocks are manufactured, using imported cement. There is also a small-scale sawmill industry.

20 LABOR

There were 6,250 persons engaged in various occupations in 1986. National government workers accounted for 40% of wage employment in 1986.

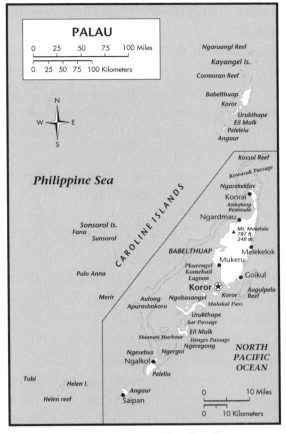

LOCATION: 131° to 135°E; 3° to 8°N.

21 AGRICULTURE

Staple subsistence crops include taros (edible roots), cassavas, sweet potatoes, bananas, and papayas. Commercial produce consists mostly of copra (dried coconut meat) and coconut oil, vegetables, and a wide variety of tropical fruits.

22 DOMESTICATED ANIMALS

Livestock is limited to pigs, chickens, ducks, cattle, and goats.

23 FISHING

Palau's marine resources are rich and diverse. The total catch was 4,068 tons in 1991. Deep-sea fishing resulted in a tuna catch of 2,706 tons in 1991.

24 FORESTRY

Palau is heavily dependent on imported forestry products, including furniture and lumber for house construction.

25 MINING

The Koror state government engages in commercial production of dredged coral from the Palau lagoon, with a production capacity of 800 cubic meters per day.

26 FOREIGN TRADE

Imports include food, beverages, and tobacco; manufactured goods; and machinery and transportation equipment. The country's limited range of exports includes shells; fresh, frozen, and smoked fish; and wooden handicrafts.

27 ENERGY AND POWER

The economy is almost totally dependent on imported petroleum for energy. Electricity is supplied from one power plant, with an installed capacity of approximately 8,000 kilowatts.

28 SOCIAL DEVELOPMENT

Social organization is based on the maternal kin group, or clan. Villages ideally consist of ten clans, with the leader of the highest ranking clan serving as village chief.

29 HEALTH

Hospital services are provided by the MacDonald Memorial Hospital in Koror, which has 60 beds.

30 HOUSING

There were 2,501 occupied houses in 1986. About 80% of all houses have water and electricity.

31 EDUCATION

Elementary education is free and compulsory for all Palauan children aged 6–14. In 1990, there were 369 students in private schools and 1,756 in public schools.

32 MEDIA

A radio station in Koror broadcasts to listeners in the outer islands. Television is limited to one channel in the Koror area.

33 TOURISM AND RECREATION

Palau is rich in live coral formations and tropical fish, making the country a popular destination for snorkeling and scuba diving. Many tourists visit the World War II battlefields, war memorials, and shrines.

34 FAMOUS PALAUANS

Lazarus E. Salii (b.1937) became the third president of Palau in September 1985.

35 BIBLIOGRAPHY

Parmentier, Richard J. *The Sacred Remains: Myth, History, and Polity in Belau.* Chicago: University of Chicago Press, 1987.

Roff, Sue Rabbitt. *Overreaching in Paradise: United States Policy in Palau Since 1945.* Juneau, Alaska: Denali Press, 1991.

PANAMA

Republic of Panama
República de Panamá

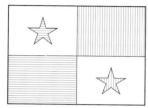

CAPITAL: Panama City (Panamá).

FLAG: The national flag is divided into quarters. The upper quarter next to the staff is white with a blue star; the upper outer quarter is red; the lower quarter next to the staff is blue; and the lower outer quarter is white with a red star.

ANTHEM: *Himno Nacional,* beginning "Alcanzamos por fin la victoria" ("We reach victory at last").

MONETARY UNIT: The balboa (B) of 100 centésimos is the national unit of account. Panama issues no paper money, and US notes are legal tender. Panama mints coins of 0.05, 0.10, 0.25, 0.50, 1 and 5 balboas which are interchangeable with US coins.

WEIGHTS AND MEASURES: The metric system is official, but British, US, and old Spanish units are also used.

HOLIDAYS: New Year's Day, 1 January; Martyrs' Day, 9 January; Labor Day, 1 May; National Revolution Day, 11 October; National Anthem Day, 1 November; All Souls' Day, 2 November; Independence from Colombia, 3 November; Flag Day, 4 November; Independence Day (Colón only), 5 November; First Call of Independence, 10 November; Independence from Spain, 28 November; Mother's Day and Immaculate Conception, 8 December; Christmas, 25 December. Movable religious holidays are Shrove Tuesday and Good Friday.

TIME: 7 AM = noon GMT.

1 LOCATION AND SIZE

The Republic of Panama, situated on the Isthmus (narrow strip of land connecting two larger areas) of Panama, has an area of 78,200 square kilometers (30,193 square miles), slightly smaller than the state of South Carolina.

The Canal Zone (1,432 square kilometers/553 square miles), over which the United States formerly exercised sovereignty, was incorporated into Panama on 1 October 1979. Panama has a total boundary length of 3,045 kilometers (1,892 miles).

Its capital city, Panama City, is located where the Panama Canal meets the Gulf of Panama.

2 TOPOGRAPHY

Panama is a country of heavily forested hills and mountain ranges. The eastern San Blas mountain chain (Cordillero de San Blas) parallels the Caribbean coastline. In the west is the Barú volcano (Volcán Barú) (3,475 meters/11,401 feet), formerly known as Chiriquí. The Panama Canal lies in the central part of the country that averages only 87 meters (285 feet) in altitude. Panama has over 300 rivers, most of them short, and more than 1,600 islands.

3 CLIMATE

The annual average temperature on both coasts is 27°C (81°F), and it ranges from 10° to 19°C (50° to 66°F) at various mountain elevations. There is little seasonal change in temperature. Humidity is quite high, averaging 80%. Rainfall averages 178 centimeters (70 inches) in Panama City and 328 centimeters (129 inches) in Colón.

4 PLANTS AND ANIMALS

Most of Panama is a thick jungle, with occasional patches of savanna or prairie. On the wet Caribbean coast, the forest is evergreen, while on the drier Pacific side it is semi-deciduous. Species of flowering plants exceed 2,000 and include the national flower, the Holy Ghost orchid. Mammals inhabiting the isthmus (narrow strip of land connecting two larger land masses) are the anteater, armadillo, bat, coati, deer, opossum, peccary, raccoon, tapir, and many varieties of monkey. Reptiles, especially alligators, are numerous along the coasts. Bird life is rich and varied, and fish abound.

5 ENVIRONMENT

Panama's soil is eroding at a rate of 2,000 tons per year. During the late 1980s and early 1990s, the nation lost 139 square miles of its forests. Air pollution from industry and transportation is also a problem in the urban centers. Water pollution from pesticides, sewage, and the oil industry directly affects 44% of rural dwellers, who do not have pure water. As of 1994, 13 of Panama's mammal species and 14 of its bird species were endangered. Of the nation's plant species, a total of 549 are threatened with extinction.

6 POPULATION

The census of 13 May 1990 showed the total population as 2,329,329, excluding residents of the former Canal Zone. The mid-1994 estimate was 2,630,791, and the United Nations projection for the year 2000 was 2,893,000. Panama's estimated population density is 33 persons per square kilometer (85 persons per square mile). Panama City, the capital, had 584,803 inhabitants in 1990.

7 MIGRATION

Immigration and emigration have been roughly in balance in recent years. In the 1990s, 134,953 residents entered the country and 149,028 left. There were 61,400 foreign-born persons in Panama that year, of whom 13,644 were Colombians.

8 ETHNIC GROUPS

The racial and cultural composition of Panama is highly diverse. According to recent estimates, some 67–70% of the inhabitants are mestizo (mixed white and Amerindian) or mulatto (mixed white and black); 14% are black (West Indians); 10–14% are white (mostly Europeans); and 5–8% are Amerindian. There is also a Chinese community of about 100,000.

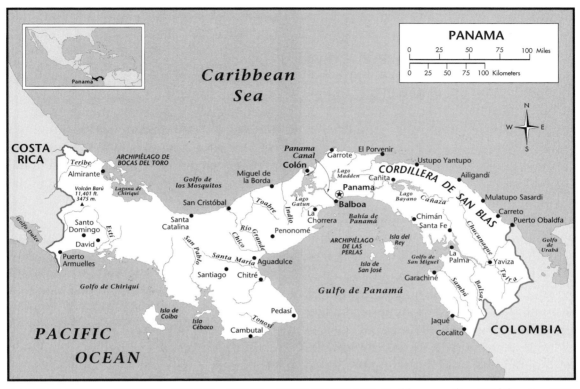

Map scale:

PANAMA

0 25 50 75 100 Miles

0 25 50 75 100 Kilometers

LOCATION: 7°12′9″ to 9°37′57″N; 77°9′24″ to 83°3′7″W. **BOUNDARY LENGTHS:** Caribbean coastline, 963 kilometers (596 miles); Colombia, 225 kilometers (140 miles); Pacific coastline, 1,527 kilometers (950 miles); Costa Rica, 330 kilometers (206 miles). **TERRITORIAL SEA LIMIT:** 200 miles.

9 LANGUAGES

Spanish, the official language of Panama, is spoken by over 90% of the people, but English is a common second language. The Amerindians use their own languages.

10 RELIGIONS

An estimated 80% of the people are Catholic, 5% Protestant, and 4.5% Muslim. There are about 25,000 Baha'is, 7,400 Hindus, 5,300 followers of Amerindian tribal religions, 3,800 Chinese folk-religionists, 3,100 Jews, and 2,800 Buddhists.

11 TRANSPORTATION

In 1991, there were 8,500 kilometers (5,283 miles) of roads, of which 32.3% were paved. The 80-kilometer (50-mile) Trans-Isthmian Highway links Colón and Panama City. In 1991, there were 150,000 registered passenger cars and 46,000 trucks and buses.

Railway lines total 238 kilometers (148 miles) of track. The Panama Railroad parallels the canal for 77 kilometers (48 miles) between Colón and Panama City.

The Panamanian merchant marine was the world's largest in 1991, with 3,040 registered ships, totaling 46.1 million gross registered tons. Panama is a crossroads for air travel within the Americas. The main airfield is Omar Torrijos International Airport. Compañía Panameña de Aviación (COPA) carried 379,400 passengers in 1992.

The Panama Canal traverses the isthmus and is 82 kilometers (51 miles) in length from deep water to deep water. In 1991, it handled cargo totaling 165.8 million tons through 14,108 transits.

12 HISTORY

The isthmus region was an area of sea trade long before Europeans explored it. It was also the meeting point of several significant Amerindian cultures: Mayan, Aztec, Chibcha, and Carib.

European Influence

In 1502, Columbus claimed Panama for Spain. In 1513, Vasco Nuñez de Balboa led soldiers across the isthmus and made the European discovery of the Pacific Ocean. Despite strong resistance by the Cuna Amerindians, the first settlements, including Panama City, were established on the coasts. In 1567, Panama was made part of the viceroyalty of Peru.

From the sixteenth until the mid-eighteenth century, the isthmus was a strategic link in Spanish trade with the west coast of South America, especially the viceregal capital of Lima. In 1740, the isthmus was placed under the jurisdiction of the newly recreated viceroyalty of New Granada.

Panama declared its independence from Spain in 1821 and joined the Republic of Gran Colombia, a short-lived union of Colombia, Venezuela, and Ecuador, founded in 1819. In 1826, Panama was the seat of the Pan American Conference called by the Liberator, Simón Bolívar. When Gran Colombia was dissolved in 1829–30, Panama still remained part of Colombia. Secessionist revolts took place in 1830 and 1831, and during 1840–41.

The Panama Canal and Independence

The discovery of gold in California in 1848 brought the isthmus into prominence as a canal site linking the Atlantic and Pacific Oceans. The United States negotiated the Hay-Herrán Treaty over canal rights with Colombia in 1903. After Colombia refused to ratify the treaty, Panama seceded from Colombia. Backed by US naval forces, Panama declared its independence on 3 November 1903.

Panama then signed a canal agreement with the United States and received a lump sum of $10 million and an annual rent of $250,000. The Hay-Bunau-Varilla Treaty (1903) permanently granted the United States an 8-kilometer (5-mile) strip of land on either side of the canal and permitted it to intervene to protect its interests in the region.

The United States intervened to establish order in 1908 (during the time the canal was under construction), in 1917 after the canal had opened to traffic, and again in 1918. In 1936, however, the United States adopted a policy of nonintervention, and in 1955, the annual rent

A tugboat assisting a tanker on the Panama Canal.

paid by the United States was raised to $1,930,000.

In the decades following World War II (1939–45), the question of sovereignty over the Canal Zone was a persistent source of conflict in Panamanian politics. In 1964, riots broke out in the Canal Zone whe Panamanians protested American neglect of a 1962 joint Panama-US flag-flying agreement. From then on, Panama sought sovereignty over the Canal Zone.

In October 1968, National Guard Brigadier General Omar Torrijos Herrera deposed the elected president and established a dictatorship.

US Signs Canal Treaties

Final agreement on the future of the canal and the Canal Zone came on 7 September 1977. General Torrijos and US president Jimmy Carter signed the Panama Canal Treaty. The treaty recognized Panama's sovereignty over the Canal Zone, but granted the United States rights to operate, maintain, and manage the canal through 31 December 1999. After that date, ownership of the canal itself would revert to Panama.

In addition, a so-called Neutrality Treaty guaranteed the neutrality of the canal and denied the United States the right of intervention into Panamanian affairs. The treaties were ratified by popular vote in Panama on 23 October 1977. After prolonged debate and extensive amendment the treaties were also passed by the US Senate in March and April 1978.

Torrijos resigned as head of government in 1978 but continued to rule behind the scenes as National Guard commander until his death in a plane crash on 31 July 1981. Over the next few years, the National Guard, now renamed the Panama Defense Forces (PDF), came under the influence of General Manuel Noriega, as a succession of civilian governments followed each other.

Noriega and Drugs

By 1987, Noriega had been accused by close associates and the United States of falsifying the 1984 election results, drug trafficking, giving aid to the Colombian and Salvadoran rebels, and providing military secrets to Cuba. The United States Senate approved legislation cutting off aid to Panama in December 1987. In February 1988, Noriega was indicted in US courts for drug trafficking. Throughout 1988 and 1989, both the United States and Panamanian opposition struggled to oust Noriega, who clung to power.

In December 1989, after a series of moves including a trade embargo by the United States calculated to bring down the Noriega regime, Noreiga declared war on the United States and ordered attacks on US military personnel. President George Bush responded quickly, ordering the US military into Panama. Noriega surren-

dered and was sent to the United States for trial.

The administration of Guillermo Endara, who became president after the downfall of Noriega, was widely criticized for the continuing poor economic conditions. In May 1994, a new president, Perez Balladares was elected.

13 GOVERNMENT

Under the constitution of 1972, Panama is a republic in which the president, assisted by a cabinet, exercises executive power. Legislative power is vested in the unicameral Legislative Assembly. The 67 members are elected for five-year terms by direct popular vote. All Panamanians 18 years of age or over have the right to vote.

Panama is divided into nine provinces, each subdivided into 65 municipal districts.

14 POLITICAL PARTIES

The coalition that came to power in 1990 consisted of President Guillermo Endara's Arnulfista Party, led by Dr. Arnulfo Escalona; the National Liberal Republican Movement (MOLIRENA), led by second vice-president Guillermo Ford; and the Christian Democratic Party (PDC), led by first vice-president Ricardo Arias. Later, Arias broke from the coalition, and the PDC, which controls the Legislative Assembly, is now the leader of the opposition.

15 JUDICIAL SYSTEM

Judicial authority rests with the Supreme Court, which is composed of nine magis-

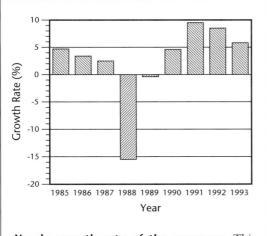

Yearly growth rate of the economy. This economic indicator tells by what percent the economy has increased or decreased when compared with the previous year.

the United States embargo and subsequent military invasion, aimed at bringing down General Manuel Noriega, who was responsible for an increase in drug trafficking. By 1992, Panama's economic growth was among the strongest in the Western Hemisphere. In 1993, the economy continued to grow, but at a slower pace.

Panama's economy is based on well-developed service industries, including the Panama Canal, banking, insurance, and government. Panama does not print any money and, therefore, lacks an independent monetary policy. The US dollar is the legal tender in the nation.

18 INCOME

In 1992, Panama's gross national product (GNP) was $6,133 million at current prices, or about $2,600 per person. For the period 1985–92, the average annual inflation rate was 1.3%, resulting in a real growth rate in GNP of –1.2% per person.

19 INDUSTRY

Industry, generally light, consists principally of food-processing and alcoholic beverage production, ceramics, tropical clothing, cigarettes, hats, furniture, shoes, soap, and edible oils. The government encourages industrialization by granting special tax breaks to new enterprises and imposing protective duties on competing foreign manufacturers. The Industrial Development Bank promotes small industries and provides credit on a long-term basis.

trates. There are 4 superior courts, 18 circuit courts, and at least 1 municipal court in each district. At the local level, two types of administrative judges, "corregidores" and "night" (or "police") judges, hear minor civil and criminal cases involving sentences under one year.

16 ARMED FORCES

The new National Police Force numbers 11,000, supported by a maritime service (350 staff, 3 patrol boats) and air service (350 staff, 14 aircraft and helos). The United States maintains troops numbering 10,500 in the Canal Zone. In 1990 Panama spent $75.5 million on defense.

17 ECONOMY

In the early 1990s, Panama rebounded from a severe recession brought about by

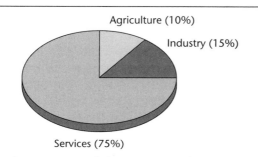

Agriculture (10%)

Industry (15%)

Services (75%)

Components of the economy. This pie chart shows how much of the country's economy is devoted to agriculture (includes forestry, hunting, and fishing), industry, or services.

20 LABOR

In 1991, the economically active population numbered 858,509. Of the employed work force of 721,800 Panamanians in 1991, government and services engaged 26.3%; commerce, 19.8%; agriculture, 22.9%; manufacturing/mining, 9.4%; construction, 3.6%; transportation and communications, 6.2%; utilities, 1.2%; business services, 4.1%; and other areas, 6.5%. The unemployment rate declined from 17% in 1990 to 15.7% in 1991.

Minimum age laws regulate child labor, and these are usually enforced, although less so in Panama's interior.

21 AGRICULTURE

About 8.6% of the total land area was classified as cultivable in 1991. Farming methods are primitive, and productivity is low. The best lands are held by large owners.

Panama provides its own bananas, sugar, rice, corn, and coffee, but imports large quantities of other foods. Agricultural production grew by 3% in 1992. Banana exports rose by 3% in 1992 to 40.1 million boxes, with over half destined for the German market. Sugar exports fell by about 13% in 1992, while coffee exports dropped by 20.4% the same year. In 1992, crop production (in tons) included raw sugar, 1,400,000; bananas, 1,110,000; rice, 165,000; corn, 95,000; and coffee, 12,000.

22 DOMESTICATED ANIMALS

The Panamanian livestock industry produces enough meat to supply domestic demand and provides hides for export. Most cattle and hogs are tended by small herders, and dairy farming has expanded in recent years. In 1992, there were 1,400,000 head of cattle, 257,000 hogs, and 9,000,000 poultry. Milk production in 1992 totaled 127,000 tons; egg production, 12,000 tons.

23 FISHING

The offshore waters of Panama abound in fish and seafood, and fisheries are a significant segment of the national economy. There is freshwater fishing in the rivers and deep-sea fishing along the Pacific and Caribbean coasts for amberjack, barracuda, bonito, corbina, dolphin, mackerel, pompano, red snapper, sailfish, sea bass, and tuna.

In 1991, the fish catch totaled 147,435 tons. In addition, 65,417 tons of anchovies were caught in 1992.

24 FORESTRY

Forests and woodland cover about 43% of the country's area but have been largely unused for forestry products because of a lack of transportation facilities. Hardwood, particularly mahogany, is produced for export, and abacá fiber, which is used in the making of marine cordage, is a valuable forest product. Estimated production of roundwood was 1.87 million cubic meters in 1991.

25 MINING

Mining is limited, but there are known deposits of copper, manganese, iron, asbestos, gold, and silver. Commercial deposits of gold and silver were discovered in the region around Santiago in 1980. Salt, produced by evaporation of seawater at Aguadulce, is a major mineral product; the total salt output was an estimated 5,000 tons in 1991.

26 FOREIGN TRADE

In 1992, total merchandise exports accounted for $700 million. Exports were mainly composed of sugar, bananas, shrimp and other seafood, coffee, sugar, clothing, and petroleum products. Imports recorded $1,600 million, including food products and petroleum. Main manufactured exports include foodstuffs, beverages and tobacco, 22%; textiles, apparel and leather, 51%; chemicals, petroleum, carbon, rubber, and plastic by-products, 17%; machinery and equipment, 3%.

As of 1992, Panama's major trading partners were as follows: the United States, Central America (Costa Rica, El Salvador, Guatemala, Honduras, and Nicaragua), and Europe for exports; the United States, Central America, Mexico, Japan, Venezuela, and Europe for imports.

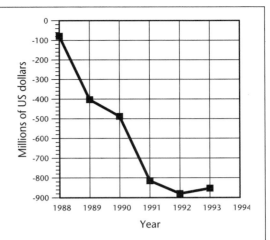

Yearly balance of trade measured in millions of US dollars. The balance of trade is the difference between what a country sells to other countries (its exports) and what it buys (its imports). If a country imports more than it exports, it has a negative balance of trade (a trade deficit). If exports exceed imports, there is a positive balance of trade (a trade surplus).

27 ENERGY AND POWER

Production of electric power totaled 2.9 billion kilowatt-hours in 1991. About 65% of Panama's electrical power capacity is hydroelectric. A geothermal region in southwest Panama has an estimated potential of 400,000 kilowatts. Some energy is also obtained from fuel wood.

The inauguration in 1982 of a trans-Panamanian pipeline assists the shipment of Alaskan crude oil to the eastern United States by allowing the loading and unloading of supertankers (large ships) on both sides of the isthmus. The pipeline's maximum capacity is 830,000 barrels per day.

28 SOCIAL DEVELOPMENT

The Social Security Fund provides medical service and hospitalization, maternity care, pensions for disability and old age, and funeral benefits. Children are cared for through a child welfare institute, which operates under the Ministry of Labor and Social Welfare. The government has made efforts to integrate the Amerindian population of the eastern Caribbean coast through land grants, basic education, and improved transportation. The social security system covered more than one million persons in the mid-1980s.

While Panama has a relatively high rate of female enrollment in higher education, many female graduates are still forced to take low-paying jobs. Only 5% of the country's managerial positions are occupied by women.

29 HEALTH

Public health services include free health examinations and medical care for the needy, health education, sanitation inspection, hospital and clinic construction, and nutrition services. In 1988, Panama had 4,131 physicians. In 1990, the population per physician was 834, and there were 2.7 hospital beds per 1,000 inhabitants. In 1992, 80% of the population had access to health care services.

Malaria has been controlled and the yellow-fever mosquito practically eliminated. Today, the principal causes of death are cancer, heart disease, cerebrovascular disease, pneumonia and bronchopneumonia, and enteritis and diarrhea. In some areas of Panama, poor sanitation, inadequate housing, and malnutrition still constitute health hazards. Average life expectancy in 1992 was 73 years.

30 HOUSING

Housing in urban areas has been a permanent problem since US construction in the Canal Zone brought a great influx of migrant laborers into Colón and Panama City. In the early 1980s, however, the shortage of low-income housing remained acute, particularly in Colón. According to the latest available information for 1980–88, total housing units numbered 448,000 with 4.9 people per dwelling.

31 EDUCATION

In 1990, illiteracy was estimated at 12% of the adult population (males, 10.6% and females, 11.7%) compared with 21% 20 years earlier. Education is free and compulsory for children aged 7 through 15. In 1990, there were 2,659 primary schools with 350,931 students. At the secondary schools there were 191,251 students.

Universities include the state-run University of Panama and Santa María la Antigua. In 1991, at all institutions of higher learning, there were 3,308 teaching staff with 58,625 students enrolled.

32 MEDIA

In 1992, there were 91 AM commercial radio broadcasting stations and 23 television channels. In that year there were 552,000 radios and 410,000 television

Selected Social Indicators

These statistics are estimates for the period 1988 to 1993. For comparison purposes, data for the United States and averages for low-income countries and high-income countries are also given.

Indicator	Panama	Low-income countries	High-income countries	United States
Per capita gross national product†	$2,600	$380	$23,680	$24,740
Population growth rate	2.0%	1.9%	0.6%	1.0%
Population growth rate in urban areas	2.6%	3.9%	0.8%	1.3%
Population per square kilometer of land	33	78	25	26
Life expectancy in years	73	62	77	76
Number of people per physician	834	>3,300	453	419
Number of pupils per teacher (primary school)	23	39	<18	20
Illiteracy rate (15 years and older)	12%	41%	<5%	<3%
Energy consumed per capita (kg of oil equivalent)	599	364	5,203	7,918

† The gross national product (GNP) is the total dollar value of all goods and services produced by a country in a year. The per capita GNP is calculated by dividing a country's GNP by its population. The World Bank defines low-income countries as those with a per capita GNP of $695 or less. High-income countries have a per capita GNP of $8,626 or more. Less than 14% of the world's 5.5 billion people live in high-income countries, while almost 60% live in low-income countries.

> = greater than   < = less than

Sources: World Bank, *Social Indicators of Development 1995,* Baltimore: Johns Hopkins University Press, 1995. Central Intelligence Agency, *World Fact Book,* Washington, D.C.: Government Printing Office, 1994.

sets. In 1993, there were 260,000 telephones, mainly in the Panama City area. Leading Panama City dailies, with their estimated 1991 circulations, are *Crítica* (40,000); *El Siglo* (36,000); *El Panama America* (32,000); and *The Star and Herald* (25,000).

33 TOURISM AND RECREATION

The government encourages tourism through the Panamanian Tourist Bureau and is promoting investment in some of the most remote parts of the country, including Coiba Island (Isla de Coiba). In 1991, 279,000 tourists arrived in Panama, 269,000 of them from the Americas. Revenues from tourism totaled an estimated $196 million.

In addition to the Panama Canal itself, tourist attractions include Panama City, beach resorts in the Pearls Archipelago (Archipélago de las Perlas), and the resorts in the mountains. Water sports, tennis, golf, and horse racing are popular.

34 FAMOUS PANAMANIANS

Outstanding political figures of the nineteenth century include Tomás Herrera (1804–54), the national hero who led the first republican movement; and Justo Arosemena (1817–96), a writer and nationalist. The most important political leader of the 20th century was Omar Torrijos Herrera (1929–81), who ruled Panama from 1969 until his death and successfully negotiated the Panama Canal treaties of 1979 with the United States.

Important poets include Tomás del Espíritu Santo (1834–62) and Ricardo Miró (1888–1940). Panamanian-born José Benjamin Quintero (b.1924) is a noted stage director in the US. Harmodio Arias (1886–1962) was the prominent owner of the newspaper *El Panamá-America*. Leading Panamanian painters include Epifanio Garay (1849–1903) and Humberto Ivaldi (1909–47). Noteworthy among Panamanian athletes is the former world light- and welter-weight boxing champion Roberto Durán (b.1949).

35 BIBLIOGRAPHY

Conniff, Michael. *Black Labor on a White Canal: Panama*. Pittsburgh, Pennsylvania: University of Pittsburgh Press, 1985.

Greene, Graham. *Getting to Know the General*. New York: Simon & Schuster, 1984.

Meditz, Sandra W., and Dennis M. Hanratty, eds. *Panama: A Country Study*. 4th ed. Washington, D.C.: Library of Congress, 1989.

Vizquez, A. *Panama*. Chicago: Children's Press, 1991.

PAPUA NEW GUINEA

Independent State of Papua New Guinea

CAPITAL: Port Moresby.

FLAG: The flag is a rectangle, divided diagonally. The upper segment is scarlet with a yellow bird of paradise; the lower segment is black with five white stars representing the Southern Cross.

ANTHEM: *O, Arise All You Sons.*

MONETARY UNIT: The kina (κ) of 100 toea is linked with the Australian dollar. There are coins of 1, 2, 5, 10, 20, and 50 toea and 1 kina, and notes of 2, 5, 10, 20, and 50 kina. κ1=US$1.0391 or US$1=κ 0.9624.

WEIGHTS AND MEASURES: The metric system is the legal standard.

HOLIDAYS: New Year's Day, 1 January; Queen's Birthday, 1st Monday in June; Remembrance Day, 23 July; Independence Day, 16 September; Christmas, 25 December; Boxing Day, 26 December. Movable religious holidays include Good Friday and Easter Monday.

TIME: 10 PM=noon GMT.

1 LOCATION AND SIZE

Situated to the north of Australia, Papua New Guinea has a total land area of 461,690 square kilometers (178,259 square miles), slightly larger than the state of California. Mainland Papua New Guinea occupies the eastern portion of the island of New Guinea, the second-largest island in the world. It shares the island with its western neighbor, a province of Indonesia. Papua New Guinea has a total boundary length of 5,972 kilometers (3,711 miles).

Papua New Guinea's capital city, Port Moresby, is located on the country's southern coast.

2 TOPOGRAPHY

The eastern half of the island of New Guinea is dominated by a massive central cordillera, or chain of mountain ranges. A second mountain chain runs parallel to it. Active and recently active volcanoes are prominent features of New Guinea landscapes. In the lowlands are many swamps and floodplains. Important rivers are the Sepik and the Fly.

The smaller islands of Papua New Guinea generally feature mountain ranges rising directly from the sea or from narrow coastal plains.

3 CLIMATE

Annual rainfall varies widely with the monsoon pattern, ranging from as little as 100 centimeters (40 inches) at Port Moresby to as much as 750 centimeters (300 inches) in other coastal regions. Most of the lowland and island areas have daily mean temperatures of about 27°C (81°F),

Photo credit: Cynthia Bassett

Villagers returning from a day of fishing.

while in the highlands temperatures may fall to 4°C (39°F) at night and rise to 32°C (90°F) in the daytime. Relative humidity is uniformly high in the lowlands at about 80%.

4 PLANTS AND ANIMALS

In low-lying coastal areas, various species of mangroves (trees that send out many dense roots) form the main vegetation, together with tropical trees such as the casuarina, sago, and palm. Most of the country is covered by rainforests, in which valuable trees such as kwila and cedar are found. Orchids, lilies, ferns, and creepers abound. There are large stands of pine at higher elevations, and at the highest altitudes, mosses, lichens, and other alpine plants grow.

Papua New Guinea supports a great variety of bird life. About 850 species have been recognized. Papua New Guinea is the major center for a number of bird families, particularly the bird of paradise, bower bird, cassowary, kingfisher, and parrot. There are about 200 species of mammals, many nocturnal. Rodents and marsupials (animals that have pouches for their young) predominate. Butterflies of Papua New Guinea are world famous for their size and vivid coloring.

5 ENVIRONMENT

Papua New Guinea's environmental concerns include pollution, global warming, and the loss of the nation's forests. Coastal waters are polluted with sewage and residue from oil spills. Some 6% of the nation's city dwellers and 30% of rural people do not have pure water. Another significant source of pollution is open-pit mining. In 1994, 5 of the nation's mammal species and 25 of its bird species were endangered, as well as 88 types of plants.

6 POPULATION

The census population in 1990 was 3,689,038. The United Nations projection for the year 2000 was 4,867,000. Estimated population density is 9 persons per square kilometer (20 per square mile). Port Moresby, the capital, had a 1990 population of 193,242.

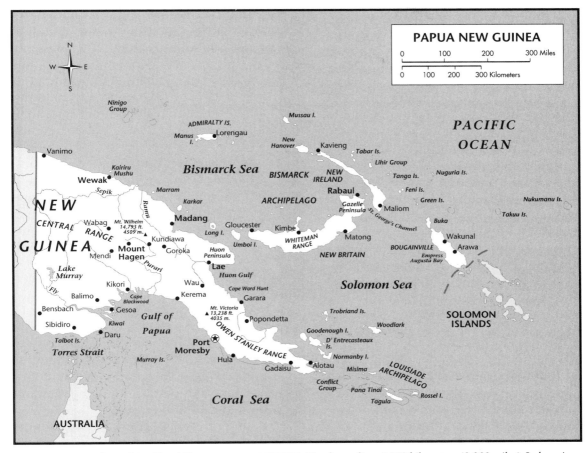

LOCATION: 140°51′ to 160°E; 0° to 12°S. **BOUNDARY LENGTHS:** Total coastline, 5,152 kilometers (3,202 miles); Indonesia, 820 kilometers (509 miles). **TERRITORIAL SEA LIMIT:** 12 miles.

7 MIGRATION

The numbers of emigrants and immigrants have been roughly equal in recent years. In 1982–86, an average of 4,079 residents left the country each year, while 5,109 persons entered intending residency. Many more came as refugees from the neighboring province of Indonesia on the island of New Guinea. In 1993, some 3,750 such immigrants were living in a camp in the west.

8 ETHNIC GROUPS

The native people are Melanesians. They are usually classified by language group, with Papuans representing the descendants of the original Australoid migration and Austronesian speakers descended from later migrants. Of the non-native population, the largest group is Australian, followed by others of European and Chinese origin.

Photo credit: Cynthia Bassett

At the annual Sing Sing, tribes gather in native dress to dance and preserve their tribal traditions.

9 LANGUAGES

There are now three official languages: English, Pidgin (a Melanesian common language with roots primarily in English and German), and Hiri Motu, another common language of Papuan origin. In all, there are more than 700 native languages.

10 RELIGIONS

Native religions, varying widely in ritual and belief, remain important in tribal societies in Papua New Guinea. More than 90% of the population are formally Christian. Of these, an estimated two-thirds are Protestants and about one-third Catholics. Baha'ism is the only other non-native faith that has gained a foothold.

11 TRANSPORTATION

Transportation is a major problem in Papua New Guinea because of the difficult terrain. Of some 19,200 kilometers (11,900 miles) of roads, only 640 kilometers (400 miles) are paved. In 1992 there were 41,300 motor vehicles. Papua New Guinea has no railroads.

The principal harbors are Madang, Port Moresby, Lae, and Rabaul. There are international shipping services by refrigerated container ships and other cargo vessels. In 1992, Papua New Guinea's national air carrier, Air Niugini, carried 764,600 international and domestic passengers. There are 19 airports.

12 HISTORY

New Guinea was first sighted by Spanish and Portuguese sailors in the early sixteenth century and was known as Isla del Oro (Island of Gold). The western part of the island was claimed by Spain in 1545 and named New Guinea for an imagined resemblance of the people to those on the West African coast. Traders began to appear in the islands in the 1850s, and the Germans sought the coconut oil trade in northern New Guinea about that time.

In 1884, Britain established a claim on the southern coast of New Guinea and adjacent islands. The Germans claimed three different parts of northern New Guinea. British New Guinea passed to Australian control in 1902 and was renamed the Territory of Papua in 1906. ("Papua" is a Malay word for the typically frizzled quality of Melanesian hair.) German New Guinea remained intact until the outbreak of World War I in 1914, when it was seized by Australian forces. In 1921, the former German New Guinea was placed under League of Nations control, administered by Australia. In 1947, it became the Trust Territory of New Guinea.

Both territories were merged into the Territory of Papua and New Guinea in 1949. Eight years later, the territory was renamed Papua New Guinea. On 1 December 1973, it was granted self-government.

Separatist movements in Papua in 1973 and secessionist activities on the island of Bougainville in 1975 flared briefly and then died out. Papua New Guinea achieved complete independence on 16 September 1975, with Michael Somare as prime minister of a coalition government.

A secessionist crisis on Bougainville dominated domestic politics during 1990–91. The Bougainville Revolutionary Army (BRA) declared the island of Bougainville to be independent from Papua New Guinea in May 1990, and in response government forces landed on the north of Bougainville in April 1991.

During 1993 the Government continued to extend its control over Bougainville, partly because of popular disapproval of human rights violations by members of the BRA. A dispute with the Solomon Islands over its support of the BRA led to an invasion by troops of the Papua New Guinea army into the Solomon Islands in April 1993.

13 GOVERNMENT

Papua New Guinea is an independent, parliamentary democracy in the Commonwealth of Nations, with a governor-general representing the British crown. Under the 1975 constitution, legislative power is vested in the National Parliament of 109 members. Voting is universal and compulsory for adults at age 18.

Papua New Guinea is divided into 20 provinces, each headed by a premier.

14 POLITICAL PARTIES

The Pangu Pati, still active, formed Papua New Guinea's first coalition government after it became independent. Eight parties have been founded since 1978. One of them, the People's Democratic Movement, formed in 1985 by former members of the Pangu Pati, won 18 seats in the 1987 elections, while the Pangu Pati captured 25. Other parties that participated in the 1992 elections were the People's Action Party, the People's Progress Party, the League for National Advancement, the United Party, the Papua Party, the National Party, and the Melanesian Alliance.

15 JUDICIAL SYSTEM

The Supreme Court is the nation's highest judicial authority and final court of appeal. Other courts are the National Court, district courts, and local courts, established to deal with minor offenses.

16 ARMED FORCES

The main armed force is the Papua New Guinea Defense Force, which in 1993 had 3,800 men, 5 large patrol boats, 1 landing craft, and 9 aircraft (3 armed). The Papua New Guinea police force has a strength of about 4,600. Australia provides 100 advisors and engineers.

17 ECONOMY

Economic activity is concentrated in two areas, agriculture and mining. New mining operations have made up for the 1989 closing of the Bougainville copper mine, which had been a chief foreign exchange earner since the early 1970s. Economic growth, which averaged 3.7% between 1985 and 1988, rose to about 10% in 1991 and 12% in 1992. Papua New Guinea's economy relies heavily on the inflow of Australian aid, which was reduced by 5% per year between 1985 and 1990 by mutual agreement.

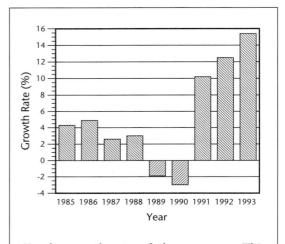

Yearly growth rate of the economy. This economic indicator tells by what percent the economy has increased or decreased when compared with the previous year.

18 INCOME

In 1992, Papua New Guinea's gross national product (GNP) was $3,846 million at current prices, or about $1,130 per person. For the period 1985–92 the average inflation rate was 4.1%, resulting in a real growth rate in GNP of –0.1%.

19 INDUSTRY

Industries are concentrated in industrial metals, timber processing, machinery, food, drinks, and tobacco. Handicraft and cottage industries have expanded.

20 LABOR

Although most of the adult population engages in productive activity, only 7% (270,000 persons) were wage earners in 1992. Wage and salary earners are concentrated in agriculture, including fishing

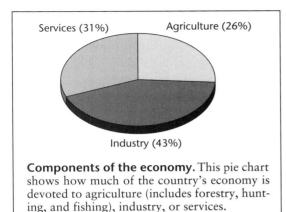

Services (31%) Agriculture (26%)

Industry (43%)

Components of the economy. This pie chart shows how much of the country's economy is devoted to agriculture (includes forestry, hunting, and fishing), industry, or services.

centrated in Agriculture, including fishing and forestry; commerce; and government and public authority employment. Legislation covers working conditions and wages, and provides for collective bargaining.

The minimum working age is 18. However, children between the ages of 11 and 18 may be employed in family-related work with parental permission, medical clearance, and a work permit. Such employment is rare except on family farms.

21 AGRICULTURE

Staple crops include yams, taros (edible roots), and other vegetables. Cash crops are increasing in rural areas, stimulated by government-financed development programs. Production by small farmers of coffee, copra (dried coconut meat), cocoa, tea, rubber, and oil palm is important for export. Main crops and 1985 output (in tons) included sweet potatoes, 475,000; sugar cane, 450,000; copra, 110,000; coffee, 47,000; cocoa, 34,000; and rubber, 4,000.

22 DOMESTICATED ANIMALS

Livestock in 1992 included an estimated 1 million hogs, 4,000 sheep, and 3 million chickens. That same year there were 105,000 head of cattle.

23 FISHING

Fish exports in 1992 were up 5.4% over 1991. In 1991, fish and fish product exports were valued at $12.4 million.

24 FORESTRY

Usable forests include a great variety of hardwood and softwood species. The total roundwood production in 1991 was 8,188,000 cubic meters, as compared with about 7,058,000 cubic meters in 1981. Production of sawn timber in 1991 was estimated at 117,000 cubic meters.

25 MINING

As of 1991, the country was the eleventh largest copper and sixth largest gold producer in the world. Gold production in 1986 was estimated at about 60,780 kilograms.

The Bougainville copper mine, one of the richest in the world, remained closed in 1991 because of civil unrest caused by Bougainville Revolutionary Army militants. All copper production now comes from another mine, which produced 204,459 tons in 1991. In the same year, production of silver totaled 124,880 kilograms.

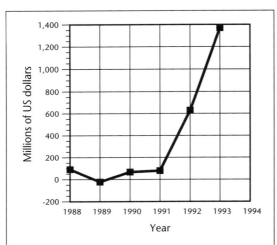

Yearly balance of trade measured in millions of US dollars. The balance of trade is the difference between what a country sells to other countries (its exports) and what it buys (its imports). If a country imports more than it exports, it has a negative balance of trade (a trade deficit). If exports exceed imports, there is a positive balance of trade (a trade surplus).

26 FOREIGN TRADE

Papua New Guinea's main exports are copper, coffee, and gold. Through most of the period when Papua New Guinea was a territory administered by Australia, the two were also major trading partners. In the 1970s, Papua New Guinea's trade with other countries, especially Japan and West Germany, increased. Today, leading trade partners are Germany, Japan, Australia, Singapore, the United States, and the United Kingdom.

27 ENERGY AND POWER

Of the total amount of electricity generated in Papua New Guinea, about one-quarter comes from hydroelectric facilities and three-quarters from thermal plants. In 1992, fuel and energy imports totaled $152 million, or 9% of total imports. In 1992, an oil project produced 14,547,900 barrels of oil. Recoverable oil reserves were estimated at 236 million barrels in 1991.

28 SOCIAL DEVELOPMENT

The National Provident Fund provides old age, disability, and survivor benefits. Workers' compensation is provided by employers. Rural communities traditionally assume communal obligations to those in need.

Women remain second-class citizens due to traditional patterns of discrimination. Intertribal warfare often involves attacks on women.

29 HEALTH

In 1990, there were 3.4 hospital beds per 1,000 people. Medical personnel in 1990 included 301 doctors and 2,447 nurses. There is about 1 doctor for every 12,754 people. In 1992, 96% of the population had access to health care services.

The main health problems are malaria, tuberculosis, leprosy, and venereal disease. Pneumonia and related respiratory infections are major risks. Life expectancy is still only 56 years.

30 HOUSING

In most urban areas, squatter settlements have been established. New housing has fallen far short of the demand, especially for medium- and low-cost units. As of 1988, the housing stock totaled 555,000,

Selected Social Indicators

These statistics are estimates for the period 1988 to 1993. For comparison purposes, data for the United States and averages for low-income countries and high-income countries, are also given.

Indicator	Papua New Guinea	Low-income countries	High-income countries	United States
Per capita gross national product†	$1,130	$380	$23,680	$24,740
Population growth rate	2.3%	1.9%	0.6%	1.0%
Population growth rate in urban areas	3.6%	3.9%	0.8%	1.3%
Population per square kilometer of land	9	78	25	26
Life expectancy in years	56	62	77	76
Number of people per physician	12,256	>3,300	453	419
Number of pupils per teacher (primary school)	31	39	<18	20
Illiteracy rate (15 years and older)	48%	41%	<5%	<3%
Energy consumed per capita (kg of oil equivalent)	238	364	5,203	7,918

† The gross national product (GNP) is the total dollar value of all goods and services produced by a country in a year. The per capita GNP is calculated by dividing a country's GNP by its population. The World Bank defines low-income countries as those with a per capita GNP of $695 or less. High-income countries have a per capita GNP of $8,626 or more. Less than 14% of the world's 5.5 billion people live in high-income countries, while almost 60% live in low-income countries.

> = greater than   < = less than

Sources: World Bank, Social Indicators of Development 1995, Baltimore: Johns Hopkins University Press, 1995. Central Intelligence Agency, World Fact Book, Washington, D.C.: Government Printing Office, 1994.

and the number of people per dwelling averaged 5.8.

31 EDUCATION

Education in Papua New Guinea is not compulsory, and only about 52% of the population is literate. Children attend state-run community schools for primary education and provincial and national high schools for secondary education. Higher education is offered by the University of Papua New Guinea in Port Moresby, the University of Technology in Lae, and the Pacific Adventist College.

32 MEDIA

There were 72,223 telephones in 1991. The National Broadcasting Commission operates three radio networks and one national television station. It broadcasts in English, Pidgin, Hiri Motu, and a dozen other native languages. In 1991 there were an estimated 288,000 radios and 9,000 television sets.

The major newspaper is the Papua New Guinea Post-Courier, which is published daily in English with a 1991 circulation of about 33,900. The twice-weekly Times of Papua Guinea is an English-language paper published in Boroko. It had a circulation of some 15,000 in 1992. *Niugini Nius*, also in Boroko, is published Tuesday–Friday (circulation 15,000) and also has a weekend edition(16,000).

33 TOURISM AND RECREATION

In 1991, 37,346 tourists visited Papua New Guinea, 46% from Australia, 16% from Europe, and 16% from the Americas. There were 2,631 hotel rooms in 1991.

Water sports, golf, tennis, and rock climbing are popular pastimes.

34 FAMOUS PAPUA NEW GUINEANS

The best known Papua New Guineans are Michael Thomas Somare (b.1936), the nation's first prime minister; Sir Albert Maori Kiki (b.1931), author of *Kiki: Ten Thousands Years in a Lifetime*; and Vincent Eri, author of *The Crocodile*.

35 BIBLIOGRAPHY

Bakker, Edie. "Return to Hunstein Forest." *National Geographic*, February 1994, 40–63.

Bulbeck, Chilla. *Australian Women in Papua New Guinea: Colonial Passages, 1920–1960*. New York: Cambridge University Press, 1992.

Fox, M. *Papua New Guinea*. Chicago: Children's Press, 1994.

Gillison, Gillian. *Between Culture and Fantasy: A New Guinea Highlands Mythology*. Chicago: University of Chicago Press, 1993.

McConnell, Fraiser. *Papua New Guinea*. Santa Barbara, Calif.: Clio Press, 1988.

Mead, Margaret. *Growing Up in New Guinea*. Middlesex: Penguin, 1973 (orig. 1930).

Theroux, Paul. "The Spell of the Trobriand Islands." *National Geographic*, July 1992, 117–136.

PARAGUAY

Republic of Paraguay
República del Paraguay

CAPITAL: Asunción.

FLAG: The national flag, officially adopted in 1842, is a tricolor of red, white, and blue horizontal stripes. The national coat of arms appears in the center of the white stripe on the obverse, and the Treasury seal in the same position on the reverse.

ANTHEM: *Himno Nacional*, beginning "Paraguayos, república o muerte" ("Paraguayans, republic or death").

MONETARY UNIT: The guaraní (G) is a paper currency of 100 céntimos. There are notes of 1, 5, 10, 50, 100, 500, 1,000, 5,000, and 10,000 guaraníes. G1 = $0.0005 (or $1 = G1,883.2).

WEIGHTS AND MEASURES: The metric system is the legal standard.

HOLIDAYS: New Year's Day, 1 January; San Blas Day, 3 February; National Defense Day, 1 March; Labor Day, 1 May; Independence Days, 14–15 May; Peace Day, 12 June; Founding of Asunción, 15 August; Constitution Day, 25 August; Victory Day (Battle of Boquerón), 29 September; Columbus Day, 12 October; All Saints' Day, 1 November; Our Lady of Caacupé, 8 December; Christmas, 25 December. Movable religious holidays are Holy Thursday, Good Friday, and Corpus Christi.

TIME: 8 AM = noon GMT.

1 LOCATION AND SIZE

One of South America's two landlocked countries, Paraguay has a total area of 406,750 square kilometers (157,047 square miles), slightly smaller than the state of California. It has a total boundary length of 3,920 kilometers (2,436 miles). Paraguay's capital city, Asunción, is located in the southwestern part of the country.

2 TOPOGRAPHY

The eastern part of Paraguay contains luxuriant hills, meadows, and forests. The western three-fifths constitute a dry, sparsely populated prairie known as the Chaco Boreal. The Paraguay River, the nation's most important waterway, divides the two sections. The Pilcomayo River flows southeast, forming the southwestern border between Argentina and Paraguay.

3 CLIMATE

Two-thirds of Paraguay is within the temperate zone, one-third in the tropical zone. Temperatures generally range from 10° to 21°C (50° to 70°F) in autumn and winter, and 26° to 37°C (79° to 99°F) in spring and summer. Rainfall averages about 200 centimeters (80 inches) a year along the

Photo credit: Anne Kalosh

Street scene in Asunción, Paraguay.

eastern frontier with Brazil, gradually diminishing toward the west to an average of 81 centimeters (32 inches) in the Chaco Boreal.

4 PLANTS AND ANIMALS

The eastern forests abound in hardwoods, including native varieties such as urunday, cedron, curupay, and lapacho. Medicinal herbs, shrubs, and trees abound, as well as some dyewoods (wood used to make dye). Yerba maté, a holly popularly used in tea, grows wild in the northeast.

Animals found in Paraguay include the jaguar, wild boar, capybara, deer, armadillo, anteater, fox, brown wolf, carpin-

cho, and tapir. Crocodiles abound, and the boa constrictor thrives in the west. The carnivorous piranha fish is common.

5 ENVIRONMENT

Paraguay's forests are threatened by the expansion of agriculture. Water pollution from industrial pollutants and sewage is also a problem: 49% of the city dwellers and 91% of the rural population do not have pure water. The nation's cities produce 0.4 million tons of solid waste per year. Some of Paraguay's cities have no facilities for waste collection. As of 1994, 5 mammal species, 34 bird species, and 15 plant species were endangered.

6 POPULATION

According to the 1992 census, Paraguay had a population of 4,123,550. A population of 5,538,000 was projected for the year 2001. Population density was was 11 persons per square kilometer (26.3 persons per square mile) in 1992. The capital city, Asunción, had an estimated population of 607,000 in 1990.

7 MIGRATION

In 1985, the immigrant population totaled 199,500; the leading immigrant groups were Germans, Japanese, Koreans, Chinese, Brazilians, and Argentines. There were 5,417 official immigrants in 1991, of whom 2,188 were Brazilians.

8 ETHNIC GROUPS

According to an estimate in the late 1980s, some 95% of the population is mestizo, principally a mixture of Spanish and Guaraní Amerindian. The others are pure

PARAGUAY

| 0 | 50 | 100 | 150 | 200 Miles |

| 0 | 50 | 100 | 150 | 200 Kilometers |

LOCATION: 19°17′ to 27°30′s; 54°30′ to 62°28′w. **BOUNDARY LENGTHS:** Brazil, 1,290 kilometers (806 miles); Argentina, 1,880 kilometers (1,170 miles); Bolivia, 750 kilometers (460 miles).

Amerindian (1–3%), black, or of European or Asian immigrant stock. However, another estimate puts mestizos at 76% and Europeans at 20%. In 1986, there were about 46,700 tribal Amerindians.

9 LANGUAGES

Paraguay is a bilingual nation. Spanish, the dominant language, is taught in the schools and is spoken by about 55% of the people. However, about 90% of Paraguayans speak Guaraní, an Amerindian language that evolved from the southern dialect of the Tupi-Guaraní group.

10 RELIGIONS

Roman Catholicism is the official religion of Paraguay, and more than 93% of all Paraguayans are Catholics. In 1985, there were an estimated 67,000 Protestants, 22,000 members of Amerindian tribal religions, and 2,000 Buddhists. In 1990, there were 900 Jews.

11 TRANSPORTATION

The inland waterways handle about 65% of Paraguay's foreign trade with Argentina, Brazil, Chile, Europe, Japan, and the United States. Asunción, the chief port, and Concepción can accommodate ocean-going vessels. In addition, Paraguay has been given free port privileges at Santos and Paranaguá, Brazil.

Road construction is another critical focus of development. In 1991, highways totaled some 21,960 kilometers (13,648 miles). In 1992, 80,000 passenger cars and 40,000 commercial vehicles were in use. Altogether there are some 970 kilometers (603 miles) of railway trackage.

The modernization of Asunción's Presidente Stroessner Airport was completed in 1980. Paraguayan Air Lines (Líneas Aéreas Paraguayas—LAP) provides both domestic and international service.

12 HISTORY

The original inhabitants of present-day Paraguay were Guaraní Amerindians. The

Photo credit: Mary A. Dempsey
Covered wagons line up at the edge of the market in Concepción.

first European known to have explored Paraguay was the Italian, Sebastian Cabot, sailing from 1526 to 1530 in the service of Spain. The first permanent Spanish settlement, Nuestra Señora de la Asunción (present-day Asunción), was founded in 1537.

The next two centuries were dominated by Jesuit missionaries, who organized Guaraní families in mission villages (*reducciones*) designed as self-sufficient communes. Amerindians were taught trades, improved methods of cultivation, the fine arts, as well as religion. Above all, they were protected from the Spanish colonists, who sought to exploit them.

As the settlements prospered and grew in number to around 30 (with over 100,000 Amerindians), the jealousy of the Spanish colonists sparked a campaign to discredit the Jesuits. Eventually, the King of Spain was turned against them, and in 1767 he expelled the Jesuits from the New World. Once they had left, the *reducciones* disappeared.

In achieving independence, Paraguay first had to fight the forces of Argentina. Paraguay declared independence from Spain in 1810 but rejected the leadership of Buenos Aires. An Argentine expedition was decisively defeated, and Paraguay deposed the last of its royal governors in 1811.

El Supremo

Since then, Paraguay has been dominated by dictatorships or near-dictatorships. The first and most famous of the dictators was José Gaspar Rodríguez de Francia (known as El Supremo). Francia isolated Paraguay from the outside world and suppressed all criticism at home. At the same time, however, he was honestly devoted to his country's welfare. Francia governed until his death in 1840. Today, he is regarded as Paraguay's "founding father."

A later dictator, Francisco Solano López, provoked quarrels with Argentina, Brazil, and Uruguay, which allied and attacked Paraguay. The War of the Triple Alliance (1865–70) was the bloodiest in Latin American history. The war was a disaster for Paraguay, which lost two-thirds of all its adult males, including López himself. Paraguay's population fell from about 600,000 to about 250,000. The war also cost Paraguay 55,000 square miles of territory, its economic well-being, and its pride.

For the next 50 years, Paraguay stagnated economically. The male population was replaced by an influx of immigrants from Italy, Spain, Germany, and Argentina. Politically, there was a succession of leaders, alternating between rival parties. Then, a long-smoldering feud with Bolivia broke into open warfare (1932–35) after oil was discovered in the Chaco Boreal, the country's desolate western region. Although outnumbered three to one, the Paraguayans, intent on avenging the defeat of 1870, conquered three-fourths of the disputed territory, most of which they retained following the peace settlement of 1938.

Paraguay had a succession of leaders in the late 1930s, some of them heroes of the war with Bolivia. Following the death of General José Felix Estigarribía in an airplane crash in 1940, General Higinio Morínigo, the minister of war, was appointed president by the cabinet. Through World War II (1939–45), Morínigo received large amounts of aid from the United States, even though he allowed widespread Axis (Germany, Italy, and Japan) activity in the country.

Stroessner Takes Over

Federico Chávez ruled from 1949 until 1954. In May 1954, General Alfredo Stroessner, commander-in-chief of the armed forces, used his cavalry to seize power. With help from the United States, he brought financial stability to an economy racked by runaway inflation, but he used terrorist methods in silencing all opposition. Stroessner won a third presidential term in February 1963, despite the constitutional stipulation that a president could be reelected only once.

Stroessner ran for reelection in 1968, 1973, 1978, 1983, and 1988, all with only token opposition permitted. On 17 September 1980, the exiled former dictator of Nicaragua, Anastasio Somoza Debayle, who had been granted asylum by the Stroessner government, was assassinated in Asunción, and Paraguay broke off relations with Nicaragua.

During the 1980s, Stroessner relaxed his hold on Paraguay. The state of siege, which had been renewed every three months since 1959, was allowed to lapse in April 1987. However, allegations of widespread human rights abuses continued.

Coup Topples Stroessner

On 3 February 1989, Stroessner's 35-year dictatorship came to an end at the hand of General Andrés Rodríguez, second in command of the Paraguayan military. Immediately after the coup, Rodríguez announced that elections would be held in May. With only three months to prepare, little opposition was mounted, and Rodríguez won easily with 75.8% of the vote.

There followed an immediate easing of restrictions on free speech and organization. Labor unions were recognized and opposition parties allowed to operate freely. Rodríguez promised and delivered elections in 1993. In an unprecedented transfer of political power from one elected government to another, Juan Carlos Wasmosy was elected to the presidency.

13 GOVERNMENT

Paraguay is a republic, with substantial powers conferred on the executive branch. The president, who is directly elected for a five-year term, is commander-in-chief of the military and conducts foreign affairs. He appoints the 11-member cabinet, most administrators, and justices of the Supreme Court. He is advised by the Council of State, consisting of the cabinet ministers, the president of the National University, the archbishop of Asunción, the president of the Central Bank, and representatives of other sectors and the military.

The 1967 constitution provided for a two-chamber legislature, consisting of the 36-member Senate and the 72-member Chamber of Deputies. Representatives must be at least 25 years of age and are elected for five-year terms. Voting is by secret ballot and is compulsory for all citizens between 18–60 years of age.

Paraguay is divided into 19 departments subdivided into districts, which, in turn, comprise municipalities and rural districts (*partidos*).

14 POLITICAL PARTIES

Since the end of the War of the Triple Alliance, two parties have dominated politics—the National Republican Association

(Asociación Nacional Republicana), generally known as the Colorado Party, and the Liberal Party.

15 JUDICIAL SYSTEM

The five-judge Supreme Court exercises both original and appeals jurisdiction. There are four appeals tribunals: civil/commercial, criminal, labor, and juvenile. There are special appeals chambers for civil and commercial cases and criminal cases. Each rural district (*partido*) has a judge appointed by the central government to settle local disputes and to try accused persons and sentence those found guilty.

16 ARMED FORCES

Paraguay's armed forces numbered 16,500 (11,000 draftees) in 1993, with about 12,500 in the army, 3,000 in the navy (including 500 marines), and 1,000 in the air force. Paraguay has compulsory military service of 18–24 months for all males between the ages of 18 and 20. Expenditures of the Ministry of Defense were $60 million in 1989.

17 ECONOMY

Landlocked Paraguay has a limited economy based principally on agriculture, livestock production, forestry, and the basic processing of materials. In recent years, the relative importance of agriculture has declined, and the value of services has risen; however, cattle-raising remains a key economic activity.

Paraguay has suffered for years from runaway inflation. The inflation rate was

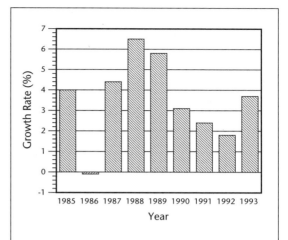

Yearly growth rate of the economy. This economic indicator tells by what percent the economy has increased or decreased when compared with the previous year.

an estimated 30% in 1986 and was estimated at 20% for 1992.

18 INCOME

In 1992, Paraguay's gross national product (GNP) was $6,038 million at current prices, or about $1,510 per person. For the period 1985–92 the average annual inflation rate was 28.5%, resulting in a real growth rate in GNP of 1.0%.

19 INDUSTRY

Among Paraguay's industrial strengths are the processing of agricultural, animal, and forestry products, mainly for export, and small-scale manufacturing of consumer goods for local needs.

Food-processing plants include slaughterhouses, flour mills, sugar mills, oil mills for the production of cottonseed and pea-

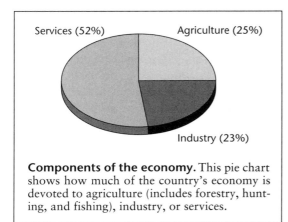

Services (52%) · Agriculture (25%) · Industry (23%)

Components of the economy. This pie chart shows how much of the country's economy is devoted to agriculture (includes forestry, hunting, and fishing), industry, or services.

The 1992 constitution provides Paraguayans in both the public and private sector the freedom to form and join unions without government interference.

Minimum age laws regulate child labor, but many children are nevertheless employed in agriculture and certain urban occupations, especially in the "informal" economy.

21 AGRICULTURE

Although land area under cultivation amounts to 5.6% of Paraguay's total land area, only 1.1% of the economically active population was engaged in agriculture in 1991. The two most widely cultivated crops are manioc (cassava) and corn, which, with meat, are the staples of the Paraguayan diet.

Cotton, tobacco, and sugarcane are among the leading cash and export crops. A national wheat program increased production to 300,000 tons in 1990, eliminating the need for wheat imports. Enough beans, lentils, sweet potatoes, peanuts, coffee, and fruits are grown for home use, and slightly more than enough rice.

Crops yielding edible oils are widely grown, and yerba maté (holly used for tea) is cultivated on plantations. Production of principal crops for 1992 (in tons) included sugar cane, 2,788,000; manioc, 2,200,000; soybeans, 1,315,000; corn, 466,000; cotton, 215,000; and rice, 50,000.

22 DOMESTICATED ANIMALS

Cattle-raising forms a significant part of the country's economy. In 1992, livestock

nut oils for domestic consumption, as well as castor, tung, coco, and palm oils for export. Related industries process the by-products of oil extraction, and mills produce yerba maté. There are numerous sawmills. A considerable but decreasing number of hides are also produced for export.

Although there is a considerable textile industry, imports still run high. Products for domestic consumption include pharmaceutical and chemical goods, finished wood and furniture, brick and tiles, cigars and cigarettes, candles, shoes, matches, soap, and small metal goods.

20 LABOR

According to 1991 estimates, the work force totaled 1,600,000, or more than one-third of the national population. In 1991, agriculture, animal husbandry, and forestry employed 44% of the work force; industry and commerce, 34%; service, 18%; and government, 4%. Unemployment was 13% in 1991.

totaled 7,800,000 head of cattle, 2,600,000 hogs, 380,000 sheep, and 350,000 horses. Beef production was about 143,000 tons. Other livestock products in 1992 included 240,000 tons of milk and 36,000 tons of eggs.

23 FISHING

Paraguay has no sizable fishing industry, and the consumption of fresh fish is low. The Paraguay River yields salmon, surubi, pacú, boga, and mandi. The catch was 13,000 tons in 1991.

24 FORESTRY

Although forest resources are immense, exploitation is limited by lack of roads and mechanized transport facilities. About half of Paraguay's total surface area consists of forest and woodland (13.3 million hectares/32.7 million acres in 1991). Roundwood cuttings totaled 8.5 million cubic meters in 1991.

25 MINING

Excellent limestone, found in large quantities along the Paraguay River north of Concepción, is quarried for the cement industry. Sandstone, mica, copper, kaolin, clay, and salt have been exploited modestly, and there are known deposits of azurite, barite, gypsum, lignite, malachite, mica, peat, pyrite, pyrolusite, soapstone, and uranium.

26 FOREIGN TRADE

Agricultural, animal, and forest products are exported, and foods, transportation equipment, machinery, chemicals, textiles, and other manufactured goods are

Photo credit: Anne Kalosh

Gaucho ropes a cebu cow at Estancia Raya Uno, Paraguay.

imported. Except for 1976 and 1977, Paraguay has had a trade deficit every year since 1965. There were reports through the 1980s of widespread smuggling.

27 ENERGY AND POWER

In 1973, Paraguay and Brazil agreed on the joint construction of the Itaipú power plant, the world's largest hydroelectric project. The plant, which began operating in 1984, produces 70% of Paraguay's electricity, or about 75 billion kilowatt hours per year. Total power production was 29,780 million kilowatt hours in 1991.

Selected Social Indicators

These statistics are estimates for the period 1988 to 1993. For comparison purposes, data for the United States and averages for low-income countries and high-income countries are also given.

Indicator	Paraguay	Low-income countries	High-income countries	United States
Per capita gross national product†	**$1,510**	$380	$23,680	$24,740
Population growth rate	**3.0%**	1.9%	0.6%	1.0%
Population growth rate in urban areas	**4.5%**	3.9%	0.8%	1.3%
Population per square kilometer of land	**11**	78	25	26
Life expectancy in years	**70**	62	77	76
Number of people per physician	**1,262**	>3,300	453	419
Number of pupils per teacher (primary school)	**23**	39	<18	20
Illiteracy rate (15 years and older)	**10%**	41%	<5%	<3%
Energy consumed per capita (kg of oil equivalent)	**214**	364	5,203	7,918

† The gross national product (GNP) is the total dollar value of all goods and services produced by a country in a year. The per capita GNP is calculated by dividing a country's GNP by its population. The World Bank defines low-income countries as those with a per capita GNP of $695 or less. High-income countries have a per capita GNP of $8,626 or more. Less than 14% of the world's 5.5 billion people live in high-income countries, while almost 60% live in low-income countries.

> = greater than   < = less than

Sources: World Bank, *Social Indicators of Development 1995*, Baltimore: Johns Hopkins University Press, 1995. Central Intelligence Agency, *World Fact Book*, Washington, D.C.: Government Printing Office, 1994.

28 SOCIAL DEVELOPMENT

Social insurance includes free medical, surgical, and hospital care for the worker and dependents; maternity care and cash benefits; sickness and accident benefits; retirement pensions at age 60; and funeral benefits. Unemployment insurance does not exist, but severance pay is provided.

Domestic violence and workplace sexual harassment remain serious problems for women.

29 HEALTH

Hospital and medical facilities are generally concentrated in Asunción and other towns. In 1990, there was 1 hospital bed for every 1,000 people. There were 2,536 doctors in 1988. In 1992 there was 1 doctor per 1,262 people. Approximately 60% of the population has access to health care services. In 1990, total health care expenditures were $160 million.

Average life expectancy is 70 years. The principal causes of death are bacillary dysentery and other intestinal diseases, heart disease, pneumonia, and cancer.

30 HOUSING

Between 1982 and 1988, the number of housing units rose to 755,000 with five people per dwelling. In 1973, a National

Paraguayan women selling chipa bread.

Housing Bank was established to finance low-income housing development.

31 EDUCATION

As of 1990, the estimated literacy rate was 90%, 88% for females and 92% for males. Elementary education is compulsory and free between the ages of 7 and 14. In 1991, there were 4,649 public and private primary schools, with 720,983 students; and 169,167 students at the secondary level with 12,218 teaching staff.

Universities include the National University of Paraguay and Nuestra Señora de la Asunción Catholic University. Total university and higher institution enrollment in 1990 was 32,884 students.

32 MEDIA

There were 47 radio stations in Paraguay in 1991, including the official stations, Radio Nacional of Asunción and Radio Encarnación, and the Catholic Radio Caritas. Paraguay also has four television stations. Radio sets in use numbered about 750,000 in 1991; television receivers 220,000. As of 1991, there were 111,514 telephones in use, most of them in Asunción.

Many opposition newspapers—notably *El Enano*, a Liberal Party daily, and *ABC Color*, an independent newspaper—have been closed down. Newspaper readership is among the lowest in Latin America.

Leading newspapers (with 1991 circulation) are *Patria* (30,000); *Hoy* (40,000); and *Ultima Hora* (40,000).

33 TOURISM AND RECREATION

In 1991, there were 293,794 tourist arrivals, with 34% from Argentina, 19% from Brazil, and 8% from Uruguay. Tourist receipts totaled $145 million. There were 4,766 rooms in hotels and other facilities, with 10,449 beds and a 30% occupancy rate.

The monuments, museums, and parks of Asunción are the main tourist attractions. Also of interest are the Amerindian markets in and around the capital, such as the famous market of Itauguá, about 30 kilometers (18 miles) from Asunción, where the makers of ñandutí lace sell their wares. Another popular tourist attraction is the world famous Iguazu Falls (Cataratas del Iguazu) at Paraguay's borders with Brazil and Argentina. Soccer (called football in Paraguay) is the country's national sport, with some 30 clubs in Asunción alone. Tennis, horse racing, boxing, basketball, and rugby football are also popular.

34 FAMOUS PARAGUAYANS

Paraguay acclaims—despite their reputations as dictators—the first three leaders of the independent nation: José Gaspar Rodríguez de Francia (El Supremo, 1761?–1840); his nephew Carlos Antonio López (1790–1862); and the latter's son Francisco Solano López (El Mariscal, 1827–70). Alfredo Stroessner (b.1912) was president of Paraguay from 1954 to 1989.

Leading writers include Juan Silvano Godoi (1850–1926), former president Juan Natalicio González (1897–1966), and Hugo Rodríguez Alcalá (b.1918). Pablo Alborno (1877–1958) and Juan Domínguez Samudio (1878–1936) were noted artists, while in music, José Asunción Flores (b.1904) is a leading figure.

35 BIBLIOGRAPHY

Dibble, Sandra. "Paraguay: Plotting a New Course." *National Geographic,* August 1992, 88–113.

Hanratty, Dennis M., and Sandra W. Meditz, eds. *Paraguay, a Country Study.* 2d ed. Washington, D.C.: Library of Congress, 1990.

Haverstock, Nathan A. *Paraguay in Pictures.* Minneapolis: Lerner Publications, 1987.

Morrison, M. *Paraguay.* Chicago: Children's Press, 1993.

Nickson, R. Andrew. *Paraguay.* Santa Barbara, Calif.: Clio, 1987.

PERU

Republic of Peru
República del Perú

CAPITAL: Lima.

FLAG: The national flag consists of red, white, and red vertical stripes, with the coat of arms centered in the white band.

ANTHEM: *Himno Nacional,* beginning "Somos libres, seámoslo siempre" ("We are free; let us remain so forever").

MONETARY UNIT: The nuevo sol (ML), a paper currency of 100 céntimos, replaced the inti on 1 July 1991 at a rate of 11,000,000 = ML1, but, in practice, both currencies are circulating. There are coins of 1, 5, 10, 20, and 50 céntimos and 1 nuevo sol, and notes of 10, 20, 50, and 100 nuevos soles and 10,000, 50,000, 100,000, 500,000, 1,000,000, and 5,000,000 intis. ML1 = $0.0005 (or $1 = ML2,160).

WEIGHTS AND MEASURES: The metric system is the legal standard.

HOLIDAYS: New Year's Day, 1 January; Labor Day, 1 May; Day of the Peasant, half-day, 24 June; Day of St. Peter and St. Paul, 29 June; Independence Days, 28–29 July; Santa Rosa de Lima (patroness of Peru), 30 August; Battle of Anzamos, 8 October; All Saints' Day, 1 November; Immaculate Conception, 8 December; Christmas, 25 December. Movable holidays include Holy Thursday and Good Friday.

TIME: 7 AM = noon GMT.

1 LOCATION AND SIZE

Peru is South America's third-largest country, with an area of 1,285,220 square kilometers (496,226 square miles), slightly smaller than the state of Alaska. It has a total boundary length of 9,354 kilometers (5,812 miles). Peru's capital city, Lima, is located on the Pacific coast.

2 TOPOGRAPHY

Peru is divided into three contrasting topographical regions: the coast, the Andean highlands, and the Amazon rainforest to the east, with 18 rivers and 200 tributaries. The Peruvian Andes are divided into three chains. The western mountain chain runs parallel to the coast and forms the Peruvian continental divide. Less regular are the Cordillera Central and Cordillera Oriental. Lake Titicaca (Lago Titicaca), the highest large navigable lake in the world (about 3,800 meters [12,500 feet] high), lies partly in Peru and partly in Bolivia. Of the 10 Peruvian peaks that rise above 5,800 meters (19,000 feet), Mt. Huascarán, 6,768 meters (22,205 feet), is the highest. The most important rivers include the Marañón, Amazon, and Ucayali.

3 CLIMATE

Average temperatures range from 21°C (70°F) in January to 10°C (50°F) in June at

Lima, on the coast. At Cusco, in the mountains, the range is only from 12°C (54°F) to 9°C (48°F), while at Iquitos, in the Amazon region, the temperature averages about 32°C (90°F) all year round.

The rainy season in the Andes extends from October to April, the reverse of the coastal climate. Temperatures vary more from day to night than seasonally. In the eastern jungle, precipitation is heavy, from 190 to 320 centimeters (75 to 125 inches) annually. A warm Pacific Ocean west-to-east current called El Niño appears near the Peruvian coast every five or six years.

4 PLANTS AND ANIMALS

Peru's several climates and contrasting surface features have produced a rich diversity of native plants and animals. Wherever the coastal desert is not barren of life, there are sparse shrubs, cacti, and algarroba (carob plant), and a few palm oases along the perennially flowing rivers from the Andes. High-altitude vegetation includes mainly grasses.

As the eastern slopes descend, glaciers are remarkably close to rainforests and tropical vegetation. The 601,000 square kilometers (232,000 square miles) of eastern jungle contain the dense native plants of the Amazon basin. Such native plants as sarsaparilla, barbasco, cinchona, coca, ipecac, vanilla, leche caspi, and curare, as well as the wild rubber tree, mahogany, and other tropical woods, thrive in this region.

The rich marine plant life off the Peruvian coast attracts a wealth of marine life, the most important of which are ancho-veta, tuna, whale, swordfish, and marlin. Characteristic of the Andes mountains are the great condor, ducks, and other wild fowl. The vizcacha, a mountain rodent, and the chinchilla are well known, as is the puma, or mountain lion.

Peru is famous for its American members of the camel family—the llama, alpaca, huarizo, and guanaco—all typical grazing animals of the highlands. The humid forests and savannas of eastern Peru contain almost half the country's species of animals, including parrots, monkeys, sloths, alligators, paiche fish, piranhas, and boa constrictors, all common to the Amazon Basin.

5 ENVIRONMENT

Peru's principal environmental problems in the mid-1990s include air pollution from industrial and transportation vehicle emissions. Peru contributed 0.5% to the world's total gas emissions. Water pollution from industrial waste, sewage, and offshore oil development is another concern. Of the nation's water, 72% is used to support farming and 9.0% for industrial activity. Some 32% of city dwellers and 76% of the rural population do not have pure water. The nation's cities produce 3 million tons of solid waste per year.

A major environmental challenge for Peru in the 1980s was how to open the selva (the country's eastern jungle region) for agricultural development without doing permanent harm to the ecology of the Amazon Basin. As of 1994, 29 of the nation's mammal species and 75 of its bird species were endangered, as well as 360 of its plant species.

LOCATION: 0°1′ to 18°20′s; 68°39′ to 81°19′w. **BOUNDARY LENGTHS:** Ecuador, 1,420 kilometers (880 miles); Colombia, 2,900 kilometers (1,800 miles); Brazil, 1,560 kilometers (975 miles); Bolivia, 900 kilometers (560 miles); Chile, 160 kilometers (100 miles); Pacific coastline, 2,414 kilometers (1,497 miles). **TERRITORIAL SEA LIMIT:** 200 miles.

6 POPULATION

The population according to the 1981 census was 17,005,210. The 1994 population was estimated at 23,383,011, and the United Nations projects a population for the year 2000 of 26,276,000. The estimated population density in 1994 was 18 persons per square kilometer (47 persons per square mile) overall. Metropolitan Lima, the capital, had about 6,869,209 inhabitants in 1995.

7 MIGRATION

Peru has not attracted large numbers of immigrants in the twentieth century, although there are Japanese as well as Chinese communities in the coastal cities. In 1991, 377,485 Peruvians left the country and 309,136 returned. The United States was the leading country of destination (38%), with Chile second. Arrivals by foreigners outnumbered departures by 7,789.

Internally, the main trend has been migration from the highlands to the coastal cities, especially Lima.

8 ETHNIC GROUPS

In the early 1990s, about 45% of the inhabitants were Amerindian, 37% mestizo (of mixed Spanish and Amerindian ancestry), 15% white, and 3% black, Asian, or other.

Of the more than 8 million Amerindians in Peru today, the main groups are the Quechua- and Aymará-speaking tribes, but there are also some other small tribes in the highlands. There are small groups of Germans, Italians, and Swiss, as well as Chinese and Japanese.

9 LANGUAGES

In 1990, over 72% of the population claimed to speak only Spanish. At least 7 million Amerindians, as well as many mestizos, speak Quechua, the native tongue of the Inca peoples, the use of which was outlawed following an Amerindian revolt in 1780. Aymará is spoken by at least 700,000 people, and various other languages are spoken by tribal groups in the Amazon Basin.

10 RELIGIONS

Although the population was about 90% Roman Catholic in the early 1990s, the practice of Catholicism in Peru is combined with Amerindian elements. Protestants numbered almost 6% in the late-1980s, and followers of tribal religions totaled perhaps another 1%. There were also an estimated 7,000 Buddhists and 3,300 Jews living in Peru.

11 TRANSPORTATION

The system of highways that was the key to the unification of the Inca Empire was not preserved by the Spanish conquerors. The lack of an adequate transportation system is still a major obstacle to economic progress.

Peru's railroad system consists of 1,884 kilometers (1,171 miles) of track in 1991. The Tacna-Arica Railway, totaling 62 kilometers (39 miles) links Peru with Chile.

In 1991, of the estimated 56,645 kilometers (35,200 miles) of existing roads, less than 10% were paved. The nation's highways are deteriorating, especially in the mountains, where landslides and guerrilla attacks often occur. In 1991, there were 399,881 automobiles and 235,663 trucks and buses. About 60% of inland freight and 90% of all passengers are carried by road.

The Amazon River with its tributaries, such as the Marañón and the Ucayali, provides a network of waterways for eastern Peru. Peru has 11 deepwater ports, and in 1991, its merchant fleet consisted of 38 vessels over 1,000 tons, with a total gross registered tonnage of 404,000. Callao is Peru's chief port.

Much of Peru would be isolated without air transport. An international airport serves the Lima-Callao area. In 1991/92, Aeroperú and Faucett Airlines flew 32.5 million kilometers (20.2 million miles) and carried 2,441,200 passengers.

12 HISTORY

Perhaps as early as 6,000 years ago, the first primitive farmers appeared in present-day Peru. Between 500 BC and AD 1000, at least five separate civilizations developed. In the thirteenth century, the extraordinary empire of the Incas was established with its capital at Cuzco (Cusco).

During the next 300 years, the Inca empire expanded to northern Ecuador, middle Chile, and the Argentine plains. With paved highways, advanced agriculture, and a complex economy, the rulers in Cuzco (Cusco) dominated a population of 8–12 million. The Incas were sun worshippers and embalmed their dead. They used a calendar and a decimal system of counting, but never developed a wheel.

Francisco Pizarro's small band of Spaniards arrived in 1532. The Inca empire was already in a weakened state due to a civil war, and it collapsed under Pizarro's pressure by the following year. Lima was established in 1535. It became the magnificent center of the Viceroyalty of Peru, which ruled over all Spanish South America except Venezuela.

Peru remained a Spanish stronghold into the nineteenth century, with little internal agitation for independence. In the end, Peru was liberated by outsiders, José de San Martín of Argentina and Simón Bolívar of Venezuela. Bolívar's victory at Ayacucho on 9 December 1824 put an end to Spanish domination on the South American continent.

Between 1826 and 1908, Peruvian presidents ruled an unstable republic plagued by rivalries between military chieftains (*caudillos*) and by a rigid class system. Between the 1850s and the mid-1880s, Peru experienced an economic boom financed by sales of guano (a valuable fertilizer created from nitrogen-rich bird droppings) to Europe. A program of road building was begun, and an American, Henry Meiggs, was hired by the government to build a railroad network in the Andes.

In the War of the Pacific (1879–84), Chile defeated the forces of Peru and Bolivia and occupied Lima from 1881 to 1883. Under various agreements, Peru was forced to give up territory, including the provinces rich in nitrate.

Peru entered the twentieth century with a constitutional democratic government and a stable economy. A period of moderate reform came to an end in 1919, when Augusto Leguía y Salcedo, who had served as constitutionally elected president during 1908–12, took power in a military coup.

In opposition to Leguía's dictatorship, the leftist American Popular Revolutionary Alliance (APRA) was formed in 1924. In 1930, the worldwide depression reached Peru. There was an uprising of Apristas (members of APRA) in 1932, but the military and its conservative allies successfully contained it. World War II (1939–45) brought the eruption in 1941 of a border war with Ecuador, which was resolved in Peru's favor. (The nearly 200-year-old border dispute still has not been settled to the satisfaction of both countries.)

In 1945, APRA was legalized by President Manuel Prado y Ugartache. Over the next 20 years, Peru had a series of governments. Civilian regimes were terminated prematurely by military coups in 1948, 1962, and 1968. The 1948 coup was followed by eight years of military rule under General Manuel A. Odría.

The 1968 coup inaugurated 10 years of military government, which implemented socialist-style economic reforms. The military also reached out to Peru's long-neglected Amerindian population, making Tupac Amaru (leader of an Amerindian revolt against the Spanish) a national symbol, and recognizing Quechua as an official national language.

Present History

Peru returned to civilian government with the elections of 1980, in which former president Fernando Belaúnde Terry was returned to office. During Belaúnde's administration, a small guerrilla group, Shining Path (*Sendero Luminoso*) began operating openly in the Andes. The government's campaign against terrorism, beginning in May 1983 and continuing through 1985, resulted in the disappearance of thousands, charges of mass killings, and the granting of unlimited power to the armed forces.

The election of 1985 was historic in two ways: it was the first peaceful transfer of power in 40 years, and it brought into office the first president from APRA since the party's founding. The economic policies of the new president, Alán García Pérez, were initially successful, but Peru's economic troubles persisted. After an initial boom, industrial production began to sag, and food shortages became common. By 1990, inflation had climbed to four-digit levels.

Meanwhile the Shining Path escalated its attacks, coming down from the mountains and striking at urban and suburban targets around Lima and Callao. In response, García authorized a set of brutal counter-rebel campaigns.

By 1990, neither APRA nor the AP (the Popular Action Party of Belaúnde) had popular support. In a surprise turn of events, Alberto Fujimori, the son of Japanese immigrants, defeated conservative novelist Mario Vargas Llosa by 57% to 34%. Fujimori immediately imposed a set of harsh economic measures designed to curb inflation. These policies caused a great deal of economic disruption but did reduce inflation to pre-1988 levels.

Photo credit: Susan D. Rock.

Courthouse in Lima.

Fujimori moved aggressively to combat the Shining Path and other guerrilla groups, but violence continued, human rights deteriorated, and the military became stronger. Fujimori also became more and more isolated politically. In April 1992, he shut down Congress and refused to recognize any judicial decisions. However, this *autogolpe* ("self-coup") received widespread popular approval and, most importantly, the military supported Fujimori's moves.

Both APRA and AP refused to take part in the 1992 elections, and Fujimori's New Majority/Change 90 group took a majority of seats.

13 GOVERNMENT

Under the 1979 constitution, the president was popularly elected for a five-year term and could not be reelected to a consecutive term. The National Congress consisted of a 60-member Senate and a 180-member Chamber of Deputies. All elected legislators had five-year terms.

After the *autogolpe* (President Fujimori's 1992 seizure of all government power), the constitution was suspended. The Constituent Assembly soon amended the 1979 constitution to allow a president to run for a second consecutive term. The document is still under revision.

Peru is divided into 148 provincial subdivisions.

14 POLITICAL PARTIES

In recent times, Peru's two main political parties have been the American Popular Revolutionary Alliance (Alianza Popular Revolucionaria Americana—APRA) and The Popular Action Party (Partido de Acción Popular, or AP).

APRA was begun in 1924 as a movement of and for Latin American workers. Outlawed in 1931 and again in 1948, and legalized in 1956, APRA has traditionally opposed the military. In 1985, for the first time, an APRA candidate, Alán García Pérez, won the presidency. APRA is boycotting any political arrangement under current president Alberto Fujimori.

The Popular Action Party (AP) was founded in 1956. Originally a reform party, it competed with APRA for the support of those favoring change in Peru. The AP won the presidency in 1963 and 1980, with Fernando Belaúnde Terry as its candidate both times.

The Popular Christian Party (Partido Popular Cristiano—PPC), the main party on the right, holds eight Assembly seats in the Fujimori government.

The largest active guerrilla party is Shining Path (Sendero Luminoso), a Communist group founded in 1964. Also active is the smaller MRTA/MIRA, formed from a merger of the Tupac Amaru Revolutionary Movement (Movimiento Revolucionario Tupac Amaru—MRTA) and the Movement of the Revolutionary Left (MIR).

15 JUDICIAL SYSTEM

Peru's highest judicial body, the 16-member Supreme Court, sits at Lima and has national jurisdiction. The nine-member Court of Constitutional Guarantees rules on human rights cases. Superior courts, sitting in the departmental capitals, hear appeals from the provincial courts, which are divided into civil, penal, and special chambers.

As of 1993, approximately 70% of the judges and prosecutors had been appointed by President Fujimori after his seizure of all government powers in 1992, and they never were confirmed by Congress. Despite constitutional reforms, many accused persons (especially those accused of drug trafficking or terrorism) may spend months or even years in prison before they are brought to trial.

16 ARMED FORCES

Two years of military service are obligatory and universal, but only a limited number of men between the ages of 20 and 25 are drafted. There are 188,000 army reservists.

The total strength of the armed forces in 1993 was 112,000 (including 69,000 draftees). Army personnel numbered 75,000, navy 22,000 (including 3,000 marines), and air force 15,000. About 84,000 men make up the national police. In 1991, Peru spent approximately $430 million on defense.

The armed forces, advised by 50 Russians, contend with approximately 5,000–8,000 armed guerrillas of the Shining Path

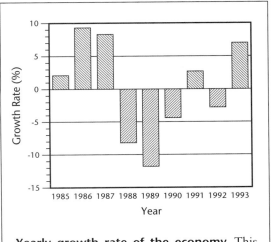

Yearly growth rate of the economy. This economic indicator tells by what percent the economy has increased or decreased when compared with the previous year.

from 139.2% in 1991 to 56.7% in 1992 to 39.5% in 1993, the lowest level in 15 years.

The government is pursuing its goal of returning all state-owned enterprises to private ownership, including major utilities and mining companies, which is scheduled for 1994.

18 INCOME

In 1992, Peru's gross national product (GNP) was $21,272 million at current prices, or about $1,490 per person. For the period 1985–92, the average annual inflation rate was 736.8%, resulting in a real growth rate in GNP of −4.3% per person.

19 INDUSTRY

Smelting and refining are among Peru's most important industries. There are also a number of foundries, cement plants, automobile assembly plants, and plants producing sulfuric acid and other industrial chemicals.

The expansion of the fish meal industry led to the creation of many related industries—factories for the production of cans, paper, jute bags, and nylon fishnet. Once a major exporter of the natural fertilizer guano, Peru now produces synthetic fertilizers high in nitrogen and related industrial chemicals.

Production of selected industrial goods in 1986 was as follows: crude steel, 298,801 tons; cement, 2,205,100 tons; wheat flour, 874,956 tons; and raw sugar, 600,209 tons; passenger cars, 7,054; tires, 914,781.

(Sendero Luminoso) and 500 terrorists of the Tupac Amaru movement.

17 ECONOMY

Since World War II, the Peruvian economy has developed rapidly, exhibiting a rate of growth that has been among the highest in Latin America. The strength of Peru's economy lies in its natural resources. Silver and gold were the prized commodities of colonial Peru. In more recent times, lead, copper, zinc, iron ore, and petroleum have become important exports.

In the early 1990s, the Peruvian economy came out of recession, as a result of an increase in foreign investment. In 1993, the economy recovered significantly, registering a growth of 7.0%. The government has continued to reduce the annual rate of inflation. Annual inflation went down

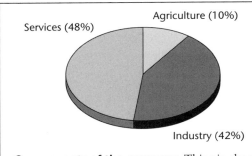

Services (48%)

Agriculture (10%)

Industry (42%)

Components of the economy. This pie chart shows how much of the country's economy is devoted to agriculture (includes forestry, hunting, and fishing), industry, or services.

into cooperative farms. Fields are communally planted and harvested, and the produce or the profits divided.

Staple crops are potatoes and corn, grown throughout Peru, but with very low yields. The leading commercial crops are rice, cotton, sugar, and barley. Production of major crops (in thousands of tons) in 1992 included sugarcane, 7,000; potatoes, 989; rice, 827; corn, 510; coffee, 85; wheat, 73; and cotton, 34. Sugar production fell by 34% during 1991/92 from the 6.1 million tons produced in 1989/90.

20 LABOR

In 1990, the employed labor force was estimated at 5.3 million, or about one-quarter of the population. Of the total, agriculture employed 28.4%; industry, 13%; services, 29.6%; and other activities, 29%. According to official statistics, the unemployment rate was 8.3% at the end of 1990, but underemployment was estimated to be 86.4%. About 5% of the total labor force was unionized in 1992.

Minimum age laws regulate child labor. Yet approximately 90% of school age children are employed, primarily in the informal economy, as a result of difficult economic circumstances.

21 AGRICULTURE

Only 3.7 million hectares (9.2 million acres), or 2.9% of the total land, was under cultivation in 1984. The area of available agricultural land per capita is one of the lowest in the nonindustrialized world. In the 1970s, large private estates were abolished and mostly reorganized

22 DOMESTICATED ANIMALS

The southern Andes mountains contain the major cattle ranges. Although 27.1 million hectares (66.9 million acres), or 21% of Peru's land area, are permanent natural pasture and meadow, areas suitable for dairy cattle are few. In 1992, the livestock population included 12 million sheep, 3.9 million head of cattle, 2.7 million hogs, 661,000 horses, 490,000 donkeys, and an estimated 62 million chickens. Livestock output in 1991 included 110,000 tons of beef, 92,000 tons of pork, 320,700 tons of poultry, 106,700 tons of eggs, and 768,000 tons of milk.

23 FISHING

The Peruvian fishing industry, primarily based on the export of fish meal, which is used in poultry feed, is among the largest in the world. Commercial deep-sea fishing off the Peruvian coast is a major enterprise.

Peruvian waters normally abound with marketable fish: bonito, mackerel, drum, sea bass, tuna, swordfish, anchoveta, herring, shad, skipjack, yellowfin, pompano, and shark. More than 50 species are caught commercially. There are over 40 fishing ports on the Peruvian coast, Callao being one of the most important. The total catch in 1991 was 6.9 million tons, including 3 million tons of anchoveta (small anchovies).

24 FORESTRY

About 61% of Peru's land area, or approximately 79 million hectares (195 million acres), is covered by tropical rainforests. The trees of commercial importance on the coastal plain are amarillo, hualtaco, and algarroba (cut for railway ties and for charcoal fuel). Lumber from planted eucalyptus is used locally in the mountains for ties and for props by the mining industry.

Eastern Peru contains Peru's only coniferous woods. Cedar, mahogany, moena, tornillo, and congona (broadleaf hardwoods) are also logged. The rainforests of the Amazon River area lowlands contain cedar, mahogany, rubber (wild and plantation), and leche caspi (a chewing-gum base). Commercially important are tagua nuts, balata, coca, fibers, and a wide range of medicinal plants. Cultivating the coca leaf (the source of cocaine) for illicit purposes was regarded as an increasing problem in the 1980s.

Mahogany is now the principal lumber export product, sent mainly to the United States and Europe. Mahogany and Spanish cedar trees supply about half of Peru's lumber output, which falls far short of the nation's needs. In 1991, production of roundwood totaled 7.9 million cubic meters.

25 MINING

Peru has long been famous for the wealth of its mines, some of which have been worked extensively for more than 300 years. Through modern techniques and equipment, a vast potential of diverse marketable minerals is gradually becoming available from previously inaccessible regions. Because many of the richest mines are found in the central Andes mountains, often above 4,300 meters (14,000 feet), their operations have been wholly dependent on the Andean Indians' adaptation to working at high altitudes.

Copper, iron, lead, and zinc, the leading metals, are mined chiefly in the central Andes. In 1991, Peru's copper output was 381,991 tons; copper accounted for 22% of Peru's $3,307 million export market in that year. In 1991, production of iron ore reached 3,593,000 tons, zinc production stood at 627,824 tons, and lead at 199,811. Minor industrial metals, such as tungsten, molybdenum, bismuth, and antimony, are extracted in various parts of Peru.

From 1987 to 1991, Peru was (on average) the world's second–largest producer of mine silver, producing 631 tons of the refined metal in 1991. Of the 30 industrial minerals mined commercially in Peru, the important ones are salt, gypsum, marble, limestone, and anthracite. Bituminous coal deposits, in immense reserves throughout

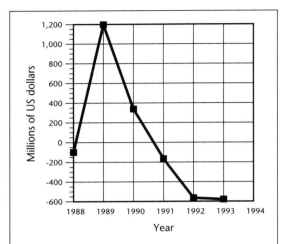

Yearly balance of trade measured in millions of US dollars. The balance of trade is the difference between what a country sells to other countries (its exports) and what it buys (its imports). If a country imports more than it exports, it has a negative balance of trade (a trade deficit). If exports exceed imports, there is a positive balance of trade (a trade surplus).

the Andes, have not been extensively developed because of difficult access.

26 FOREIGN TRADE

Minerals, fish meal, and cotton are traditionally the chief exports; other exports, such as manufactured goods and processed foodstuffs, claimed under 20% of all exports.

As of 1994, the United States continued to be Peru's largest trading partner. United States exports to Peru rose to over $1 billion in 1992, making up 25% of Peru's imports. Main imports from the United States include cereals, refined oil, machinery parts, chemicals, and electrical machinery. Principal exports to the United

States included mineral fuel oil, refined silver and jewelry, lead ore, and concentrated coffee. United States imports from Peru totaled about $739 million in 1992.

In 1993, Peruvian exports remained nearly unchanged; imports decreased slightly.

27 ENERGY AND POWER

Electric power production increased to 14,828 million kilowatt hours in 1991. Consumption of electricity in 1991 averaged about 674 kilowatt hours per person, low by Latin American standards. Almost 75% of the population is without electricity.

In the 1970s, Peru's Upper Amazon River Basin was developed into a major petroleum source; the nation's petroleum export revenues increased from $52.2 million in 1977 to $646 million in 1985. The 853-kilometer (530-mile) trans-Andean pipeline, with a capacity of 200,000 barrels a day, was completed in 1977.

28 SOCIAL DEVELOPMENT

Workers receive benefits covering disability, medical attention, hospitalization, maternity, old age, retirement, and widows' and orphans' benefits. Working mothers are entitled to maternity leave of 90 days at 100% pay.

Women are often kept from leadership roles in the public and private sectors by the force of tradition, although they are legally equal under the constitution.

Selected Social Indicators

These statistics are estimates for the period 1988 to 1993. For comparison purposes, data for the United States and averages for low-income countries and high-income countries are also given.

Indicator	Peru	Low-income countries	High-income countries	United States
Per capita gross national product†	**$1,490**	$380	$23,680	$24,740
Population growth rate	**2.0%**	1.9%	0.6%	1.0%
Population growth rate in urban areas	**2.7%**	3.9%	0.8%	1.3%
Population per square kilometer of land	**18**	78	25	26
Life expectancy in years	**66**	62	77	76
Number of people per physician	**943**	>3,300	453	419
Number of pupils per teacher (primary school)	**28**	39	<18	20
Illiteracy rate (15 years and older)	**15%**	41%	<5%	<3%
Energy consumed per capita (kg of oil equivalent)	**332**	364	5,203	7,918

† The gross national product (GNP) is the total dollar value of all goods and services produced by a country in a year. The per capita GNP is calculated by dividing a country's GNP by its population. The World Bank defines low-income countries as those with a per capita GNP of $695 or less. High-income countries have a per capita GNP of $8,626 or more. Less than 14% of the world's 5.5 billion people live in high-income countries, while almost 60% live in low-income countries.

> = greater than   < = less than

Sources: World Bank, *Social Indicators of Development 1995,* Baltimore: Johns Hopkins University Press, 1995. Central Intelligence Agency, *World Fact Book,* Washington, D.C.: Government Printing Office, 1994.

29 HEALTH

Although Peru has made significant advances toward reducing epidemic disease, improving sanitation, and expanding medical facilities, much remains to be done. Health services are concentrated around metropolitan Lima. In 1990, there were 32,434 hospital beds at a rate of 1.5 per 1,000 people. There is one physician per 943 people, and about 75% of the population had access to health care services. Health care expenditures in 1990 were $1,065 million.

Leading causes of death in 1990 were communicable diseases and maternal/peri- natal causes, noncommunicable diseases, and injuries. There were about 26,000 war-related deaths in Peru from 1983 to 1992. Average life expectancy is estimated at 66 years.

30 HOUSING

Successive governments since the 1950s have recognized the importance of slum clearance and public housing programs in combating disease and high mortality rates. Most housing development programs carried out by the government and by private enterprise have been in the Lima area. In rural areas, a conservative estimate of the housing shortage runs to a

Photo credit: Corel Corporation.

Peruvians traveling by reed boats on Lake Titicaca.

minimum of 700,000. The total housing stock numbered 4,906,000 in 1985.

31 EDUCATION

Education is free and compulsory for children aged 6 to 15. In 1990, the adult literacy rate was estimated at 85% (91.5% for men and 78.7% for women). A 1972 law established Quechua and Aymará as languages of instruction for non-Spanish-speaking Amerindians, especially in the lowest grades.

In 1990 there were 27,970 primary schools, with 4,019,483 pupils and 143,025 teachers. There are about 29 students per teacher in the primary schools. The number of secondary school students in 1990 was 743,569 students, with 58,131 teachers. The total higher education enrollment in 1983 reached 394,000. There is a national university in practically every major city; the oldest is the National University of San Marcos of Lima, originally founded in 1551.

32 MEDIA

In 1992, there were 140 television broadcast stations and about 2.1 million sets. There were 273 radio stations, and the number of radio receivers exceeded 5.6 million. In 1991, there were 736,203 telephones, more than two-thirds of them in Lima.

The leading Lima dailies—among them *El Comercio* (1991 circulation 126,800), *Ojo* (309,100), and *Expreso* (124,300)—are the most important newspapers and are flown daily to provincial towns. The official government publication is *El Peruano* (35,000), a daily gazette in which laws, decrees, and brief government announcements appear.

Freedom of the press has been restricted since the political crackdown by President Fujimori in April 1992, and journalists have been arrested by the government.

33 TOURISM AND RECREATION

Tourists, as well as scholars, are especially drawn to the wealth of archaeological remains on the coast and in the highlands. Inca ruins may be seen at Cuzco (Cusco), and Machu Picchu (Machupicchu), as well as on Lake Titicaca (Lago Titicaca) islands.

The northern coastal waters are famous for big-game fishing. In Lake Titicaca (Lago Titicaca), trout average 10 kilograms (22 pounds), and trout weighing as much as 21 kilograms (46 pounds) have been caught. Other tourist attractions include beaches and water sports. Several state parks offer mountain climbing, cross-country skiing, and white-water rafting. The most popular sports are soccer (which is called football), baseball, basketball, and bullfighting.

In 1991, 232,012 tourists visited Peru, 20% from the United States and 30% from South America. Earnings from tourism were $277 million. There were 35,142 hotel rooms with 62,081 beds.

34 FAMOUS PERUVIANS

The Inca Huayna Capac (1450?–1525 AD) reigned from 1487 and extended the Inca Empire, encouraging public works and fine arts. On his death he left the empire to his two sons, Huáscar (1495?–1533) and Atahualpa (1500?–1533); Huáscar was executed by his half-brother, and Atahualpa, the last of the great Incas, was executed by the Spanish conquistador Francisco Pizarro (1470?–1541).

Acknowledged as America's first great writer, Garcilaso de la Vega (El Inca, 1539?–1616), son of a Spanish conquistador and an Inca princess, preserved in his *Royal Commentaries of the Incas* authentic descriptions of his ancestral empire and its traditions. Tupac Amaru II (José Gabriel Condorcanqui, 1742–81), partly descended from the Incas, led a revolt against Spanish rule in 1780 in which he was defeated, captured, and executed.

The hero of the War of Independence, Mariano Melgar (1792–1815), was also a poet and composer whose regional songs (*yaravís*) are still popular. Marshal Ramón Castilla (1797–1867) distinguished himself in two great presidential terms (1845–51, 1855–62), introducing railways and the telegraph, emancipating the slaves, modernizing Lima, and developing the important guano industry. Ricardo Palma (1833–1919) is considered Peru's greatest literary figure; a critic, historian, and storyteller, he originated the genre called tradición, and wrote the 10-volume *Tradi-*

187

ciones Peruanas. José María Valle-Riestra (1858–1925) was an important composer.

In the modern era, Jorge Chávez (1887–1910) made the first solo flight across the Alps in 1910. Santos Chocano (1875–1934), César Vallejo (1895–1938), and José María Eguren (1882–1942) are considered Peru's finest modern poets. The novelist Mario Vargas Llosa (b.1936) was the first Latin American president of PEN, an international writers' organization. Peru's best-known contemporary painter is Fernando de Szyszlo (b.1925). Yma Sumac (b.1928) is an internationally known singer.

Víctor Raúl Haya de la Torre (1895–1979) founded APRA in 1924 as a Latin American workers' movement; it became Peru's most significant political force. General Juan Velasco Alvarado (1910–77), who led the military coup of 1968, ruled as president of Peru until his own ouster by a bloodless coup in 1975. General Francisco Morales Bermúdez Cerruti (b.1921), president during 1975–80, prepared the country for a return to civilian rule. Fernando Belaúnde Terry (b.1913), founder of the Popular Action Party, served as president during 1963–68 and again during 1980–85. Alán García Pérez (b.1949) was elected president in 1985. In 1982, Javier Pérez de Cuéllar (b.1920) became secretary-general of the United Nations.

35 BIBLIOGRAPHY

Bingham, Hiram. *Lost City of the Incas: The Story of Machu Picchu and Its Builders.* New York: Duell, Sloan & Pearce, 1949.

Fisher, John Robert. *Peru.* Santa Barbara, Calif.: Clio Press, 1989.

Hemming, John. *The Conquest of the Incas.* New York: Harcourt Brace Jovanovich, 1970.

Hudson, Rex A., ed. *Peru in Pictures.* Minneapolis: Lerner, 1987.

Lepthien, E. *Peru.* Chicago: Children's Press, 1992.

Long, Michael E. "Modern-day Echoes of Peru's Past." *National Geographic,* June 1990, 34–49.

PHILIPPINES

Republic of the Philippines
Republika ng Pilipinas

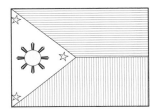

CAPITAL: Manila.

FLAG: The national flag consists of a white equilateral triangle at the hoist, with a blue stripe extending from its upper side and a red stripe extending from its lower side. Inside each angle of the triangle is a yellow five-pointed star, and in its center is a yellow sun with eight rays.

ANTHEM: *Bayang Magiliw (Nation Beloved)*.

MONETARY UNIT: The peso (P) is divided into 100 centavos. There are coins of 1, 5, 10, 25, and 50 centavos and 1 and 2 pesos, and notes of 5, 10, 20, 50, 100, and 500 pesos. P1 = $0.0363 (or $1 = P27.565).

WEIGHTS AND MEASURES: The metric system is the legal standard, but some local measures are also used.

HOLIDAYS: New Year's Day, 1 January; Freedom Day, 25 February; Labor Day, 1 May; Heroes' Day, 6 May; Independence Day (from Spain), 12 June; Thanksgiving, 21 September; All Saints' Day, 1 November; Bonifacio Day, 30 November; Christmas, 25 December; Rizal Day, 30 December; Last Day of the Year, 31 December. Movable religious holidays include Holy Thursday and Good Friday.

TIME: 8 PM = noon GMT.

1 LOCATION AND SIZE

The Republic of the Philippines consists of a group of 7,107 islands situated southeast of mainland Asia and separated from it by the South China Sea. The total land area is approximately 300,000 square kilometers (115,831 square miles), 67% of which is contained within the two largest islands: Luzon, 105,708 square kilometers (40,814 square miles), and Mindanao, 95,586 square kilometers (36,906 square miles). Comparatively, the area occupied by the Philippines is slightly larger than the state of Arizona. The Philippines has a total coastline of 36,289 kilometers (22,549 miles).

The Philippines' capital city, Manila, is located on the island of Luzon.

2 TOPOGRAPHY

The land is extremely varied, with volcanic mountain masses forming the cores of most of the larger islands. Mt. Apo, in Mindanao, is the highest point in the Philippines (elevation 2,954 meters/9,692 feet). A number of volcanoes are active, and the islands have been subject to destructive earthquakes. Lowlands are generally narrow coastal strips except for larger plains in Luzon and Mindanao, and others on other islands. Rivers are short and generally seasonal in flow. Important rivers are the Cagayan in Luzon and the

Pulangi and Agusan in Mindanao. Flooding is a frequent hazard.

3 CLIMATE

Except in the higher mountains, temperatures remain warm, the annual average ranging from about 26° to 28°C (79° to 82°F). The average annual rainfall in the Philippines exceeds 250 centimeters (100 inches). Annual normal relative humidity averages 80%. Violent tropical storms (*baguios*), or typhoons, are frequent. On 5 November 1991 a typhoon hit central Philippines, killing 3,000 people.

4 PLANTS AND ANIMALS

Forests cover almost one-half of the land area and are typically tropical, with vines and other climbing plants. Open grasslands, ranging up to 2.4 meters (8 feet) in height, occupy one-fourth of the land area. They are not naturally occurring, but rather the aftermath of slash-and-burn agriculture. The diverse native plants include 8,500 species of flowering plants, 1,000 kinds of ferns, and 800 species of orchids.

Common mammals include the wild hog, deer, wild carabao (water buffalo), monkey, civet cat, and various rodents. There are about 500 species of birds, among the more numerous being the megapodes (turkey-like wildfowl), button quail, jungle fowl, peacock pheasant, dove, pigeon, parrot, and hornbill. Reptilian life is represented by 100 species. There are crocodiles, and the larger snakes include the python and several varieties of cobra.

5 ENVIRONMENT

Pollution from industrial sources and mining operations is a significant environmental problem in the Philippines. The nation's cities create 5.4 million tons of solid waste per year, and 38 of the country's rivers contain high levels of toxic contaminants. Of the nation's available water, 61% is used to support farming and 21% is used for industrial activity. About 28% of the nation's rural dwellers do not have pure water, while only about 7% of the city dwellers do not have pure water.

Also threatened are the coastal mangrove swamps, which serve as important fish breeding grounds, and offshore corals, about 50% of which are rated dead or dying as a result of pollution and dynamiting by fishermen. The nation is also vulnerable to typhoons, earthquakes, floods, and volcanic activity that can present devastating environmental problems.

In 1994, 12 of the nation's mammal species and 39 bird species were endangered, and 159 plant species were threatened with extinction.

6 POPULATION

The 1990 census reported the population at 60,559,116. Average population density was about 211 persons per square kilometer (547 per square mile). The projected population for the year 2000 was 76,091,000. Created in 1975, metropolitan Manila—with a 1990 population of 7,929,000—includes four cities: Manila proper (1,601,234 at the 1990 census), Quezon City (1,669,776), Caloocan City

(763,415), Pasay City (368,366) and 13 surrounding municipalities.

7 MIGRATION

The rapid growth of the Philippine population has led to considerable internal migration. On Luzon, frontierlike settlements have pushed into the more remote areas. Mindoro and Palawan islands also have attracted numerous settlers, and hundreds of thousands of land-hungry Filipinos have relocated to less densely populated Mindanao.

There also has been a massive movement to metropolitan Manila, especially from central Luzon. Emigration abroad is substantial. In 1989 it came to 55,703. Emigration to the United States particularly has been considerable: as of the 1990 US census, 1,406,770 Americans (chiefly in California and Hawaii) claimed Filipino ancestry. Over 500,000 Philippine citizens were working abroad in the late 1980s and early 1990s, mainly in the Middle East, but also in Hong Kong and Singapore.

8 ETHNIC GROUPS

Filipinos of Malay (Malayan and Indonesian) stock constitute about 90% of the total population. They are divided into nine main ethnic groups: Tagalog, Ilocanos, Pampanguenos, Pangasinans, Bicolanos, Cebuanos, Boholanos, Ilongos, and the Waray-Waray. The Chinese minority numbered about 600,000 in 1990. Numerous smaller ethnic groups inhabit the interiors of the islands, including the Igorot of Luzon and the Bukidnon,

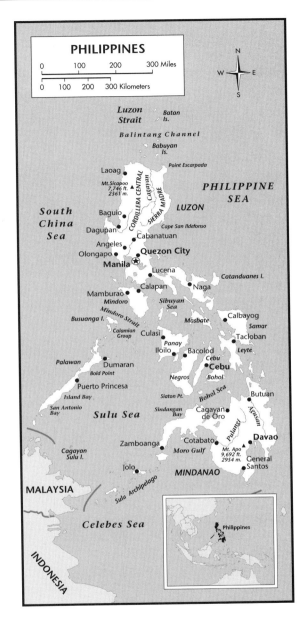

LOCATION: 4°23′ to 21°25′N; 116° to 127°E. **TERRITORIAL SEA LIMIT:** 12 miles.

Manobo, and Tiruray of Mindanao. There were 73 hill tribes in 1986.

9 LANGUAGES

There are two official languages: Pilipino (based on Tagalog), the national language adopted in 1946 and understood by a majority of Filipinos; and English, which is also widely spoken and understood. More than 80 native languages and dialects (basically of Malay-Indonesian origin) are spoken. Besides Tagalog, which is spoken around Manila, the principal languages include Cebuano (spoken in the Visayas), Ilocano (spoken in northern Luzon), and Panay-Hiligaynon.

10 RELIGIONS

The Philippines is the only predominantly Christian country in Asia. Most of the population (about 83%) belongs to the Roman Catholic Church. Members of the Filipino Independent Church (Aglipayan) constitute about 3.9% of the population. Muslims, commonly called Moros by non-Muslims, represent about 5%, and various Protestant churches, 4%. Tribal religionists, mainly in the more inaccessible mountainous areas of Luzon and Mindanao, constitute about 0.7%, Buddhists about 0.2%, Baha'is about 0.1%, and Chinese folk religionists about 0.1%. There are also small communities of Hindus and Jews.

11 TRANSPORTATION

The total length of roadways in 1991 was 156,000 kilometers (96,938 miles). There were 456,606 passenger cars (including jeepneys, or minibuses) in 1991, nearly

Photo credit: Susan D. Rock.

Boatmen with their canoes.

half of them registered in Manila. There were also 158,828 commercial vehicles, 138,138 trucks, and 20,690 buses. In 1991 there were 378 kilometers (235 miles) of common-carrier railroad track, which plays only a minor role in transportation.

Water transportation is of great importance for inter-island and intra-island transportation. Manila is the busiest Philippine port in international shipping, followed by Cebu and Iloilo. In 1991, the merchant fleet totaled 536 ships with 7.9 million gross registered tons, eleventh in the world.

Philippine Air Lines (PAL), the national airline, provides domestic and international flights. The Benigno S. Aquino International Airport is the principal international air terminal. Five airports serve international flights.

12 HISTORY

Evidence of human habitation dates back some 250,000 years. In more recent times, the Philippine Islands are thought to have been settled by Negritos, who crossed then existing land bridges from Borneo and Sumatra some 30,000 years ago. These peoples were later outnumbered by waves of Malays, who arrived from the south, at first by land and later on boats called *barangays,* a name also applied to their communities.

By the fourteenth century, Arab traders introduced Islam to the southern islands. Commercial and political ties also linked various parts of the island group with Indonesia, Southeast Asia, India, China, and Japan. Ferdinand Magellan, a Portuguese-born navigator sailing for Spain, made the European discovery of the Philippines on 15 March 1521. The Spanish conquest of the islands was completed by 1571, made easier by the almost complete conversion of the natives to Christianity by that time. The Philippines, as a province of New Spain, was administered from Mexico.

The Struggle for Independence

Although Spain governed the islands until the end of the nineteenth century, its rule was constantly threatened by the Portuguese, the Dutch, the English, the Chinese, and the Filipinos themselves.

Filipino aspirations for independence, suppressed by conservative Spanish rule, climaxed in the unsuccessful rebellion of 1896–98. José Rizal, the most revered Filipino patriot, was executed, but General Emilio Aguinaldo and his forces continued the war. During the Spanish-American War (1898), Aguinaldo declared independence from Spain on 12 June. When the war ended, the United States acquired the Philippines from Spain for $20,000,000. American rule replaced that of the Spanish, but Philippine nationalists continued to fight for independence.

Over the long term, the effect of American administration was to make the Philippines an arm of the US economy, as a supplier of raw materials to and a buyer of finished goods from the American mainland. In the face of the continued nationalist drive for independence, the US Congress passed a series of bills that ensured a degree of Philippine self-rule. The Tydings-McDuffie Independence Law of 1934 instituted commonwealth government and further called for complete independence in 1944.

World War II

On 8 December 1941, Japan invaded the Philippines, which then became the site of the most bitter and decisive battles fought in the Pacific during World War II. By May 1942, the Japanese had achieved full possession of the islands. United States forces, led by General Douglas MacArthur, recaptured the Philippines in early

1945, following the Battle of Leyte Gulf, the largest naval engagement in history. In September 1945, Japan surrendered.

Independence

On 4 July 1946, the Republic of the Philippines was inaugurated, with Manuel A. Roxas y Acuña as its first president. Both casualties and damage in the Philippines from World War II were extensive, and rehabilitation was the major problem of the new state. Communist guerrillas, called Hukbalahaps, were threatening the republic, and their revolutionary demands were countered by land reforms and military action.

In 1965, Ferdinand Edralin Marcos was elected president, and reelected in 1969 by a record majority of 62%. Unable to run for a third term in 1973, President Marcos placed the entire country under martial law, charging that the nation was threatened by a "full-scale armed insurrection and rebellion." Marcos arrested many of his political opponents, some of whom remained in detention for years.

Throughout the 1970s, Marcos tightened his control of the government through purges of opponents, promotion of favorites, and delegation of leadership of several key programs—including the governorship of metropolitan Manila—to his wife, Imelda Romualdez Marcos.

Although Marcos made headway against the southern guerrillas, his human-rights abuses cost him the support of the powerful Roman Catholic Church. Pope John Paul II came to Manila in February 1981 and protested the violation of basic human rights. In June 1981, Marcos was elected for a new six-year term as president under an amended constitution preserving most of the powers he had exercised under martial rule. In 1983 Benigno S. Aquino, Jr., a long-time critic of Marcos, was shot at the Manila airport which was later named in his honor. Aquino was assassinated as he returned from self-exile in the United States to lead the opposition in the 1984 legislative elections.

In 1985, political pressures were mounting on Marcos. He was forced to call for an election in February 1986. Later that month a military revolt grew into a popular rebellion that ousted the long-time leader. United States President Ronald Reagan offered Marcos asylum, and Marcos went into exile in Hawaii.

After Marcos

On 25 February 1986, Corazon Aquino, widow of Benigno Aquino, assumed the presidency. On 11 May 1987, she was elected in the first free elections in nearly two decades, held under a new constitution. On 20 December 1987 one of the worst ocean disasters in history occurred when an overcrowded passenger ship collided with an oil tanker off Mindoro Island and at least 1,500 people perished. On 28 September 1989 former President Ferdinand Marcos died in Honolulu. Aquino refused to allow him to be buried in the Philippines.

Under pressure from communist rebels, Aquino removed US military bases from the Philippines in 1989. In September

1990 Aquino said it was time to consider an "orderly withdrawal" of US forces from the Philippines. Within a year the Philippines was struck by three major natural disasters. In July 1990 an earthquake measuring 7.7 on the Richter scale struck. The epicenter was 55 miles north of Manila and more than 1,600 people were killed. A super-typhoon devastated the central islands in November 1990. An even more destructive natural disaster occurred on 12 June 1991 when Mount Pinatubo (in Zambales province near Olangapo), a volcano dormant for more than 500 years, violently erupted.

On 30 June 1992 Fidel Ramos succeeded Corazon Aquino as president of the Philippines. Ramos, a Methodist and the Philippine's first non-Catholic president, considers the country's population growth rate as an obstacle to development. Catholics have protested the Ramos administration's birth control policies and the public health promotion of prophylactics to limit the spread of AIDS.

Domestic violence by the Muslim population continued throughout the 1980s. In January 1994 the government signed a cease-fire agreement with the Moro National Liberation Front ending 20 years of guerrilla war. Conflicting claims to the Spratly Islands in the South China Sea are a source of tension between the Philippines and the People's Republic of China.

13 GOVERNMENT

Under the constitution of 11 February 1987, the Philippines is a democratic republican state. Executive power is vested in a president elected by popular vote for a six-year term, with no eligibility for reelection. The president is assisted by a vice-president, elected for a six-year term, with eligibility for one immediate reelection, and a cabinet, which can include the vice-president.

Legislative power rests with a two-chamber legislature. The Senate has 24 members elected for six-year terms. A House of Representatives is elected from single-member districts for three-year terms. In 1991, 200 members were elected and up to 50 more may be appointed by the president.

In 1991, the Philippines was divided into 73 provinces and approximately 1,500 municipalities. Each municipality was further divided into communities (*barangays*).

14 POLITICAL PARTIES

After assuming the presidency in 1986, Corazon Aquino formally organized the People's Power Movement (Lakas Ng Bayan), the successor to the party of her late husband, Benigno Aquino. In the congressional elections of May 1987, Aquino's popularity gave her party a sweep in the polls, making it the major party in the country.

In 1993 there were over a dozen recognized political organizations and six parties organized in opposition to the government.

On 26 August 1994, President Fidel Ramos announced a new political coalition that would produce the most powerful political group in the Philippines. Ramos's Lakas-National Union of Christian Democrats (Lakas/NUCD) teamed with the Democratic Filipino Struggle (Laban ng Demokratikong Pilipino, Laban).

15 JUDICIAL SYSTEM

Under the 1973 constitution, the Supreme Court, composed of a chief justice and 14 associate justices, was the highest judicial body of the state, with supervisory authority over the lower courts. The entire court system was modified in 1981, with the creation of new regional courts of trials and of appeals. Philippine courts functioned without juries.

The Constitution calls for an independent judiciary, and defendants in criminal cases are afforded the right to counsel.

16 ARMED FORCES

The all-volunteer active armed forces numbered 106,500 in mid-1993, and reserves 131,000. The army, with 68,000 members, had 8 infantry divisions and 6 specialized brigades. The navy had a total of 23,000 members (including 8,500 marines and 2,000 in the coast guard), with 1 frigate (warship) and 42 patrol and coastal combatants. The air force had a strength of 15,500, with 49 combat aircraft and 94 armed helicopters. The Philippine national police totaled 90,000, and the Citizen Armed Forces had 45,000 personnel. Estimated defense expenditures in 1991 were $1 billion.

17 ECONOMY

The Philippines is primarily an agricultural nation, raising crops for domestic use and export. It is the world's largest pro-

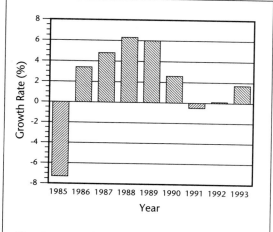

Yearly growth rate of the economy. This economic indicator tells by what percent the economy has increased or decreased when compared with the previous year.

ducer of coconuts and manila hemp (*abacá*). Manufacturing, which has expanded and diversified since political independence, depends on imported raw materials. Mining, once centered on gold, is now diversified, with chromite, copper, and iron providing important earnings. The economy is heavily dependent on foreign trade.

Throughout 1990–92 slow economic growth plagued the Philippines. Inadequate transport and communications networks and prolonged drought reduced industrial and agricultural expansion. Widespread unemployment and underemployment characterize the Philippine labor market. High rates of labor migration abroad (686,137 in 1992) provide some relief and account for a substantial portion of the country's foreign exchange earnings.

Since 1990 the most visible problem for the economy has been the shortage of electric power. In 1992 the water level of a lake in Mindanao fell, causing a 50% reduction in the power supply to Mindanao. In Manila, the industrial hub, power outages often last from four to six hours per day. In 1993 the inflation rate continued to decline and the return to economic growth was expected to accelerate through the 1990s.

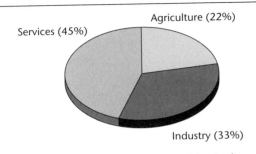

Components of the economy. This pie chart shows how much of the country's economy is devoted to agriculture (includes forestry, hunting, and fishing), industry, or services.

18 INCOME

In 1992, Philippines' gross national product (GNP) was $49,462 million at current prices, or about $850 per person. For the period 1985–92 the average inflation rate was 10.1%, resulting in a real growth rate in GNP of 1.9% per person.

19 INDUSTRY

Industry is concentrated in the Manila area. The leading manufactured goods (by value) are foods, tobacco products, chemicals and pharmaceuticals, beverages, wood products, and apparel.

In 1990 most industrial output was concentrated in a few large firms. Although small- and medium-sized businesses accounted for 80% of manufacturing employment, they accounted for only 25% of the value of manufactured goods.

Food manufacturing has remained the primary industry, accounting for some 37% of total manufacturing output in 1992. Petroleum and coal products (17.9%), chemicals and chemical products

(6.6%), and apparel and footwear (6%) were next in importance.

20 LABOR

The Philippines had an employed labor force estimated at 21.9 million in 1992, of whom 45% were engaged in agriculture, forestry, and fishing. In 1992, the unemployment rate was estimated at 8.6% overall, with a much higher rate (about 26%) in metropolitan Manila.

Strikes are prohibited in such essential services as transportation, communications, and health care. In 1990, 12.1% of the labor force was unionized. Overseas employment is a very important part of the Philippines' income. Pay sent home by overseas workers in 1990 was the second largest source of foreign exchange, and overseas workers account for 40% of each year's new workers in the labor market.

The law prohibits employment of children under the age of 15. Despite the law, many children are employed in hazardous jobs, or under unacceptable conditions. A raid on a sardine factory in Manila found 27 children under age 17 at work there. They had been working for over a year without pay and without being allowed to leave.

21 AGRICULTURE

About one-third of the total land area can be cultivated. Three-fourths of the cultivated area is devoted to crops for consumption and one-fourth to commercial crops, mainly for export. Roughly half the cultivated land is devoted to the two main subsistence crops, palay (unhusked rice) and corn.

Production of palay in 1992 was 9,129,000 tons. The Philippines has produced enough corn to meet its needs since the late 1970s. Production of animal feed lags behind the demand, so imports are still necessary. Corn output in 1992 was 4,570,000 tons. Lesser food crops include sweet potatoes, beans, cassava, peanuts, and various fruits and vegetables.

Commercial agriculture, dominated by large plantations, centers on coconuts and copra, sugarcane, tobacco, bananas, and pineapples. Coconuts are the most important export crop, accounting for 20% of world production. In 1992, 8,465,000 tons of coconuts were produced. Copra (dried coconut meat) production, in which the Philippines leads the world, rose from 1,470,000 tons in 1965 to an estimated 1,670,000 tons in 1992.

Sugarcane production provided the country's single largest export item until 1978, when output and prices fell. Production was forecast at only 27.3 million tons in 1992. Exports of sugarcane were 1% of total exports in 1992. Pineapple production rose to 1.17 million tons in 1992. Production of coffee was 110,000 tons, and 3,900,000 tons of bananas were produced that year.

22 DOMESTICATED ANIMALS

Animal farming never has been important, because meat consumption is very low in the Philippines. The carabao, or water buffalo, are the principal pack animals, particularly in the rice paddies. Hogs are the chief meat animals (except in Muslim sections). The Philippines produces enough pork and poultry to meet its needs, but imports of beef and dairy products are still necessary. In 1992 there were 1.6 million head of cattle, 2.5 million buffaloes, and 8 million hogs. In 1992 there were 63 million chickens.

23 FISHING

Fish is the primary source of protein in the Filipino diet. Some 2,000 species abound in Philippine waters. Despite more than a doubling in output since the 1960s, the fishing industry remains relatively undeveloped, and large quantities of fish are imported. In 1991, the catch totaled 2,311,797 tons.

Anchovy, mackerel, sea bass, red snapper, sardines, herring, mullet, barracuda, pompano, tuna, bonito, and shark are the most plentiful. Pearl shells (including cultured pearls), sponges, sea cucumbers (trepang), shark fins, and sea turtles are exported.

24 FORESTRY

Forests are an important economic resource in the Philippines. As of 1991, 34% of the land area was forest and woodland. In 1991, the production of roundwood totaled 38.7 million cubic meters. Among other forest products are bamboo, rattan, resins, tannin, and firewood. Rubber output totaled 82,000 tons in 1985.

25 MINING

Mining and related processing activities are promoted by the government as part of the Philippines' industrialization effort. Copper (150,000 tons produced in 1991) is the leading mineral, followed by gold (24,938 kilograms/27.5 tons in 1991), manganese ore (14,000 tons in 1991), and nickel (18,400 tons of metal content in 1991).

The Philippines reportedly has the world's largest source of refractory chromite and produces sizable quantities of metallurgic chromite. Chromite ore production in 1991 totaled 184,010 tons. Silver, lead, and zinc also are produced for export. Clays, limestone, pyrites, guano, silica sands, and salt are produced for local consumption. Coal production rose from 331,000 tons in 1981 to 1,267,102 tons in 1991.

26 FOREIGN TRADE

In 1992 the top export products were garments, semiconductors and electronic microcircuits, crude coconut oil, bars and copper rods, and bananas and plantains. In 1992 the top import products were mineral fuels/lubricants and related mate-

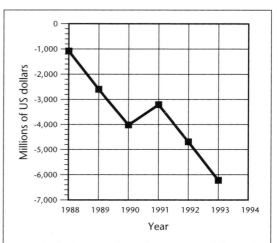

Yearly balance of trade measured in millions of US dollars. The balance of trade is the difference between what a country sells to other countries (its exports) and what it buys (its imports). If a country imports more than it exports, it has a negative balance of trade (a trade deficit). If exports exceed imports there is a positive balance of trade (a trade surplus).

rials, non-electrical machinery, electrical machinery, base metals and metal products, and transport equipment.

The United States and Japan continued through 1992 to be the Philippines' primary trading partners. Also important were Germany, Hong Kong, and the United Kingdom.

27 ENERGY AND POWER

Domestic oil production was 1.5 million barrels in 1991. The Philippine government has developed an alternative energy program, including, for example, the use of "alcogas" (gasohol) and "cocodiesel" (coconut oil in diesel fuels). With the recent discovery of oil off the shores of the western island of Palawan, more drilling and deep-sea exploration is expected.

Brownouts and power outages were common in 1993. Total electrical output in 1991 was 22,484 million kilowatt hours, of which 51% was conventional thermal, 23% was hydropower, and 26% was geothermal.

28 SOCIAL DEVELOPMENT

The government social program includes the settlement of landless families in new areas, building of rural roads, schools, and medical clinics, and the distribution of relief supplies to the needy.

The Social Security System (SSS) covers employees of private firms in industrial and agricultural production. Government employees are covered under the Government Service Insurance System (GSIS). The system's benefits include compensation for confinement due to injury or illness, pensions for temporary incapacity, insurance payments to families in case of death, old age pensions, and benefits to widows and orphans.

A medical care plan (Medicare) provides hospital, surgical, medicinal, and medical-expense benefits to members and their dependents. Women are eligible for paid maternity leaves of six weeks for the first four births.

The government has actively promoted family planning, and despite opposition from Roman Catholic traditionalists (including Pope John Paul II in his February 1981 visit), the program has met with significant success. The fertility rate in the late 1980s was 3.9 per 1,000 people,

down from 5 per 1,000 people in the late 1970s.

Most, but not all, of the legal rights enjoyed by men are extended to women. Restrictions on property ownership were removed by a 1992 law.

29 HEALTH

In 1991, there were 1,663 hospitals and 31,375 physicians. There is about 1 doctor per 2,000 people in 1992. Nearly 75% of the population had access to health care services in 1992.

Pulmonary infections (tuberculosis, pneumonia, bronchitis) are prevalent, but malaria is virtually unknown in larger cities and is being eliminated in the countryside. Malnutrition remains a health problem, despite government assistance in the form of Nutripaks, consisting of native foods such as mung beans and powdered shrimp, made available for infants, children, and pregnant women. Average life expectancy is about 67 years.

30 HOUSING

Tens of thousands of *barrios* (districts) are scattered throughout the Philippines, each consisting of a double row of small cottages strung out along a single road. Each cottage is generally built on stilts and has a thatched roof, veranda, and small yard. From 1984 to 1987, an annual average of about 103,150 units were built by private builders with minimal assistance from the government. The total number of dwellings in 1992 was 10,550,000.

Selected Social Indicators

These statistics are estimates for the period 1988 to 1993. For comparison purposes, data for the United States and averages for low-income countries and high-income countries are also given.

Indicator	Philippines	Low-income countries	High-income countries	United States
Per capita gross national product†	$850	$380	$23,680	$24,740
Population growth rate	2.2%	1.9%	0.6%	1.0%
Population growth rate in urban areas	4.3%	3.9%	0.8%	1.3%
Population per square kilometer of land	211	78	25	26
Life expectancy in years	67	62	77	76
Number of people per physician	>2,000	>3,300	453	419
Number of pupils per teacher (primary school)	33	39	<18	20
Illiteracy rate (15 years and older)	10%	41%	<5%	<3%
Energy consumed per capita (kg of oil equivalent)	328	364	5,203	7,918

† The gross national product (GNP) is the total dollar value of all goods and services produced by a country in a year. The per capita GNP is calculated by dividing a country's GNP by its population. The World Bank defines low-income countries as those with a per capita GNP of $695 or less. High-income countries have a per capita GNP of $8,626 or more. Less than 14% of the world's 5.5 billion people live in high-income countries, while almost 60% live in low-income countries.

> = greater than   < = less than

Sources: World Bank, *Social Indicators of Development 1995*, Baltimore: Johns Hopkins University Press, 1995. Central Intelligence Agency, *World Fact Book*, Washington, D.C.: Government Printing Office, 1994.

31 EDUCATION

Education is free and compulsory in the primary schools and is coeducational. English is the main medium of instruction, although Pilipino or the local dialect is used for instruction in the lower primary grades. In 1990, about 90% of adults were literate (men: 90.0% and women: 89.5%).

In 1991, 34,081 primary schools had an enrollment of 10,558,105 students and secondary schools had 4,208,151 students. The same year, there were 316,182 primary school teachers and 129,700 secondary school teachers. For the period 1988–93, there was an average of 33 students per teacher in primary schools.

The University of the Philippines is the leading institution of higher learning. In addition, there are some 50 other universities, including the University of Santo Tomás, founded in 1611 and run by Dominican friars. In 1991, universities and all higher level institutions had 1,656,815 students.

32 MEDIA

In 1991 there were 986,117 telephones. Radio and television are operated by both government agencies and private busi-

Photo credit: Susan D. Rock.

Girl Scouts at Ft. Santiago, Manila.

nesses. In 1989, there were 322 radio stations, 5 major television networks, and 33 television broadcasting stations. In 1991, there were 8,810,000 radios and 2,800,000 television sets.

Under martial law, censorship of the press, radio, and television was imposed by the government under Ferdinand Marcos. Many reporters, editors, and publishers were arrested during this period. Censorship was ended in 1986 under the Corazon Aquino administration. In 1991 there were some 38 daily newspapers, as compared with 6 during the Marcos era. The following were among the leading dailies published in metropolitan Manila (with estimated 1991 circulations): *People's Journal* (345,000); *Manila Times* (275,000); *Manila Bulletin* (275,000); *Philippine Daily Inquirer* (165,000); and *Balita* (150,900).

33 TOURISM AND RECREATION

The increase in tourism that followed the ouster of Ferdinand Marcos was dampened by the national disasters of the early 1990s. In 1991 visitor arrivals dropped 7.1% between 1990 and 1991. That year, 849,000 tourists arrived, 452,000 from Southeast Asia and 216,000 from the Americas. The Japanese were the top visitors (20.8%) and US visitors were the next largest group. Hong Kong, Taiwan, and

Australia were other important sources of visitors. Revenues from tourism totaled $1.28 billion.

Hotels in Manila meet international standards. A convention center and several major new hotels were added in Manila in the mid-1970s. In 1991, there were 13,262 hotel rooms with a 64.7% occupancy rate.

Manila remains the chief tourist attraction. Other points of interest are the 2,000-year-old rice terraces north of Baguio; Vigan, the old Spanish capital; Cebu, the oldest city; numerous beaches and mountain wilderness areas; and homes formerly owned by the Marcoses.

Basketball is the national sport, followed in popularity by baseball and soccer. Jai-alai is popular in Manila and Cebu. Cockfighting is legal and often televised.

34 FAMOUS FILIPINOS

Filipinos have made their most important marks in the political arena. Foremost are José Rizal (1861–96), a distinguished novelist, poet, physician, linguist, statesman, and national hero; and Emilio Aguinaldo y Famy (1869–1964), the commander of the revolutionary forces and president of the revolutionary First Philippine Republic (1899).

Notable Filipinos of this century include Manuel Luis Quezon y Molina (1878–1944), the first Commonwealth president; Ramón Magsaysay (1907–57), a distinguished leader in the struggle with the Hukbalahap Communist rebels; and Carlos Peña Rómulo (1899–1985), a Pulitzer Prize-winning author and diplomat and the president of the fourth UN General Assembly.

Ferdinand Edralin Marcos (b.1917–89), who won distinction as a guerrilla fighter during the Japanese occupation, was the dominant political figure in the Philippines from his first election to the presidency in November 1965 to his removal in February 1986. His wife, Imelda Romualdez Marcos (b.1930), emerged as a powerful force within her husband's government during the 1970s. Leading critics of the Marcos government during the late 1970s and early 1980s were Benigno S. Aquino, Jr. (1933–83) and Jaime Sin (b.1928), who became the archbishop of Manila in 1974 and a cardinal in 1976. Maria Corazon Cojuangco Aquino (b.1933), the widow of Benigno, opposed Marcos for the presidency in February 1986 and took office when he went into exile in the same month.

Lorenzo Ruiz (fl.17th cent.) was canonized, along with 15 companion martyrs, as the first Filipino saint. Fernando M. Guerrero (1873–1929) was the greatest Philippine poet in Spanish. Two painters of note were Juan Luna y Novicio (1857–99) and Félix Resurrección Hidalgo y Padilla (1853–1913). Contemporary writers who have won recognition include Claro M. Recto (1890–1960), José García Villa (b.1914), and Carlos Bulosan (1914–56). José A. Estella (1870–1945) is the best-known Filipino composer. Filipino prizefighters have included two world champions, Pancho Villa (Francisco Guilledo, 1901–25) and Ceferino García (1910–81).

35 BIBLIOGRAPHY

Brands, H. W. *Bound to Empire: The United States and the Philippines*. New York: Oxford University Press, 1992.

Bresnan, John, ed. *Crisis in the Philippines: The Marcos Era and Beyond*. Princeton, N.J.: Princeton University Press, 1986.

Davis, Leonard. *The Philippines: People, Poverty, and Politics*. New York: St. Martin's, 1987.

Dolan, Ronald E., ed. *Philippines: A Country Study*. 4th ed. Washington, D.C.: Library of Congress, 1993.

Lepthien, E. *The Philippines*. Chicago: Children's Press, 1986.

O'Brien, Niall. *Revolution from the Heart*. New York: Oxford University Press, 1987.

Pedrosa, Carmen Navarro. *Imelda Marcos*. New York: St. Martin's, 1987.

Richardson, Jim. *Philippines*. Santa Barbara, Calif.: Clio Press, 1989.

POLAND

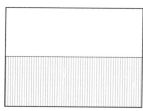

Polish People's Republic

Polska Rzeczpospolita Ludowa

CAPITAL: Warsaw (Warszawa).

FLAG: The national flag consists of two horizontal stripes, the upper white and the lower red.

ANTHEM: *Jeszcze Polska nie zginela (Poland Is Not Yet Lost).*

MONETARY UNIT: The zloty (z) is a paper currency of 100 groszy. There are coins of 1, 2, 5, 10, 20, and 50 groszy and 1, 2, 5, 10, 20, 50, and 100 zlotys, and notes of 10, 20, 50, 100, 200, 500, 1,000, 2,000, 5,000, 10,000, 20,000, 50,000, 100,000, 200,000, 500,000, 1,000,000, and 2,000,000 zlotys. z1 = $0.00004 (or $1 = z22,119).

WEIGHTS AND MEASURES: The metric system is the legal standard.

HOLIDAYS: New Year's Day, 1 January; Labor Day, 1 May; National Day, 3 May; Victory Day, 9 May; All Saints' Day, 1 November; Christmas, 25–26 December. Movable holidays are Easter Monday and Corpus Christi.

TIME: 1 PM = noon GMT.

1 LOCATION AND SIZE

Situated in Eastern Europe, the Polish People's Republic has an area of 312,680 square kilometers (120,726 square miles), slightly smaller than the state of New Mexico. Its total boundary length is 3,605 kilometers (2,240 miles). Poland's capital city, Warsaw, is located in the east central part of the country.

2 TOPOGRAPHY

Poland's average altitude is 173 meters (568 feet); 75.4% of the land is less than 200 meters (656 feet) above sea level. The highest point, Mount Rysy (2,499 meters/ 8,199 feet), is located on the Slovakian border. The principal topographic regions are a central lowland; the Baltic highland in the north, a region with many lakes and sandy soils; and the coastland, a narrow lowland with bays and lakes.

Several important navigable rivers drain into the Baltic Sea, among them the Vistula (Wista), the Oder (Odra), the Bug, and the Warta. There are some 9,300 lakes in the northern lake region.

3 CLIMATE

Only the southern areas are humid. Summers are cool, and winters range from moderately cold to cold. The average mean temperature is about 7°C (45°F). Temperatures in Warsaw range, on average, from –6° to –1°C (21°–30°F) in January and from 13° to 24°C (55°–75°F) in July.

Precipitation is greatest during the summer months. Annual rainfall ranges from about 50 centimeters (20 inches) in the lowlands to 135 centimeters (53 inches) in the mountains. The overall average is about 64 centimeters (25 inches).

4 PLANTS AND ANIMALS

Coniferous (cone-bearing) trees, especially pine, account for 70% of the forests. Deciduous species include birch, beech, and elm. Lynx, wildcat, European bison, moose, wild horse (tarpan), and wild goat are among the few remaining large mammals. Birds, fish, and insects are plentiful.

5 ENVIRONMENT

In 1989, 11% of the nation was considered endangered due to extreme levels of pollution and environmental damage. Poland has yet to recover from the overuse of forests during World War II and the loss of about 1.6 million hectares (4 million acres) of forestland after the war. Air pollution is caused by hazardous concentrations of airborne dust, carbon dioxide, and nitrogen compounds.

Approximately 24% of Poland's water is used to support farming and 60% is for industrial purposes. About 6% of city dwellers and 28% of rural people do not have pure water. According to a December 1985 government report, more than 90% of river waters are too polluted for safe human consumption.

In 1994, 4 mammal species, 16 bird species, and 16 types of plants were endangered.

6 POPULATION

According to the 1988 census, Poland's population was 37,879,000. As of mid-1994, the population was estimated at 38,513,000. A population of 39,508,000 is projected for the year 2000. In 1988, density was 122 persons per square kilometer (314 per square mile), with 61.2% of the population living in urban areas. Warsaw, the capital and principal city, had an estimated population of 1,653,300 at the end of 1991.

7 MIGRATION

Poland suffered a net population loss of nearly 11,000,000 between 1939 and 1949 through war losses, deportations, voluntary emigrations, and population transfers arising out of territorial changes. From the 1950s through the 1980s, Germans leaving for Germany constituted the bulk of emigrants. Jews also left in substantial numbers for Israel, both in the immediate postwar years and during the 1950s and 1960s.

Another emigration wave occurred after the declaration of martial law in December 1981. According to official figures, total external migration was 233,600 during 1981–89. It was about 16,000 in 1991. Of the 20,977 emigrants, 14,502 went to Germany. These official figures seriously underestimate real emigration, however. Germany, for example, recorded 145,643 immigrants from Poland in 1991.

8 ETHNIC GROUPS

Before World War II (1939–45), over 30% of the people living within the boundaries of Poland were non-Poles. According to the 1931 census, Polish was the mother tongue of 69% of Poland's 32 million people, Ukrainian and Ruthenian

POLAND

0   50   100 Miles

0   50   100 Kilometers

LOCATION: 14°7′ to 24°8′E; 49° to 54°50′N. **BOUNDARY LENGTHS:** Baltic coastline, 491 kilometers (304 miles); Russia, 432 kilometers (268 miles); Lithuania 91 kilometers (56 miles); Belarus, 605 kilometers (378 miles); and Ukraine, 428 kilometers (265 miles); Czech Republic, 658 kilometers (408 miles); Slovakia, 444 kilometers (275 miles); Germany, 456 kilometers (286 miles). **TERRITORIAL SEA LIMIT:** 12 miles.

14%, Belorussian 5.3%, and German 2.3%. Yiddish speakers also constituted a significant minority, and there were smaller numbers of Lithuanian, Czech, and Slovak speakers.

As a result of World War II, and of the boundary changes and population transfers that followed, only about 2% of Poland's population today is non-Polish.

Ukrainians, Lithuanians, Belorussians, Germans, Gypsies, and Slovaks are the most numerous minorities.

9 LANGUAGES

Polish, the universal language, is one of the western Slavic languages using the Latin alphabet. It is easily distinguishable from other Slavic languages by the frequent grouping of consonants. Among the several dialects are Great Polish, Kuyavian, Little Polish, Silesian, and Mazovian. Some language experts consider that Kashubian, spoken along the Baltic, is not a Polish dialect but a separate language. Many Poles speak English, French, German, or Russian, and understand other Slavic languages in varying degrees.

10 RELIGIONS

Poland is one of the world's most strongly Roman Catholic countries. During the period of Communist domination that began in 1945, Catholicism suffered extreme repression by the state. However, it lessened over time, especially after the archbishop of Kraków, Karol Cardinal Wojtyla, became Pope John Paul II in 1978. According to both state and other sources in 1993, 95% of Poles are Roman Catholics. In 1990, about 870,000 people were Russian Orthodox, and about 10,000 belonged to various Protestant groups.

On the eve of World War II, an estimated 3,351,000 Jews lived in Poland, more than in any other country. They constituted about 10% of the Polish population and nearly 20% of world Jewry. During the course of the Nazi occupation (1939–45), nearly 3,000,000 Polish Jews were killed, many of them in extermination camps such as Auschwitz (Oświecim), near Kraków.

At the end of the war, only about 55,000 Jews remained in Poland. However, returnees, mostly from the Soviet Union, raised the total Jewish population to 250,000 in 1946. The establishment of the state of Israel in 1948, combined with a series of anti-Semitic outbreaks in Poland, caused most Jews to emigrate. By 1990, Poland had only 3,800 Jews.

11 TRANSPORTATION

In 1991, the operational rail network of Poland was 27,041 kilometers (16,803 miles) in length. In 1992, the Polish railroads carried 201.7 million tons of freight.

There is a dense road and highway network. In 1991, there were a total of nearly 300,000 kilometers (186,400 miles) of roads. However, improvement and repair have not kept up with increased usage. In 1991 there were 6,112,171 passenger cars and 1,238,409 commercial vehicles.

At the beginning of 1991, Poland had 230 merchant ships, totaling 2,950,000 gross registered tons. The major ports are Szczecin, Gdynia, Gdańsk, and Swinoujście, which together handled 44.2 million metric tons of cargo in 1990. There are 3,997 kilometers (2,484 miles) of navigable rivers and canals. The main inland waterways are the Oder (Odra), the Wista, and the Warta.

Polish Air Transport (Polskie Linie Lotnicze—LOT) is a state enterprise, with Warsaw's Okecie International Airport as the center. In 1991, LOT's 27 aircraft carried 1,051,200 passengers.

12 HISTORY

The land now known as Poland was thinly populated in prehistoric times. Slavic tribes are believed to have begun settling Poland more than 2,000 years ago, but by AD 800, the population was probably no more than 1 million. Rulers of the Piast dynasty united the Polish tribes of the Vistula (Wista) and Oder (Odra) basins about the middle of the tenth century. In 966, Mieszko I, a member of this dynasty, was baptized, and Poland became a Christian nation.

During the next three centuries, Poland was continually involved in conflicts with the Germans to the west and with the Eastern Slavs and the Mongol invaders to the east. In 1386, a Polish-Lithuanian union was created through a royal marriage. This gave birth to the Jagellonian dynasty. The union extended from the Baltic to the Black Sea and held control over other territories in Central Europe, notably West Prussia and Pomerania.

Although the sixteenth century marked the golden age of Polish literature and scholarship, its political reforms contributed to the nation's eventual decline. The Polish nobility (*szlachta*) had gradually gained influence and power at the expense of the king. They placed such severe limitations on the monarchy that national unity could not be maintained.

A Russian, Prussian, and Austrian agreement led to the first partitioning of Poland in 1772. The second (1793) and third (1795) partitions led to the end of Poland as an independent nation. Galicia, now divided between present-day Poland and Ukraine, was ruled by Austria-Hungary, northwestern Poland by Prussia, and the Ukraine and eastern and central Poland by Russia. The Poles rebelled in 1830 and 1863 against the powerful rulers, but each rebellion was suppressed.

With the Russian Revolution of 1917 and the defeat of the Central Powers in World War I, Poland regained its independence. On 18 November 1918, Józef Pilsudski, leader of the prewar independence movement, formed a civilian government.

Germany Invades Poland

Poland struggled through the next two decades troubled by economic decay and political instability, and by growing pressures from its Soviet and German neighbors. Following the Nazi-Soviet Pact in 1939, Germany invaded Poland on 1 September, overrunning the country in eight days. Meanwhile, the Soviet Union occupied the Lithuanian region on 17 September. These invasions took place even though Poland had nonaggression treaties with both the Soviet Union and Germany.

By 1941, Nazi (German party led by Adolph Hitler) forces were brutally oppressing large segments of the Polish population while looting Poland's industries and major resources. Ghettos (quarters where Jews were forced to live) were set up in Warsaw and other cities, and numerous concentration camps were established on Polish territory, including the extermination camp at Auschwitz, where at least 1 million people perished between 1940 and 1944.

Poland as a whole suffered tremendous losses of life and property during World War II. An estimated 6 million Poles were killed, half of them Jews. The remaining population suffered near starvation throughout the Nazi occupation.

On 17 January 1945, Warsaw was liberated by the Soviet and Polish armies. The Provisional Government of National Unity was formally recognized by the United States and United Kingdom in July 1945. The Communists and the Socialists merged in December 1948 to form the Polish United Workers' Party (PZPR). The PZPR consistently followed a pro-Soviet policy. It shunned the Marshall Plan (plan to rebuild Europe after World War II) and, in its first two decades, renounced all dealings with the Western powers.

Poland Under Communist Rule

The first decade of Communist rule was dominated by tensions with the Roman Catholic Church and the question of Soviet influence. In response to worker riots in Poznań on 28–29 July 1956, a new Polish government, headed by Wladyslaw Gomulka introduced new freedoms, including improved relations with the Church. By the late 1950s, however, the reform movement had been halted, and the government took a harder line against dissent. In 1968 there were student demonstrations and further government crackdowns.

Following a drought in 1969 and an exceptionally severe winter, demonstrations by shipyard workers in Gdańsk broke out on 16 December 1970 protesting economic conditions. After widespread violence, in which at least 44 people were killed, the government, under a new leader, Edward Gierek, modified its economic policies and reinstated Church control over thousands of religious properties in northwestern Poland.

During the 1970s, Gierek's government vigorously pursued a policy of détente (harmony) with the West. At home, however, the economic situation kept growing worse, and Polish nationalism continued to rise. In an historic public ceremony on 31 August 1980, government officials agreed to allow workers the right to form independent trade unions and the right to strike. The independent labor movement Solidarity, headed by Lech Walesa, the leader of the Gdańsk workers, emerged in early September and soon claimed a membership of about 10 million.

On 13 December 1980, after union leaders in Gdańsk called for a national referendum on forming a non-Communist government in Poland, General Wojciech Jaruzelski, prime minister since February, declared martial law. Almost the whole leadership of Solidarity, including Walesa, was arrested, and the union was suspended.

In the following years, martial law was gradually eased, and the Jaruzelski government restored order on the political level. However, continued declines in the standard of living led to waves of strikes throughout Poland in spring and fall 1988, paralyzing the nation. The demands of strikers, most led by Solidarity, began to become political as well as economic.

Democracy Takes Over

By April 1989, the government agreed to establish a Senate with the seats to be filled by open election. In addition, 35% of the seats in the existing parliament, the Sejm, were also made subject to direct

Photo credit: AP/Wide World Photos

A father and daughter celebrate the relegalization of Solidarity outside a Warsaw courtroom. The father wears a shirt with the words "I'll be back soon" written in the format of the Solidarity logo, which was used to circumvent a government ban on union symbols imposed after the 1981 martial-law crackdown.

election. In elections in June 1989, 99 of the 100 seats in the Senate went to Solidarity members. Tadeusz Mazowiecki took office on 24 August 1989 as the first non-Communist prime minister in the eastern bloc (Communist nations in eastern Europe).

Across eastern Europe that autumn, other Communist countries were quietly breaking loose of the influence of the Soviet Union. This wave of "velvet revolutions" sped up the de-Sovietization of the Polish government. Local elections were held in May 1990, further weakening the Communists' grip on power. On 9 December 1990 Lech Walesa, the leader of the

Solidarity labor movement, was elected president.

After 1990, the number of political parties grew rapidly, weakening the impact that any one party or group of parties was able to have. This resulted in coalition governments without strong powers, giving Poland five prime ministers and four governments in 1991–93.

In addition, once the Communists had been removed from power, splits became more apparent between the 40% of Poland which is rural, and the 60% which is urban. Also important were growing tensions between intellectuals and the powerful Catholic Church, which moved to take close control over social issues like abortion, school curriculum, and women's role in society.

However, local elections held 19 June 1994 suggested that fears of a return to Communism under the new government were unfounded. The government of Polish Peasant Party leader Waldemar Pawlak, and his Democratic Left Alliance partner, Aleksander Kwasniewski, remains generally committed to democracy and economic change. In addition, President Walesa announced his intention, despite his low popularity, to fight for a second term of office when presidential elections were next held in December 1995.

13 GOVERNMENT

Without a new formal constitution, Poland has been functioning on a much-amended form of its Communist-era constitution. A package of amendments passed in October 1992 are collectively called the "Little Constitution." A 1990 agreement made the presidency a popularly elected post, rather than one of parliamentary appointment.

The present system combines a presidential and a parliamentary system. The president is directly elected, for a term of six years. The post includes traditional executive duties and powers, such as the duty to sign into law or veto legislation, but also retains many legislative powers, including the right to introduce bills and draft legal amendments.

The parliament consists of two houses: the Sejm, or lower house, with 460 seats;

and the Senate, with 100 seats. Seats are filled on the basis of party lists. The government, which appoints the Council of Ministers, is drawn from the party with majority parliamentary representation. In the absence of such a majority, coalitions are necessary.

Under the Communists, Poland was divided into 49 administrative districts, called *voivods*. The 1989 Solidarity government replaced these with the *gmina*, or local authority, which chooses its own council and officials. In 1994, there were 2,383 of these local councils.

14 POLITICAL PARTIES

After the restrictions of their Communist past, the Poles formed a rich variety of political parties. These ranged across the full political spectrum, including even such strange groups as the Polish Beerdrinkers' Party. A full 69 parties participated in the 1991 parliamentary elections, of which 29 gained seats, none of them with more than 14% of the total vote.

By 1993, however, the political scene was showing signs of stabilizing. Only 35 parties took part in that election, and only 5 received seats.

The local elections of 1994 showed Poland dividing into three basic political groupings. On the right in that election were two large coalitions made up of parties including the Christian National Union, the Center Alliance, the Movement for the Republic, the Peasant Alliance, the Conservative Coalition, the Conservative Party, the Party of Christian Democrats, and the Christian-Peasant Alliance. These parties generally favor a major role for the Catholic Church, and tend to draw their support from Poland's rural areas.

The center is dominated by Freedom Union (UW), which was formed in April 1994 when the Liberal Democratic Congress merged with the Democratic Union. Its position is taken from the intellectual wing of the original Solidarity, favoring radical economic change, while being less concerned with immediate impact upon workers.

The left, which was almost entirely defeated in 1991, has shown remarkable strength. The two major parties are the Democratic Left Alliance (SLD) and the Polish Peasant Party (PSL).

15 JUDICIAL SYSTEM

The Supreme Court, the highest judicial body, functions primarily as a court of appeal. Its judges are elected by the Council of State for five-year terms. It is divided into criminal, civil, military, and labor and social insurance chambers. In addition, there are regional courts, as well as special courts such as military tribunals, children's courts, and courts for cases involving social insurance.

In general the Poles have been reluctant to remove Communist-era judges, but fears about the fair-mindedness of people who served the earlier regime damage the public's belief in the judiciary. A 1993 law makes it possible for the Ministry of Justice to recall a judge determined by a disciplinary commission to have failed to exercise "court independence."

16 ARMED FORCES

The conscription (forced military service, or draft) law of January 1959 provides for registration at 18 and service (18 months) at age 20. Polish armed forces numbered 296,500 (167,400 draftees) in 1993, including 195,000 in 13 army divisions and 10 specialized brigades. Navy personnel totaled 19,300. The air force had 83,000 men and 424 combat aircraft of Soviet design. The reserve had about 435,000 active members in 1993. The Ministry of Interior had 20,000 troops and border guards. Defense expenditures for 1991, as officially reported, amounted to $2.4 billion. Arms exports during 1981–91 were valued at $7 billion and imports at $8 billion.

Poland provides 1,100 servicemen to seven different nations as observers.

17 ECONOMY

Until recently, Poland had a centrally planned economy that was primarily state-controlled. Since World War II, agriculture's dominant place in the economy has been shrinking. Poland, with its sizable coastline, has become a maritime nation of some importance, having developed three major ports on the Baltic Sea and a greatly expanded shipbuilding industry, which in 1991 produced 53 ships.

Since the government abandoned central planning, Poland has struggled with the transformation of over 8,000 state-owned enterprises into workable private corporations. By 1992, private businesses accounted for almost half of economic activity.

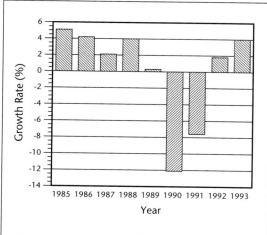

Yearly growth rate of the economy. This economic indicator tells by what percent the economy has increased or decreased when compared with the previous year.

Consumer prices shot up almost 600% in 1990, another 70% in 1991, 43% in 1992, and 35% in 1993. Unemployment rose to 15.7% at the end of 1993.

18 INCOME

In 1992, the gross national product was $75,268 million at current prices, or about $2,260 per person. For the period 1985–92 the average inflation rate was 124.2%, resulting in a real growth rate in gross national product of −1.9% per person.

19 INDUSTRY

Leading industries in 1993 included food processing (21.5% of total output), fuel (16.2%), metals and metal products (8.9%), and chemicals (5.8%). With the destabilizing effects of the breakup of the bloc of Communist countries in Europe and central planning, industrial production fell by 26% in 1990 and 12% in 1991. It grew by 5.6% in 1993, however.

Poland produced 9.9 million tons of steel in 1993. Sulfur is another important industrial commodity. Sulfur production in 1993 totaled 1,901 tons. The cement industry turned out 12.3 million tons during the same year. All these totals were lower than in the 1980s, however. In 1993, Poland produced 401,000 automatic washing machines, 584,000 refrigerators and freezers, 841,000 television sets, 307,000 radios, and 21,000 tape recorders and dictaphones.

20 LABOR

The labor force in 1992 totaled 17,529,000 persons, with 21.4% of the workers engaged in agriculture. By the end of 1991, the total unemployment rate rose from 11.4% to 13.6%, and climbed to 14.6% by mid-1993, amounting to 2.7 million Poles without work. The long-term goal of the government was 10% employee ownership of private enterprises.

A key chapter in Polish labor history began in August 1980, when, after a series of strikes in Gdańsk and elsewhere, the government authorized the formation of independent labor unions. On 5 September, a new national labor movement, called Solidarity, was born. The goals of Solidarity included a five-day work week, worker self-management, an easing of censorship, and other economic and political reforms. All existing labor organizations were outlawed on 8 October 1982, but in 1989, Solidarity was legalized once again.

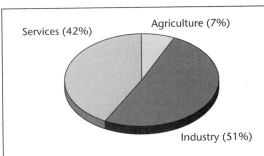

Components of the economy. This pie chart shows how much of the country's economy is devoted to agriculture (includes forestry, hunting, and fishing), industry, or services.

- Services (42%)
- Agriculture (7%)
- Industry (51%)

The minimum age for employment is 15. Young people between the ages of 15 and 18 may be employed if they have completed basic schooling and if the work involved can be defined as vocational training. The minimum age is raised to 18 for work involving a potential health hazard.

21 AGRICULTURE

About 62% of Poland's land is agricultural. Of this area, 78% is cultivated. In 1992, agriculture declined by 16.9% due to the effects of a serious drought throughout Central Europe, which led to crop losses as high as 25%.

In 1992, the principal crops and their yields (in thousands of tons) were potatoes, 23,388; meadow hay, 15,098; sugar beets, 11,052; wheat, 7,368; rye, 3,981; barley, 2,819; and oats, 1,236. Yields have been poor because of infertile soil, insufficient use of fertilizers, and inadequate mechanization, in addition to the drought.

22 DOMESTICATED ANIMALS

The government has encouraged the development of livestock production through increased feed supply and other measures. In 1992, there were 22.1 million pigs, 8.2 million head of cattle, 1.9 million sheep, 900,000 horses, and 58 million poultry.

A severe drought in 1992 adversely affected grain prices, causing livestock herds to shrink throughout the first half of 1993. Livestock products in 1992 included 2,989,000 tons of meat (down from 3,068,000 tons in 1991), 12.8 million tons of milk, and 389,000 tons of eggs.

23 FISHING

Sea fishing is conducted in the Baltic and North seas and in the Atlantic, and there are inland fisheries in lakes, ponds, and rivers. The 1992 saltwater catch was 409,389 tons, mostly herring and cod. Freshwater fishing yielded about 48,000 tons.

24 FORESTRY

As of 1991, 29% of Poland's land was forested. Pine, larch, spruce, and fir are the most important varieties of trees. The Wielkopolski National Forest, a reservation, is famous for its thousand-year-old oak trees. In 1991, wood amounting to 12.7 million cubic meters from coniferous trees and 4.3 million cubic meters from broad-leaved trees was produced. In 1992, production of wood and paper increased by 13.9% over 1991.

[25] MINING

In 1991, abandonment of state price controls and financial assistance, and the gradual shift to private ownership resulted in lower production of most mineral commodities. The acquisition of former German territories in 1945 enriched Poland with hard coal and, to a lesser extent, zinc and lead.

The most important raw material is hard coal. Poland's coal industry was the seventh largest in the world in 1991. The 1991 output consisted of 209 million tons of hard coal, 140 million tons of which were bituminous, and 69 million tons were lignite. Estimated hard-coal reserves total 65.5 billion tons of bituminous, and 12.8 billion tons of lignite.

In 1991, Poland ranked seventh in the world in mine output of copper, with 390,000 tons; ninth in refined copper production, with a reported 378,000 tons; eleventh in mine output of zinc, at 175,000 tons; seventh in silver mine output, at a reported 899,000 kilograms; and fifth in sulfur, with 3.8 million tons.

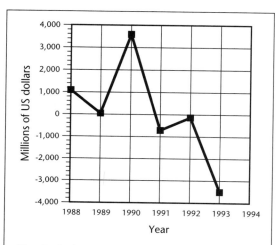

Yearly balance of trade measured in millions of US dollars. The balance of trade is the difference between what a country sells to other countries (its exports) and what it buys (its imports). If a country imports more than it exports, it has a negative balance of trade (a trade deficit). If exports exceed imports there is a positive balance of trade (a trade surplus).

[26] FOREIGN TRADE

Germany is Poland's most important supplier and customer, accounting for 23.9% of Poland's imports and 31.4% of its exports in 1992. The former Soviet Union was once Poland's leading trade partner. After the breakup of the Soviet Union, Poland continued to trade with Russia. But Russia fell to the rank of distant second trade partner in the 1990s as hard currency replaced barter-type arrangements.

Principal exports for 1992 and 1993 included mineral fuels; chemicals and products; machinery and transport equipment; and food and live animals. Principal trade partners in 1992 were Germany, Russia, France, the United Kingdom, the Netherlands, and Romania.

[27] ENERGY AND POWER

The main domestic energy sources are coal, lignite, and peat. Rivers remain a largely untapped source of power. In 1991, production totaled 134,696 million kilowatt hours. In 1991, about 77% of Poland's total energy requirement was fulfilled by coal. In 1992, Poland produced about 198 million tons of coal. Poland is

Selected Social Indicators

These statistics are estimates for the period 1988 to 1993. For comparison purposes, data for the United States and averages for low-income countries and high-income countries are also given.

Indicator	Poland	Low-income countries	High-income countries	United States
Per capita gross national product†	**$2,260**	$380	$23,680	$24,740
Population growth rate	**0.2%**	1.9%	0.6%	1.0%
Population growth rate in urban areas	**0.9%**	3.9%	0.8%	1.3%
Population per square kilometer of land	**122**	78	25	26
Life expectancy in years	**71**	62	77	76
Number of people per physician	**450**	>3,300	453	419
Number of pupils per teacher (primary school)	**16**	39	<18	20
Illiteracy rate (15 years and older)	**<2%**	41%	<5%	<3%
Energy consumed per capita (kg of oil equivalent)	**2,390**	364	5,203	7,918

† The gross national product (GNP) is the total dollar value of all goods and services produced by a country in a year. The per capita GNP is calculated by dividing a country's GNP by its population. The World Bank defines low-income countries as those with a per capita GNP of $695 or less. High-income countries have a per capita GNP of $8,626 or more. Less than 14% of the world's 5.5 billion people live in high-income countries, while almost 60% live in low-income countries.

> = greater than   < = less than

Sources: World Bank, *Social Indicators of Development 1995*, Baltimore: Johns Hopkins University Press, 1995. Central Intelligence Agency, *World Fact Book*, Washington, D.C.: Government Printing Office, 1994.

the world's seventh largest coal producer and exporter. Poland has no oil deposits but produces over one-third of its natural gas needs. Natural gas production was 3,900 million cubic meters in 1992. Poland is increasingly looking toward the Middle East for its oil supply, due to the current uncertain economic and political climate in the republics of the former Soviet Union.

28 SOCIAL DEVELOPMENT

A social insurance institute administers social security programs through a network of branch offices. Social security, including social insurance and medical care, covers nearly the entire population.

Old age, disability, and survivors' pensions are provided, as well as family allowances, sickness benefits, maternity benefits, workers' compensation, and unemployment. Special family allowances have been a part of the social security program since 1947 and are paid for each child after the first. Maternity benefits include full wages for a total of 16–18 weeks.

In 1985, women accounted for 45% of the labor force. The law prohibits women from working in 90 occupations, and a greater proportion of women than men are unemployed.

29 HEALTH

In 1990, Poland had 81,674 physicians (about 1 doctor for every 450 people) and 200,783 nurses. About 54% of the physicians and 81% of the dentists were women. In 1991, there were 56.8 hospital beds per 10,000 population. Health care suffers from a lack of medicines, many of which must be imported from the West. Total health care expenditures in 1990 were $3,157.

Life expectancy in 1992 averaged 71 years. Leading causes of death were: communicable diseases and maternal/perinatal causes; noncommunicable diseases; and injuries.

30 HOUSING

Almost 40% of all urban dwelling space was destroyed during World War II. Although investment in public housing has increased, the housing shortage remains critical. In the mid-1980s, the average wait for an apartment was about 15 years. As of 1992, there was a shortage of 1.3 million housing units, a figure that was expected to grow to 2.4 million by the year 2000. In 1991, 130,000 new housing units were constructed.

31 EDUCATION

Practically the entire Polish population is literate. Primary, secondary, and most university and other education is free. The school system, which is centralized, consists of an 8-year primary school followed by either a 4-year secondary general education school, 5-year technical school, or basic 3-year vocational training school.

In 1991 there were 18,323 primary schools with 5,305,000 students and 328,900 teachers, and 1,131 general secondary schools with 494,000 students. There are about 17 primary school students per teacher. Some 1,722,000 students attended 9,413 vocational schools, studying technology, agriculture, forestry, economy, education, health services, and the arts. Another 394,313 students attended 98 institutions of higher learning in 1990–91.

Of the 98 third-level institutions, 11 are universities, 18 are polytechnical schools, 17 are art schools, 11 are medical academies, and 3 are theological academies. Jagiellonian University, among the oldest in Europe, was established at Kraków in 1364. Other prominent universities are the Warsaw University, the Higher Theater School (Warsaw), and the Academy of Fine Arts (Kracow).

32 MEDIA

In 1991 the three radio networks were Polskie Radio, Radio Solidarnesc, and Radio Z, and television programming was broadcast by Telewizja Polskie. There were 54 radio stations and 40 TV stations. In 1991 there were 11.3 million television sets and 16.6 million radios. During the same year there were 4,830,216 telephones.

In 1991 there were 45 daily newspapers. The largest Polish dailies, with 1991 circulations, were *Gazeta Wyborcza* (510,000); *Zycie Warszawy* (250,000);

Rzeczpespolita (216,000); *Express Wieczorny* (120,000); *Trybuna* (110,000); and *Sztandar Mlodych* (102,000).

33 TOURISM AND RECREATION

The number of foreign visitors was approximately 11.3 million in 1991. There were 43,688 hotel rooms with 88,392 beds.

The main tourist attractions include the historic city of Kraków, which suffered little war damage; the resort towns of Zakopane in the mountains of the south, and Sopot, on the Baltic; and the restored Old Town in Warsaw, as well as the capital's museums and Palace of Science and Culture. Camping, hiking, and soccer are among the most popular recreational activities.

34 FAMOUS POLES

Figures prominent in Polish history include Mieszko I (fl.10th century), who led Poland to Christianity; his son and successor, Boleslaw I ("the Brave," d.1025), the first king of sovereign Poland; and Casimir III ("the Great," 1309–70), who sponsored domestic reforms. Tadeusz Andrzej Bonawentura Kościuszko (1746–1817) and Kazimierz Pulaski (1747–79) served with colonial forces during the American Revolution.

Polish public life since World War II has been dominated by Communist leaders Wladyslaw Gomulka (1905–82), Edward Gierek (b.1913), and General Wojciech Jaruzelski (b.1923). Karol Wojtyla (b.1920) was archbishop of Kraków from 1963 until he became Pope as John Paul II in 1978. Lech Walesa (b.1943), leader of the Solidarity movement during 1980–81, was a Nobel Peace Prize laureate in 1983 and has been President of Poland since 1990.

Henryk Sienkiewicz (1846–1916), Poland's first Nobel Prize winner (1905), is internationally famous for *Quo Vadis?* A Pole who achieved stature as an English novelist was Joseph Conrad (Józef Teodor Konrad Korzeniowski, 1857–1924). The best-known modern authors are novelist and short-story writer Isaac Bashevis Singer (1904–91), a Nobel Prize winner in 1978 and a US resident since 1935; science-fiction writer Stanislaw Lem (b.1921); the dissident novelist Jerzy Andrzejewski (1909–83); the poet Czeslaw Milosz (b.1911), a Nobel Prize winner in 1980 and resident of the US since 1960; and novelist Jerzy Kosinski (b.1933), who has lived in the US since 1957 and writes in English.

The greatest Polish composer was Frédéric Chopin (1810–49), born in Warsaw, who lived in Paris after 1831. Other prominent musicians include the pianist Ignacy Jan Paderewski (1860–1941), also his country's first prime minister following World War I; the great harpsichordist Wanda Landowska (1877–1959); the renowned pianist Arthur Rubinstein (1887–1982); and the composer Karol Szymanowski (1883–1937). Witold Lutoslawski (b.1913) and Krzysztof Penderecki (b.1933) are internationally known contemporary composers.

In the second half of the 19th century, Polish realism reached its height in the historical paintings of Jan Matejko (1838–93) and his contemporaries. Andrzej Wajda (b.1926) and Roman Polański (b.1933), who has lived abroad since the mid-1960s, are famous film directors, and Jerzy Grotowski (b.1933) is a well-known stage director.

The outstanding scientist and scholar Nicolaus Copernicus (Nikolaj Kopernik, 1473–1543) is world renowned. Among Poland's brilliant scientists are Maria Sklodowska-Curie (1867–1934), a co-discoverer of radium and the recipient of two Nobel Prizes, and Casimir Funk (1884–1967), the discoverer of vitamins.

35 BIBLIOGRAPHY

Davies, Norman. *Heart of Europe: A Short History of Poland.* New York: Oxford University Press, 1984.

Szulc, Tad. "Poland: The Hope That Never Dies." *National Geographic,* January 1988, 80–121.

Goodwyn, Lawrence. *Breaking the Barrier: the Rise of Solidarity in Poland.* New York: Oxford University Press, 1991.

Greene, C. *Poland.* Chicago: Children's Press, 1983.

Sanford, George. *Poland.* Santa Barbara, Calif.: Clio Press, 1993.

Walesa, Lech. *The Struggle and the Triumph: An Autobiography.* New York: Arcade, 1992.

PORTUGAL

Portuguese Republic
República Portuguesa

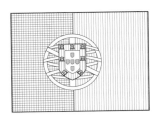

CAPITAL: Lisbon (Lisboa).

FLAG: The national flag, adopted in 1911, consists of a green field at the hoist and a larger red field. At the junction of the two, in yellow, red, blue, and white, is the national coat of arms.

ANTHEM: *A Portuguesa (The Portuguese).*

MONETARY UNIT: The escudo (E) is a paper currency of 100 centavos. There are coins of 1, 2.5, 5, 10, 20, 50, 100, and 200 escudos, and notes of 500, 1,000, 2,000, 5,000 and 10,000 escudos. E1 = $0.0057 (or $1 = E174.12).

WEIGHTS AND MEASURES: The metric system is the legal standard.

HOLIDAYS: New Year's Day, 1 January; Carnival Day, 15 February; Anniversary of the Revolution, 25 April; Labor Day, 1 May; National Day, 10 June; Assumption, 15 August; Republic Day, 5 October; All Saints' Day, 1 November; Independence Day, 1 December; Immaculate Conception, 8 December; Christmas, 25 December. Movable religious holidays include Carnival Day, Good Friday, and Corpus Christi.

TIME: GMT.

1 LOCATION AND SIZE

The westernmost country of Europe, Portugal occupies most of the western coast of the Iberian Peninsula; it shares the peninsula with Spain. Portugal has an area of 92,080 square kilometers (35,552 square miles), including the Azores Archipelago (island chain) and the islands of Madeira and Porto Santo. The area occupied by Portugal is slightly smaller than the state of Indiana. Portugal has a total boundary length of 3,007 kilometers (1,868 miles).

Portugal's capital city, Lisbon, is located on Portugal's west coast.

2 TOPOGRAPHY

Portugal's land area exhibits sharp contrasts. The north is largely lowland or land of medium altitude. The principal mountain ranges are the Serra do Caramulo and the Serra da Podrela, all north of the Tagus River. The uplands contain Portugal's highest peak, Estrela, at 1,993 meters (6,539 feet). The larger rivers—the Minho, the Douro, the Tagus, and the Guadiana—all start in Spain.

3 CLIMATE

The north has cool summers and rainy winters (average annual rainfall 125–150 centimeters/50–60 inches), with occasional snowfall. Central Portugal has hot summers and cool, rainy winters, with 50–75 centimeters (20–30 inches) average annual rainfall. The southern climate is very dry, with rainfall not exceeding 50 centimeters (20 inches) along the coast. In

Photo credit: Susan D. Rock

A cobble-stoned neighborhood in Lisbon.

Lisbon, the average temperature is about 21°C (70°F) in July and 4°C (39°F) in January.

4 PLANTS AND ANIMALS

Three types of vegetation can be found in Portugal: the green forests of eucalyptus, pine, and chestnut in the north; the open dry grasslands, interrupted by cork trees and other types of evergreen oak, in the central areas; and the dry grasslands and evergreen brush in the south. Few wild animals remain in Portugal. The coastal waters abound with fish. Sardines and tuna are among the most common.

5 ENVIRONMENT

Air and water pollution are significant environmental problems especially in Portugal's urban centers.

The nation's water supply is threatened by pollutants from the oil and cellulose industries. Portugal uses 48% of its usable water to support farming and 37% for industrial activity. In total, the nation's cities produce 2.6 million tons of solid waste.

In 1994, 6 of Portugal's mammal species and 18 of its bird species were endangered, as well as 240 plant species.

6 POPULATION

According to the 1991 census, the population of Portugal, including the Azores and Madeira, was 9,862,056. It was estimated by the US Bureau of the Census at 10,484,248 in mid-1994. The United Nations projection for the year 2000, however, is 9,932,000. Average population density in 1991 was 107 persons per square kilometer (277 per square mile). About two-thirds of the people lived in the coastal fourth of the country. Lisbon (Lisboa), the capital and principal city, had a metropolitan-area population of 1,851,063 in 1991.

7 MIGRATION

When Portugal's African colonies gained independence in 1975, an estimated 800,000 Portuguese settlers returned to Portugal. Since then at least 25,000 return from abroad each year, from other European countries or the United States. Some 4,000,000 Portuguese are living abroad,

PORTUGAL

PORTUGAL

0   25   50   75   100 Miles

0   25   50   75   100 Kilometers

ATLANTIC OCEAN

Graciosa

Faial   *Terceira*

São Jorge

Pico

São Miguel

Ponta Delgada

AZORES

0   75   150 Miles

0   75   150 Kilometers

Santa Maria

0   30 Miles

0   30 Kilometers

Porto Santo

Madeira   **ATLANTIC OCEAN**

Funchal

Desertas

MADEIRA ISLANDS

ATLANTIC OCEAN

Minho

Lima

Viana do Castelo   **Braga**   Bragança   Chaves

SERRA DA PODRELA   Zamora

Guimarães   *Tâmega*   Vila Real   Fermoselle

Porto   *Douro*

Pedroso   Meda

Aveiro   **SERRA DO CARAMULO**   Viseu

Guarda   Ciudad Rodrigo

Mondego   Estrela ▲ 6,539 ft. 1993 m.

Coimbra   Covilhã

Cabo Mondego   Figueira da Foz   Plasencia

Zêzere

Leiria   Sertã   Castelo Branco

Cabo Carvoeiro

Peniche   Santarém   *Tagus*   Sor   Portalegre   Valencia de Alcántara

S P A I N

Coruche   *Seda*

Sorraia   Mora   Mérida

Lisbon (Lisboa) ★   Barreiro   Elvas

Almada   **Setúbal**   Évora

Cabo Espichel

Baía de Setúbal   *Guadiana*

Cabo de Sines   Sines   *Sado*   Beja   Fregenal de la Sierra

Villa Nova de Milfontes   *Chança*   *Guadalquivir*

SERRA DE MONCHIQUE   **SERRA DO MALHÃO**

Portimão   Faro

Cabo de São Vicente   Sagres   *Cabo de Santa Maria*   *Golfo de Cadíz*

N W E S

Portugal

LOCATION: 36°57′39″ to 42°9′8″N; 6°11′10″ to 9°29′45″W. **BOUNDARY LENGTHS:** Spain, 1,214 kilometers (755 miles); Atlantic coastline, 1,793 kilometers (1,113 miles). **TERRITORIAL SEA LIMIT:** 12 miles.

mainly in France, Germany, Brazil, South Africa, Canada, Venezuela, and the United States. There were 121,513 legally registered foreigners in 1991, including 52,037 Africans.

8 ETHNIC GROUPS

The Portuguese people represent a mixture of various ethnic strains. In the north are traces of Celtic influence. In the south, Arab and Berber influence is considerable. Other groups—Lusitanians, Phoenicians, Carthaginians, Romans, Visigoths, and Jews—also left their mark on the Portuguese people. The present-day Portuguese population all comes from the same ethnic background, with no national minorities.

9 LANGUAGES

Portuguese, the national language, evolved from ancient dialects of Latin. Portuguese is also the official language of Brazil and the former African provinces. Spanish, French, and English are the most common second languages.

10 RELIGIONS

In 1993, about 94% of the population was Roman Catholic. There were also some 80,000 Protestants, about 15,000 Muslims, and about 2,000 Jews.

An estimated 100,000, who live mainly in the north, are officially Roman Catholics but observe some Jewish practices. These are descendants of the Marranos, a Spanish term for those who outwardly converted to Christianity but secretly practiced Judaism after the expulsion of all practicing Jews from Spain and Portugal at the end of the fifteenth century.

11 TRANSPORTATION

The railway system totals 3,614 kilometers (2,246 miles) of track. The length of usable highways in 1991 was 74,000 kilometers (45,880 miles). Bus service links all Portuguese cities, towns, and important villages. In 1991 there were 2,448,200 motor vehicles registered in continental Portugal, including 1,800,000 passenger cars, and 648,200 trucks, buses, and other commercial vehicles.

As of 1 January 1992, the Portuguese merchant fleet had 47 oceangoing vessels of over 1,000 gross tons, totaling 673,000 gross registered tons. The chief ports are Lisbon (the largest), Porto, and Sines.

Because of their geographical position, Lisbon's Portela Airport and Santa Maria in the Azores are of great importance in international aviation. The most important aviation company in Portugal is Transportes Aereos Portugueses (TAP), which was nationalized in 1975 and carried 4,145,000 passengers in 1992.

12 HISTORY

Portugal derives its name from ancient Portus Cale (now Porto), at the mouth of the Douro River, where the Portuguese monarchy began. The country's early history is the same as that of the other Iberian peoples (people of Portugal and Spain). In the first century, Lusitanians, as the ancient Portuguese were known, were overrun by Celts, Romans, Visigoths, and Moors one after the other. Alfonso I (Alfonso Henriques) became king and achieved independence for Portugal in 1143, beginning the Burgundy dynasty. By

The tile roofs of Porto, a city famous for port wine.

the mid-thirteenth century, the present boundaries of Portugal were established, and Lisbon became the capital.

In the fifteenth century, Prince Henry the Navigator (Henrique o Navegador) founded a nautical school at Sagres, where he gathered the world's best navigators, geographers, and astronomers. This began Portugal's golden age with the series of voyages that led to the formation of the Portuguese Empire. For two centuries Portuguese explorers sailed most of the world's seas. They made the European discovery of the Cape of Good Hope in Africa, Brazil in South America, and Labrador on the coast of Canada. They founded Portugal's overseas provinces in western and eastern Africa, India, Southeast Asia, and Brazil, pouring the vast riches of the empire into their homeland.

In 1580–81, Philip II of Spain, claiming the throne, conquered Portugal and acquired its empire. Portugal's national independence was restored by the revolution of 1640 and the rise of John IV, founder of the Bragança dynasty, to the Portuguese throne. John IV ushered in Portugal's silver age, the seventeenth and eighteenth centuries, when the wealth of Brazil once more made Lisbon one of the most brilliant of European capitals.

The city was largely destroyed by a great earthquake in 1755 but was soon rebuilt. During the Napoleonic wars, Portugal was the base of British operations against the French in the Iberian Peninsula. The royal family, however, withdrew to Brazil, and from 1807 to 1821, Rio de Janeiro was the seat of the Portuguese monarchy. In 1822, Brazil, ruled by Pedro, the son of King John VI of Portugal, formally declared its independence.

The Bragança dynasty, which had ruled Portugal since 1640, came to an end with the revolution of 1910, when the monarchy was replaced by a republican regime. Lack of stability under the new republic led to a military dictatorship in 1926. Marshal António Carmona served as president from 1926 to 1951. António de Oliveira Salazar became Portugal's prime minister in 1932 and proclaimed a new constitution the following year which consolidated his rule.

During World War II, Portugal supported the Allies but did not take part in combat. It later became a member of the North Atlantic Treaty Organization (NATO).

Despite its reduced status as a European power, Portugal attempted to maintain its overseas empire, especially its resource-rich African provinces. The United Nations General Assembly passed a resolution in 1965 calling for a worldwide economic and arms boycott of Portugal in order to force it to grant independence to its African dependencies. Meanwhile, guerrilla movements in Angola, Mozambique, and Guinea-Bissau were met by a steadily increasing commitment of Portuguese troops and supplies.

Salazar, who had served as prime minister of Portugal since 1932, was followed in 1968 by Marcello Caetano. The refusal of the Caetano regime to adopt democratic and economic reforms, coupled with growing discontent over the costly colonial war in Africa, led to a military takeover by the left-wing Armed Forces Movement in April 1974. Democratic liberties were immediately granted and opposition political parties legalized. A decolonization program was also begun, resulting in the independence of all of Portugal's African provinces by November 1975.

Continued differences between right and left—and between Communist and Socialist factions on the left—led to numerous temporary governments after the 1974 takeover. In April 1975, general elections were held for a Constituent Assembly, whose task was to draw up a new constitution. In April 1976 General António dos Santos Ramalho Eanes was elected president, and the leader of the Portuguese Socialist Party, Mário Alberto Nobre Lopes Soares, became prime minister. This government fell apart in 1978 and was replaced by a temporary cabinet.

After a series of different coalitions, the Socialist Party won a 35% plurality in the parliamentary elections of April 1983, and Soares was again named prime minister, forming a coalition government with the center-right Social Democratic Party (Partido Social Democratico—PSD). Political unrest increased after the election, including, in 1984, urban terrorism. In the following year, Portugal entered the European Community, boosting the economy.

The PSD was returned to power in 1991 and Mario Soares was reelected president for a second five-year term on 13 January 1991. Economic recession, government deficits, and regional development have been major concerns in the 1990s.

13 GOVERNMENT

According to the 1976 constitution as amended, the president appoints the prime minister and, at the prime minister's proposal, other members of the government. The main lawmaking body is the single-chamber Assembly of the Republic. Its members (230 in 1994) are directly elected to four-year terms.

Portugal is divided into 22 districts.

14 POLITICAL PARTIES

After the 1974 revolution, various left-wing parties that had functioned underground or in exile were recognized. Among these was the Portuguese Communist Party (Partido Comunista Português—PCP), which is Portugal's oldest political party; the Portuguese Socialist Party (Partido Socialista Português—PSP); and the Popular Democratic Party (Partido Popular Democrático—PPD).

In October 1985, former President Eanes's centrist Democratic Renewal Party (Partido Renovador Democrático—PRD) entered the ballot for the first time, taking 18% of the vote.

15 JUDICIAL SYSTEM

Justice is administered by ordinary and special courts, including the Supreme

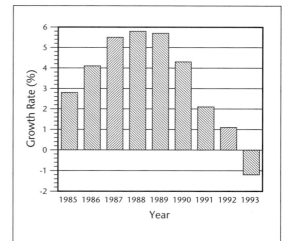

Yearly growth rate of the economy. This economic indicator tells by what percent the economy has increased or decreased when compared with the previous year.

Court of Justice in Lisbon, four courts of appeal, district courts, and special courts.

16 ARMED FORCES

The armed forces are maintained by compulsory service, with terms of 8–12 months for all services. As of 1993, the army had 32,700 personnel (24,800 draftees), the navy 15,300 (including 2,500 marines), and the air force, 10,300 personnel and 83 combat aircraft. The defense budget in 1991 was $1.7 billion. The United States maintains an important airbase in the Azores, and the North Atlantic Treaty Organization (NATO) has one headquarters at Lisbon.

17 ECONOMY

Despite the economic progress recorded since World War II, Portugal remains one of the poorest countries in Europe. The largest industries are clothing, textiles, footwear, and food processing. Two traditional Portuguese foreign exchange sources are income from tourism and payments to Portugal by emigrant workers in western Europe.

Portugal's economy was helped by entry into the European Community (EC) in 1985. Inflation has been a problem, with consumer prices rising by an average of 12.1% a year between 1985 and 1992. Unemployment fell from 8.7% in 1985 to 4.1% in 1992, but rose to 5.5% in 1993.

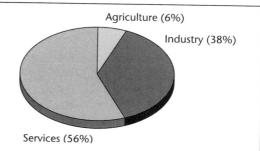

Components of the economy. This pie chart shows how much of the country's economy is devoted to agriculture (includes forestry, hunting, and fishing), industry, or services.

18 INCOME

In 1992, Portugal's gross national product was $73,336 million at current prices, or about $9,130 per person. For the period 1985–92 the average inflation rate was 13.6%, resulting in a real growth rate in gross national product of 5.5% per person.

19 INDUSTRY

Portuguese industry is mainly light. The development of heavy industry has been hampered by a shortage of electric power. Manufactured goods in 1991 included 7,342,000 tons of cement, 1,619,000 tons of wood pulp, 537,000 tons of crude steel for ingots, 1,037,000 tons of paper and paperboard, 1,522,000 radio receivers, and 318,000 television sets.

20 LABOR

The labor force in Portugal, including the Azores and Madeira, at the end of 1992 totaled 4,737,200, of whom 194,100 (or 4.1%) were unemployed. Manufacturing employed 1,126,100 persons (23.8% of the total labor force); agriculture, 536,600 (11.2%); and services, 1,290,900 (27.3%).

The minimum age for employment is 15. As of 1997, it will be raised to 16 to correspond with the completion of 9 years of compulsory schooling. It is believed that businesses in the textile, shoe, and construction industries illegally use child workers. However, since much of this work is done in private homes, it is difficult for the government to control the situation. Possibly as many as 35,000 children between the ages of 12 and 15 are illegally employed in Portugal. Fines have been raised, and the law enforced more strictly, but the government lacks resources to effectively cope with the situation.

21 AGRICULTURE

Agriculture is the main problem area of Portugal's economy. Yields are less than one-third of the European average, with a severe drought in 1991/92 only worsening the problem. Estimates of agriculture production in 1992 included potatoes, 1,293,000 tons; tomatoes, 700,000 tons; corn, 616,000 tons; wheat, 301,000 tons; olives, 221,000 tons; rice, 155,000 tons; and rye, 80,000 tons. Production of olive oil reached 40,000 tons in 1991. Wine production totaled 724,000 tons in 1992.

22 DOMESTICATED ANIMALS

In 1992, the livestock population included 5,847,000 sheep, 2,580,000 hogs, 1,370,000 head of cattle, 862,000 goats, 250,000 donkeys and mules, 18,000,000 chickens and 6,000,000 turkeys. In 1992, Portugal produced about 1,547,000 tons of milk, 55,824 tons of cheese, and 531,000 tons of meat.

23 FISHING

Portuguese fishing consists of coastal fishing, with sardines as the most important catch; trawl fishing on the high seas; and cod fishing on the Grand Banks. The total catch was 325,349 tons in 1991.

24 FORESTRY

With about 32% of the total land area forested, Portugal is an important producer of forestry products. The country is the world's leading producer of cork, ordinarily supplying about half the world output. Portugal is also an important producer of resin and turpentine. Various pine species account for most lumber exports.

25 MINING

Portugal is moderately rich in minerals. Production in 1991 included iron pyrites, 138,760 tons; anthracite, 237,000 tons; tungsten, 1,400 tons; and tin, 10,360 tons

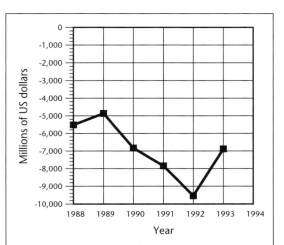

Yearly balance of trade measured in millions of US dollars. The balance of trade is the difference between what a country sells to other countries (its exports) and what it buys (its imports). If a country imports more than it exports, it has a negative balance of trade (a trade deficit). If exports exceed imports there is a positive balance of trade (a trade surplus).

(up from 63 tons in 1989). Output of copper ore was reported at 654,129 tons.

26 FOREIGN TRADE

The principal exports are raw and processed cork, textiles and clothing, footwear, electrical machinery, and road vehicles and parts. Imports include fuels, foodstuffs, raw materials, machinery and equipment, and chemicals. Portugal's principal trade partners in 1991 were France, Germany, Italy, the United Kingdom, Spain, and the Netherlands.

27 ENERGY AND POWER

Total production of electric power (including the Azores and Madeira) was

Selected Social Indicators

These statistics are estimates for the period 1988 to 1993. For comparison purposes, data for the United States and averages for low-income countries and high-income countries are also given.

Indicator	Portugal	Low-income countries	High-income countries	United States
Per capita gross national product†	**$9,130**	$380	$23,680	$24,740
Population growth rate	**-0.1%**	1.9%	0.6%	1.0%
Population growth rate in urban areas	**1.1%**	3.9%	0.8%	1.3%
Population per square kilometer of land	**107**	78	25	26
Life expectancy in years	**75**	62	77	76
Number of people per physician	**402**	>3,300	453	419
Number of pupils per teacher (primary school)	**14**	39	<18	20
Illiteracy rate (15 years and older)	**15%**	41%	<5%	<3%
Energy consumed per capita (kg of oil equivalent)	**1,781**	364	5,203	7,918

† The gross national product (GNP) is the total dollar value of all goods and services produced by a country in a year. The per capita GNP is calculated by dividing a country's GNP by its population. The World Bank defines low-income countries as those with a per capita GNP of $695 or less. High-income countries have a per capita GNP of $8,626 or more. Less than 14% of the world's 5.5 billion people live in high-income countries, while almost 60% live in low-income countries.

> = greater than   < = less than

Sources: World Bank, *Social Indicators of Development 1995,* Baltimore: Johns Hopkins University Press, 1995. Central Intelligence Agency, *World Fact Book,* Washington, D.C.: Government Printing Office, 1994.

29,871 million kilowatt hours in 1991 (compared with 6,215 million kilowatt hours in 1968), 31% from hydroelectric sources. Portugal lacks adequate fuel resources, and large quantities of coal and oil are imported, especially as the electricity sector is switching away from oil. There are no gas or oil reserves and no nuclear power plants in Portugal.

28 SOCIAL DEVELOPMENT

The government-run social security system provides old-age, disability, sickness, and unemployment benefits, family allowances, and health and medical care. The system is funded by payroll contributions from employers and employees.

According to law, women must receive equal pay for equal work. Human rights conditions improved substantially after the 1974 takeover.

29 HEALTH

The Santa Maria Hospital in Lisbon is the largest hospital in Portugal. In 1990, there were 28,016 doctors (about 1 doctor for every 402 people), and 4.2 hospital beds per 1,000 people. Total health care expenditures in 1990 were $3,970 million.

Average life expectancy in 1992 was 75 years. The leading causes of death are circulatory disorders, cancer, and respiratory disorders. Statistics for 1990 indicated that major causes of death were: communicable diseases and maternal/perinatal causes; noncommunicable diseases; and injuries.

30 HOUSING

In the early 1990s, Portugal built an average of 40,000 housing units annually. The total number of housing units in 1991 was 3,630,000. In May 1993, the government announced a $2 billion program designed to clear urban slums, which included the construction of 20,000 low-income units in Lisbon by the year 2000.

31 EDUCATION

In 1990, adult literacy rates were an estimated 85% (88.8% for men and 81.5% for women). Primary level education is compulsory for six years through 1996. In 1997, a law requires nine years of compulsory education. Secondary level education is in two stages of three years each.

In 1991 primary schools had 998,529 pupils. There are about 14 students per teacher. At the secondary level, during 1990, there were 64,513 teachers and 670,035 pupils. In 1990, total enrollment in institutions of higher learning was 185,762, with 14,432 instructors.

32 MEDIA

The government broadcasting network, Radiodifusão Portuguesa, and Radio Renascenca, a religious network, operate AM and FM stations. In 1991, Portugal

Photo credit: Susan D. Rock

School children out for a walk in Lisbon.

had about 2.2 million radios. The state-owned television network, Radiotelevisão Portuguesa, offers color broadcasts on two channels. There were 1.8 million television sets in 1991, and 2,258,315 telephones.

In 1991, 28 daily newspapers were published in Portugal, including the islands. The principal daily newspapers (with their estimated 1991 circulations) include *Correo da Manhá* (78,000); *Jornal de Noticias* (75,500); *Diario de Noticias* (70,000); *Publico* (66,500); and *A Capital* (48,400).

[33] TOURISM AND RECREATION

Tourism has become a major contributor of foreign exchange earnings ($3.7 billion in 1991). In 1991, the number of tourists was 8,656,956. Of these, 47% came from Spain, 13% from the United Kingdom, 9% from Germany, and 7% from France. There were 82,575 hotel rooms with a 41.7% occupancy rate.

Portugal's historic cities—Lisbon, Porto, Coimbra, and others—offer numerous museums, old churches, and castles. Most villages still celebrate market days with dances and other festivities. There are more than 800 kilometers (500 miles) of beaches. The Portuguese bullfight (differing from the Spanish variety in that the bulls are not killed) is a popular spectator sport. The bullfight season lasts from Easter Sunday to October. Soccer is popular as both a participant and a spectator sport.

[34] FAMOUS PORTUGUESE

Prince Henry the Navigator (Henrique Navegador, 1394–1460) laid the foundations of the Portuguese empire. Among the leaders in overseas exploration were Bartholomeu Dias (1450?–1500), the first European to round the Cape of Good Hope, and Vasco da Gama (1469–1524), who founded Portuguese India in 1498. Ferdinand Magellan (Fernão de Magalhães, 1480?–1521) led the first Spanish expedition to sail around the world.

Portugal's greatest writer was Luis Vas de Camões (1524?–80), the author of *Os Lusiadas,* the Portuguese national epic. Portugal's leading painter was Nuno Gonçalves (fl.1450–80). Among the noted Portuguese of more recent times are the novelist Camilo Castelo Branco, viscount of Correia-Botelho (1825–90), and the painter Domingos António de Sequeira (1768–1837).

António de Oliveira Salazar (1889–1970), prime minister for more than 30 years, was Portugal's best-known modern leader. The main political leaders of the late 1970s and early 1980s were the Socialist Mário Alberto Nobre Lopes Soares (b.1924), prime minister in 1976–78 and 1983–85 and president since 1986; Francisco Sá Carneiro (1934–80), prime minister in 1979–80; and economics professor Aníbal Cavaco Silva (b.1939), prime minister since 1985.

[35] BIBLIOGRAPHY

Cross, E., and W. Cross. *Portugal.* Chicago: Children's Press, 1986.

Kaplan, Marion. *The Portuguese: The Land and its People.* London: Viking, 1991.

Livermore, Harold Victor. *A New History of Portugal.* 2d ed. New York: Cambridge University Press, 1977.

McCarry, John. "Madeira Toasts the Future." *National Geographic,* November 1994, 90–113.

Severy, Merle. "Portugal's Sea Road to the East." *National Geographic,* November 1992, 56–93.

Solstein, Eric, ed. *Portugal: A Country.* 2d ed. Washington, D.C.: Library of Congress, 1993.

GLOSSARY

aboriginal: The first known inhabitants of a country. A species of animals or plants which originated within a given area.

acid rain: Rain (or snow) that has become slightly acid by mixing with industrial air pollution.

adobe: A brick made from sun-dried heavy clay mixed with straw, used in building houses. A house made of adobe bricks.

adult literacy: The ability of adults to read and write.

afforestation: The act of turning arable land into forest or woodland.

agrarian economy: An economy where agriculture is the dominant form of economic activity. A society where agriculture dominates the day-to-day activities of the population is called an agrarian society.

air link: Refers to scheduled air service that allows people and goods to travel between two places on a regular basis.

airborne industrial pollutant: Pollution caused by industry that is supported or carried by the air.

allies: Groups or persons who are united in a common purpose. Typically used to describe nations that have joined together to fight a common enemy in war.

In World War I, the term Allies described the nations that fought against Germany and its allies. In World War II, Allies described the United Kingdom, United States, the USSR and their allies, who fought against the Axis Powers of Germany, Italy, and Japan.

aloe: A plant particularly abundant in the southern part of Africa, where leaves of some species are made into ropes, fishing lines, bow strings, and hammocks. It is also a symbolic plant in the Islamic world; anyone who returns from a pilgrimage to Mecca (Mekkah) hangs aloe over his door as a token that he has performed the journey.

Altaic language family: A family of languages spoken in portions of northern and eastern Europe, and nearly the whole of northern and central Asia, together with some other regions. The family is divided into five branches: the Ugrian or Finno-Hungarian, Smoyed, Turkish, Mongolian, and Tunguse.

althing: A legislative assembly.

amendment: A change or addition to a document.

Amerindian: A contraction of the two words, American Indian. It describes native peoples of North, South, or Central America.

amnesty: An act of forgiveness or pardon, usually taken by a government, toward persons for crimes they may have committed.

Anglican: Pertaining to or connected with the Church of England.

animism: The belief that natural objects and phenomena have souls or innate spiritual powers.

annual growth rate: The rate at which something grows over a period of 12 months.

annual inflation rate: The rate of inflation in prices over the course of a year.

anthracite coal: Also called hard coal, it is usually 90 to 95 percent carbon, and burns cleanly, almost without a flame.

anti-Semitism: Agitation, persecution, or discrimination (physical, emotional, economic, political, or otherwise) directed against the Jews.

apartheid: The past governmental policy in the Republic of South Africa of separating the races in society.

appeasement: To bring to a state of peace.

appellate: Refers to an appeal of a court decision to a high authority.

applied science: Scientific techniques employed to achieve results that solve practical problems.

aquaculture: The culture or "farming" of aquatic plants or other natural produce, as in the raising of catfish in "farms."

aquatic resources: Resources that come from, grow in, or live in water, including fish and plants.

aquifer: An underground layer of porous rock, sand, or gravel that holds water.

arable land: Land that can be cultivated by plowing and used for growing crops.

arbitration: A process whereby disputes are settled by a designated person, called the arbitrator, instead of by a court of law.

archipelago: Any body of water abounding with islands, or the islands themselves collectively.

archives: A place where records or a collection of important documents are kept.

arctic climate: Cold, frigid weather similar to that experienced at or near the north pole.

aristocracy: A small minority that controls the government of a nation, typically on the basis of inherited wealth.

armistice: An agreement or truce which ends military conflict in anticipation of a peace treaty.

artesian well: A type of well where the water rises to the surface and overflows.

ASEAN *see* Association of Southeast Asian Nations

Association of Southeast Asian Nations: ASEAN was established in 1967 to promote political, economic, and social cooperation among its six member countries: Indonesia, Malaysia, the Philippines, Singapore, Thailand, and Brunei. ASEAN headquarters are in Jakarta, Indonesia. In January 1992, ASEAN agreed to create the ASEAN Free Trade Area (AFTA).

atheist: A person who denies the existence of God or of a supreme intelligent being.

atoll: A coral island, consisting of a strip or ring of coral surrounding a central lagoon.

atomic weapons: Weapons whose extremely violent explosive power comes from the splitting of the nuclei of atoms (usually uranium or plutonium) by neutrons in a rapid chain reaction. These weapons may be referred to as atom bombs, hydrogen bombs, or H-bombs.

austerity measures: Steps taken by a government to conserve money or resources during an economically difficult time, such as cutting back on federally funded programs.

Australoid: Pertains to the type of aborigines, or earliest inhabitants, of Australia.

Austronesian language: A family of languages which includes practically all the languages of the Pacific Islands—Indonesian, Melanesian, Polynesian, and Micronesian sub-families. Does not include Australian or Papuan languages.

authoritarianism: A form of government in which a person or group attempts to rule with absolute authority without the representation of the citizens.

autonomous state: A country which is completely self-governing, as opposed to being a dependency or part of another country.

autonomy: The state of existing as a self-governing entity. For instance, when a country gains its independence from another country, it gains autonomy.

average inflation rate: The average rate at which the general prices of goods and services increase over the period of a year.

average life expectancy: In any given society, the average age attained by persons at the time of death.

Axis Powers: The countries aligned against the Allied Nations in World War II, originally applied to Nazi Germany and Fascist Italy (Rome-Berlin Axis), and later extended to include Japan.

bagasse: Plant residue left after a product, such as juice, has been extracted.

Baha'i: The follower of a religious sect founded by Mirza Husayn Ali in Iran in 1863.

Baltic states. The three formerly communist countries of Estonia, Latvia, and Lithuania that border on the Baltic Sea.

Bantu language group: A name applied to the languages spoken in central and south Africa.

banyan tree: An East Indian fig tree. Individual trees develop roots from the branches that descend to the ground and become trunks. These roots support and nourish the crown of the tree.

Baptist: A member of a Protestant denomination that practices adult baptism by complete immersion in water.

barren land: Unproductive land, partly or entirely treeless.

barter: Trade practice where merchandise is exchanged directly for other merchandise or services without use of money.

bedrock: Solid rock lying under loose earth.

bicameral legislature: A legislative body consisting of two chambers, such as the U.S. House of Representatives and the U.S. Senate.

bill of rights: A written statement containing the list of privileges and powers to be granted to a body of people, usually introduced when a government or other organization is forming.

bituminous coal: Soft coal; coal which burns with a bright-yellow flame.

black market: A system of trade where goods are sold illegally, often for excessively inflated prices. This type of trade usually develops to avoid paying taxes or tariffs levied by the government, or to get around import or export restrictions on products.

bloodless coup: The sudden takeover of a country's government by hostile means but without killing anyone in the process.

boat people: Used to describe individuals (refugees) who attempt to flee their country by boat.

bog: Wet, soft, and spongy ground where the soil is composed mainly of decayed or decaying vegetable matter.

Bolshevik Revolution. A revolution in 1917 in Russia when a wing of the Russian Social Democratic party seized power. The Bolsheviks advocated the violent overthrow of capitalism.

bonded labor: Workers bound to service without pay; slaves.

border dispute: A disagreement between two countries as to the exact location or length of the dividing line between them.

Brahman: A member (by heredity) of the highest caste among the Hindus, usually assigned to the priesthood.

broadleaf forest: A forest composed mainly of broad-leaf (deciduous) trees.

Buddhism: A religious system common in India and eastern Asia. Founded by and based upon the teachings of Siddhartha Gautama, Buddhism asserts that suffering is an inescapable part of life. Deliverance can only be achieved through the practice of charity, temperance, justice, honesty, and truth.

buffer state: A small country that lies between two larger, possibly hostile countries, considered to be a neutralizing force between them.

bureaucracy: A system of government that is characterized by division into bureaus of administration with their own divisional heads. Also refers to the inflexible procedures of such a system that often result in delay.

Byzantine Empire: An empire centered in the city of Byzantium, now Istanbul in present-day Turkey.

CACM *see* Central American Common Market.

candlewood: A name given to several species of trees and shrubs found in the British West Indies, northern Mexico, and the southwestern United States. The plants are characterized by a very resinous wood.

canton: A territory or small division or state within a country.

capital punishment: The ultimate act of punishment for a crime, the death penalty.

capitalism: An economic system in which goods and services and the means to produce and sell them are privately owned, and prices and wages are determined by market forces.

Caribbean Community and Common Market (CARICOM): Founded in 1973 and with its headquarters in Georgetown, Guyana, CARICOM seeks the establishment of a common trade policy and increased cooperation in the Caribbean region. Includes 13 English-speaking Caribbean nations: Antigua and Barbuda, the Bahamas, Barbados, Belize, Dominica, Grenada, Guyana, Jamaica, Montserrat, Saint Kitts-Nevis, Saint Lucia, St. Vincent/ Grenadines, and Trinidad and Tobago.

CARICOM *see* Caribbean Community and Common Market.

carnivore: Flesh-eating animal or plant.

carob: The common English name for a plant that is similar to and sometimes used as a substitute for chocolate.

cartel: An organization of independent producers formed to regulate the production, pricing, or marketing practices of its members in order to limit competition and maximize their market power.

cash crop: A crop that is grown to be sold rather than kept for private use.

cassation: The reversal or annulling of a final judgment by the supreme authority.

cassava: The name of several species of stout herbs, extensively cultivated for food.

caste system: One of the artificial divisions or social classes into which the Hindus are rigidly separated according to the religious law of Brahmanism. Membership in a caste is hereditary, and the privileges and disabilities of each caste are transmitted by inheritance.

Caucasian: The white race of human beings, as determined by genealogy and physical features.

Caucasoid: Belonging to the racial group characterized by light skin pigmentation. Commonly called the "white race."

cease-fire: An official declaration of the end to the use of military force or active hostilities, even if only temporary.

CEMA *see* Council for Mutual Economic Assistance.

censorship: The practice of withholding certain items of news that may cast a country in an unfavorable light or give away secrets to the enemy.

census: An official counting of the inhabitants of a state or country with details of sex and age, family, occupation, possessions, etc.

Central American Common Market (CACM): Established in 1962, a trade alliance of five Central American nations. Participating are Costa Rica, El Salvador, Guatemala, Honduras, and Nicaragua.

Central Powers: In World War I, Germany and Austria-Hungary, and their allies, Turkey and Bulgaria.

centrally planned economy: An economic system all aspects of which are supervised and regulated by the government.

centrist position: Refers to opinions held by members of a moderate political group; that is, views that are somewhere in the middle of popular thought between conservative and liberal.

cession: Withdrawal from or yielding to physical force.

chancellor: A high-ranking government official. In some countries it is the prime minister.

cholera: An acute infectious disease characterized by severe diarrhea, vomiting, and, often, death.

Christianity: The religion founded by Jesus Christ, based on the Bible as holy scripture.

Church of England: The national and established church in England. The Church of England claims continuity with the branch of the Catholic Church that existed in England before the Reformation. Under Henry VIII, the spiritual supremacy and jurisdiction of the Pope were abolished, and the sovereign (king or queen) was declared head of the church.

circuit court: A court that convenes in two or more locations within its appointed district.

CIS *see* Commonwealth of Independent States

city-state: An independent state consisting of a city and its surrounding territory.

civil court: A court whose proceedings include determinations of rights of individual citizens, in contrast to criminal proceedings regarding individuals or the public.

civil jurisdiction: The authority to enforce the laws in civil matters brought before the court.

civil law: The law developed by a nation or state for the conduct of daily life of its own people.

civil rights: The privileges of all individuals to be treated as equals under the laws of their country; specifically, the rights given by certain amendments to the U.S. Constitution.

civil unrest: The feeling of uneasiness due to an unstable political climate, or actions taken as a result of it.

civil war: A war between groups of citizens of the same country who have different opinions or agendas. The Civil War of the United States was the conflict between the states of the North and South from 1861 to 1865.

climatic belt: A region or zone where a particular type of climate prevails.

Club du Sahel: The Club du Sahel is an informal coalition which seeks to reverse the effects of drought and the desertification in the eight Sahelian zone countries: Burkina Faso, Chad, Gambia, Mali, Mauritania, Niger, Senegal, and the Cape Verde Islands. Headquarters are in Ouagadougou, Burkina Faso.

CMEA see Council for Mutual Economic Assistance.

coalition government: A government combining differing factions within a country, usually temporary.

coastal belt: A coastal plain area of lowlands and somewhat higher ridges that run parallel to the coast.

coastal plain: A fairly level area of land along the coast of a land mass.

coca: A shrub native to South America, the leaves of which produce organic compounds that are used in the production of cocaine.

coke: The solid product of the carbonization of coal, bearing the same relation to coal that charcoal does to wood.

cold war: Refers to conflict over ideological differences that is carried on by words and diplomatic actions, not by military action. The term is usually used to refer to the tension that existed between the United States and the USSR from the 1950s until the breakup of the USSR in 1991.

collective bargaining: The negotiations between workers who are members of a union and their employer for the purpose of deciding work rules and policies regarding wages, hours, etc.

collective farm: A large farm formed from many small farms and supervised by the government; usually found in communist countries.

collective farming: The system of farming on a collective where all workers share in the income of the farm.

colloquial: Belonging to ordinary, everyday speech: often especially applied to common words and phrases which are not used in formal speech.

colonial period: The period of time when a country forms colonies in and extends control over a foreign area.

colonist: Any member of a colony or one who helps settle a new colony.

colony: A group of people who settle in a new area far from their original country, but still under the jurisdiction of that country. Also refers to the newly settled area itself.

COMECON see Council for Mutual Economic Assistance.

commerce: The trading of goods (buying and selling), especially on a large scale, between cities, states, and countries.

commercial catch: The amount of marketable fish, usually measured in tons, caught in a particular period of time.

commercial crop: Any marketable agricultural crop.

commission: A group of people designated to collectively do a job, including a government agency with certain law-making powers. Also, the power given to an individual or group to perform certain duties.

commodity: Any items, such as goods or services, that are bought or sold, or agricultural products that are traded or marketed.

common law: A legal system based on custom and decisions and opinions of the law courts. The basic system of law of England and the United States.

common market: An economic union among countries that is formed to remove trade barriers (tariffs) among those countries, increasing economic cooperation. The European Community is a notable example of a common market.

commonwealth: A commonwealth is a free association of sovereign independent states that has no charter, treaty, or constitution. The association promotes cooperation, consultation, and mutual assistance among members.

Commonwealth of Independent States: The CIS was established in December 1991 as an association of 11 republics of the former Soviet Union. The members include: Russia, Ukraine, Belarus (formerly Byelorussia), Moldova (formerly Moldavia), Armenia, Azerbaijan, Uzbekistan, Turkmenistan, Tajikistan, Kazakhstan, and Kirgizstan (formerly Kirghizia). The Baltic states—Estonia, Latvia, Lithuania—did not join. Georgia maintained observer status before joining the CIS in November 1993.

Commonwealth of Nations: Voluntary association of the United Kingdom and its present dependencies and associated states, as well as certain former dependencies and their dependent territories. The term was first used officially in 1926 and is embodied in the Statute of Westminster (1931). Within the Commonwealth, whose secretariat (established in 1965) is located in London, England, are numerous subgroups devoted to economic and technical cooperation.

commune: An organization of people living together in a community who share the ownership and use of property. Also refers to a small governmental district of a country, especially in Europe.

communism: A form of government whose system requires common ownership of property for the use of all citizens. All profits are to be equally distributed and prices on goods and services are usually set by the state. Also, communism refers directly to the official doctrine of the former U.S.S.R.

compulsory: Required by law or other regulation.

compulsory education: The mandatory requirement for children to attend school until they have reached a certain age or grade level.

conciliation: A process of bringing together opposing sides of a disagreement for the purpose of compromise. Or, a way of settling an international dispute in which the disagreement is submitted to an independent committee that will examine the facts and advise the participants of a possible solution.

concordat: An agreement, compact, or convention, especially between church and state.

confederation: An alliance or league formed for the purpose of promoting the common interests of its members.

Confucianism: The system of ethics and politics taught by the Chinese philosopher Confucius.

coniferous forest: A forest consisting mainly of pine, fir, and cypress trees.

conifers: Cone-bearing plants. Mostly evergreen trees and shrubs which produce cones.

conscription: To be required to join the military by law. Also known as the draft. Service personnel who join the military because of the legal requirement are called conscripts or draftees.

conservative party: A political group whose philosophy tends to be based on established traditions and not supportive of rapid change.

constituency: The registered voters in a governmental district, or a group of people that supports a position or a candidate.

constituent assembly: A group of people that has the power to determine the election of a political representative or create a constitution.

constitution: The written laws and basic rights of citizens of a country or members of an organized group.

constitutional monarchy: A system of government in which the hereditary sovereign (king or queen, usually) rules according to a written constitution.

constitutional republic: A system of government with an elected chief of state and elected representation, with a written constitution containing its governing principles. The United States is a constitutional republic.

consumer goods: Items that are bought to satisfy personal needs or wants of individuals.

continental climate: The climate of a part of the continent; the characteristics and peculiarities of the climate are a result of the land itself and its location.

continental shelf: A plain extending from the continental coast and varying in width that typically ends in a steep slope to the ocean floor.

copra: The dried meat of the coconut; it is frequently used as an ingredient of curry, and to produce coconut oil. Also written *cobra, coprah,* and *copperah.*

Coptic Christians: Members of the Coptic Church of Egypt, formerly of Ethiopia.

cordillera: A continuous ridge, range, or chain of mountains.

corvette: A small warship that is often used as an escort ship because it is easier to maneuver than larger ships like destroyers.

Council for Mutual Economic Assistance (CMEA): Also known as Comecon, the alliance of socialist economies was established on 25 January 1949 and abolished 1 January 1991. It included Afghanistan*, Albania, Angola*, Bulgaria, Cuba, Czechoslovakia, Ethiopia*, East Germany, Hungary, Laos*, Mongolia, Mozambique*, Nicaragua*, Poland, Romania, USSR, Vietnam, Yemen*, and Yugoslavia. Nations marked with an asterisk were observers only.

counterinsurgency operations: Organized military activity designed to stop rebellion against an established government.

county: A territorial division or administrative unit within a state or country.

coup d'ètat or coup: A sudden, violent overthrow of a government or its leader.

court of appeal: An appellate court, having the power of review after a case has been decided in a lower court.

court of first appeal: The next highest court to the court which has decided a case, to which that case may be presented for review.

court of last appeal: The highest court, in which a decision is not subject to review by any higher court. In the United States, it could be the Supreme Court of an individual state or the U.S. Supreme Court.

cricket (sport): A game played by two teams with a ball and bat, with two wickets (staked target) being defended by a batsman. Common in the United Kingdom and Commonwealth of Nations countries.

criminal law: The branch of law that deals primarily with crimes and their punishments.

crown colony: A colony established by a commonwealth over which the monarch has some control, as in colonies established by the United Kingdom's Commonwealth of Nations.

Crusades: Military expeditions by European Christian armies in the eleventh, twelfth, and thirteenth centuries to win land controlled by the Muslims in the middle east.

cultivable land: Land that can be prepared for the production of crops.

Cultural Revolution: An extreme reform movement in China from 1966 to 1976; its goal was to combat liberalization by restoring the ideas of Mao Zedong.

Cushitic language group: A group of Hamitic languages that are spoken in Ethiopia and other areas of eastern Africa.

customs union: An agreement between two or more countries to remove trade barriers with each other and to establish common tariff and nontariff policies with respect to imports from countries outside of the agreement.

cyclone: Any atmospheric movement, general or local, in which the wind blows spirally around and in towards a center. In the northern hemisphere, the cyclonic movement is usually counter-clockwise, and in the southern hemisphere, it is clockwise.

Cyrillic alphabet: An alphabet adopted by the Slavic people and invented by Cyril and Methodius in the ninth century as an alphabet that was easier for the copyist to write. The Russian alphabet is a slight modification of it.

decentralization: The redistribution of power in a government from one large central authority to a wider range of smaller local authorities.

deciduous species: Any species that sheds or casts off a part of itself after a definite period of time. More commonly used in reference to plants that shed their leaves on a yearly basis as opposed to those (evergreens) that retain them.

declaration of independence: A formal written document stating the intent of a group of persons to become fully self-governing.

deficit: The amount of money that is in excess between spending and income.

deficit spending: The process in which a government spends money on goods and services in excess of its income.

deforestation: The removal or clearing of a forest.

deity: A being with the attributes, nature, and essence of a god; a divinity.

delta: Triangular-shaped deposits of soil formed at the mouths of large rivers.

demarcate: To mark off from adjoining land or territory; set the limits or boundaries of.

demilitarized zone (DMZ): An area surrounded by a combat zone that has had military troops and weapons removed.

demobilize: To disband or discharge military troops.

democracy: A form of government in which the power lies in the hands of the people, who can govern directly, or can be governed indirectly by representatives elected by its citizens.

denationalize: To remove from government ownership or control.

deportation: To carry away or remove from one country to another, or to a distant place.

depression: A hollow; a surface that has sunken or fallen in.

deregulation: The act of reversing controls and restrictions on prices of goods, bank interest, and the like.

desalinization plant: A facility that produces freshwater by removing the salt from saltwater.

desegregation: The act of removing restrictions on people of a particular race that keep them socially, economically, and, sometimes, physically, separate from other groups.

desertification: The process of becoming a desert as a result of climatic changes, land mismanagement, or both.

détente: The official lessening of tension between countries in conflict.

devaluation: The official lowering of the value of a country's currency in relation to the value of gold or the currencies of other countries.

developed countries: Countries which have a high standard of living and a well-developed industrial base.

development assistance: Government programs intended to finance and promote the growth of new industries.

dialect: One of a number of regional or related modes of speech regarded as descending from a common origin.

dictatorship: A form of government in which all the power is retained by an absolute leader or tyrant. There are no rights granted to the people to elect their own representatives.

diplomatic relations: The relationship between countries as conducted by representatives of each government.

direct election: The process of selecting a representative to the government by balloting of the voting public, in contrast to selection by an elected representative of the people.

disarmament: The reduction or depletion of the number of weapons or the size of armed forces.

dissident: A person whose political opinions differ from the majority to the point of rejection.

dogma: A principle, maxim, or tenet held as being firmly established.

domain: The area of land governed by a particular ruler or government, sometimes referring to the ultimate control of that territory.

domestic spending: Money spent by a country's government on goods used, investments, running of the government, and exports and imports.

dominion: A self-governing nation that recognizes the British monarch as chief of state.

dormant volcano: A volcano that has not exhibited any signs of activity for an extended period of time.

dowry: The sum of the property or money that a bride brings to her groom at their marriage.

draft constitution: The preliminary written plans for the new constitution of a country forming a new government.

Druze: A member of a Muslim sect based in Syria, living chiefly in the mountain regions of Lebanon.

dual nationality: The status of an individual who can claim citizenship in two or more countries.

duchy: Any territory under the rule of a duke or duchess.

due process: In law, the application of the legal process to which every citizen has a right, which cannot be denied.

durable goods: Goods or products which are expected to last and perform for several years, such as cars and washing machines.

duty: A tax imposed on imports by the customs authority of a country. Duties are generally based on the value of the goods (*ad valorem* duties), some other factors such as weight or quantity (specific duties), or a combination of value and other factors (compound duties).

dyewoods: Any wood from which dye is extracted.

dynasty: A family line of sovereigns who rule in succession, and the time during which they reign.

earned income: The money paid to an individual in wages or salary.

Eastern Orthodox: The outgrowth of the original Eastern Church of the Eastern Roman Empire, consisting of eastern Europe, western Asia, and Egypt.

EC *see* European Community

ecclesiastical: Pertaining or relating to the church.

echidna: A spiny, toothless anteater of Australia, Tasmania, and New Guinea.

ecological balance: The condition of a healthy, well-functioning ecosystem, which includes all the plants and animals in a natural community together with their environment.

ecology: The branch of science that studies organisms in relationship to other organisms and to their environment.

economic depression: A prolonged period in which there is high unemployment, low production, falling prices, and general business failure.

economically active population: That portion of the people who are employed for wages and are consumers of goods and services.

ecotourism: Broad term that encompasses nature, adventure, and ethnic tourism; responsible or wilderness-sensitive tourism; soft-path or small-scale tourism; low-impact tourism; and sustainable tourism. Scientific, educational, or academic tourism (such as biotourism, archetourism, and geotourism) are also forms of ecotourism.

elected assembly: The persons that comprise a legislative body of a government who received their positions by direct election.

electoral system: A system of choosing government officials by votes cast by qualified citizens.

electoral vote: The votes of the members of the electoral college.

electorate: The people who are qualified to vote in an election.

emancipation: The freeing of persons from any kind of bondage or slavery.

embargo: A legal restriction on commercial ships to enter a country's ports, or any legal restriction of trade.

emigration: Moving from one country or region to another for the purpose of residence.

empire: A group of territories ruled by one sovereign or supreme ruler. Also, the period of time under that rule.

enclave: A territory belonging to one nation that is surrounded by that of another nation.

encroachment: The act of intruding, trespassing, or entering on the rights or possessions of another.

endangered species: A plant or animal species whose existence as a whole is threatened with extinction.

endemic: Anything that is peculiar to and characteristic of a locality or region.

Enlightenment: An intellectual movement of the late seventeenth and eighteenth centuries in which scientific thinking gained a strong foothold and old beliefs were challenged. The idea of absolute monarchy was questioned and people were gradually given more individual rights.

enteric disease: An intestinal disease.

epidemic: As applied to disease, any disease that is temporarily prevalent among people in one place at the same time.

Episcopal: Belonging to or vested in bishops or prelates; characteristic of or pertaining to a bishop or bishops.

ethnolinguistic group: A classification of related languages based on common ethnic origin.

EU *see* European Union

European Community: A regional organization created in 1958. Its purpose is to eliminate customs duties and other trade barriers in Europe. It promotes a common external tariff against other countries, a Common Agricultural Policy (CAP), and guarantees of free movement of labor and capital. The original six members were Belgium, France, West Germany, Italy, Luxembourg, and the Netherlands. Denmark, Ireland, and the United Kingdom became members in 1973; Greece joined in 1981; Spain and Portugal in 1986. Other nations continue to join.

European Union: The EU is an umbrella reference to the European Community (EC) and to two European integration efforts introduced by the Maastricht Treaty: Common Foreign and Security Policy (including defense) and Justice and Home Affairs (principally cooperation between police and other authorities on crime, terrorism, and immigration issues).

exports: Goods sold to foreign buyers.

external migration: The movement of people from their native country to another country, as opposed to internal migration, which is the movement of people from one area of a country to another in the same country.

fallout: The precipitation of particles from the atmosphere, often the result of a ground disturbance by volcanic activity or a nuclear explosion.

family planning: The use of birth control to determine the number of children a married couple will have.

Fascism: A political philosophy that holds the good of the nation as more important than the needs of the individual. Fascism also stands for a dictatorial leader and strong oppression of opposition or dissent.

federal: Pertaining to a union of states whose governments are subordinate to a central government.

federation: A union of states or other groups under the authority of a central government.

fetishism: The practice of worshipping a material object that is believed to have mysterious powers residing in it, or is the representation of a deity to which worship may be paid and from which supernatural aid is expected.

feudal estate: The property owned by a lord in medieval Europe under the feudal system.

feudal society: In medieval times, an economic and social structure in which persons could hold land given to them by a lord (nobleman) in return for service to that lord.

final jurisdiction: The final authority in the decision of a legal matter. In the United States, the Supreme Court would have final jurisdiction.

Finno-Ugric language group: A subfamily of languages spoken in northeastern Europe, including Finnish, Hungarian, Estonian, and Lapp.

fiscal year: The twelve months between the settling of financial accounts, not necessarily corresponding to a calendar year beginning on January 1.

fjord: A deep indentation of the land forming a comparatively narrow arm of the sea with more or less steep slopes or cliffs on each side.

fly: The part of a flag opposite and parallel to the one nearest the flagpole.

fodder: Food for cattle, horses, and sheep, such as hay, straw, and other kinds of vegetables.

folk religion: A religion with origins and traditions among the common people of a nation or region that is relevant to their particular life-style.

foreign exchange: Foreign currency that allows foreign countries to conduct financial transactions or settle debts with one another.

foreign policy: The course of action that one government chooses to adopt in relation to a foreign country.

Former Soviet Union: The FSU is a collective reference to republics comprising the former Soviet Union. The term, which has been used as both including and excluding the Baltic republics (Estonia, Latvia, and Lithuania), includes the other 12 republics: Russia, Ukraine, Belarus, Moldova, Armenia, Azerbaijan, Uzbekistan, Turkmenistan, Tajikistan, Kazakhstan, Kyrgizstan, and Georgia.

fossil fuels: Any mineral or mineral substance formed by the decomposition of organic matter buried beneath the earth's surface and used as a fuel.

free enterprise: The system of economics in which private business may be conducted with minimum interference by the government.

free-market economy: An economic system that relies on the market, as opposed to government planners, to set the prices for wages and products.

frigate. A medium-sized warship.

fundamentalist: A person who holds religious beliefs based on the complete acceptance of the words of the Bible or other holy scripture as the truth. For instance, a fundamentalist would believe the story of creation exactly as it is told in the Bible and would reject the idea of evolution.

game reserve: An area of land reserved for wild animals that are hunted for sport or for food.

GDP *see* gross domestic product.

Germanic language group: A large branch of the Indo-European family of languages including German itself, the Scandinavian languages, Dutch, Yiddish, Modern English, Modern Scottish, Afrikaans, and others. The group also includes extinct languages such as Gothic, Old High German, Old Saxon, Old English, Middle English, and the like.

GLOSSARY

glasnost: President Mikhail Gorbachev's frank revelations in the 1980s about the state of the economy and politics in the Soviet Union; his policy of openness.

global greenhouse gas emissions: Gases released into the atmosphere that contribute to the greenhouse effect, a condition in which the earth's excess heat cannot escape.

global warming: Also called the greenhouse effect. The theorized gradual warming of the earth's climate as a result of the burning of fossil fuels, the use of man-made chemicals, deforestation, etc.

GMT *see* Greenwich Mean Time.

GNP *see* gross national product.

grand duchy: A territory ruled by a nobleman, called a grand duke, who ranks just below a king.

Greek Catholic: A person who is a member of an Orthodox Eastern Church.

Greek Orthodox: The official church of Greece, a self-governing branch of the Orthodox Eastern Church.

Greenwich (Mean) Time: Mean solar time of the meridian at Greenwich, England, used as the basis for standard time throughout most of the world. The world is divided into 24 time zones, and all are related to the prime, or Greenwich mean, zone.

gross domestic product: A measure of the market value of all goods and services produced within the boundaries of a nation, regardless of asset ownership. Unlike gross national product, GDP excludes receipts from that nation's business operations in foreign countries.

gross national product: A measure of the market value of goods and services produced by the labor and property of a nation. Includes receipts from that nation's business operation in foreign countries

groundwater: Water located below the earth's surface, the source from which wells and springs draw their water.

guano: The excrement of seabirds and bats found in various areas around the world. Gathered commercially and sold as a fertilizer.

guerrilla: A member of a small radical military organization that uses unconventional tactics to take their enemies by surprise.

gymnasium: A secondary school, primarily in Europe, that prepares students for university.

hardwoods: The name given to deciduous trees, such as cherry, oak, maple, and mahogany.

harem: In a Muslim household, refers to the women (wives, concubines, and servants in ancient times) who live there and also to the area of the home they live in.

harmattan: An intensely dry, dusty wind felt along the coast of Africa between Cape Verde and Cape Lopez. It prevails at intervals during the months of December, January, and February.

heavy industry: Industries that use heavy or large machinery to produce goods, such as automobile manufacturing.

hoist: The part of a flag nearest the flagpole.

Holocaust: The mass slaughter of European civilians, the vast majority Jews, by the Nazis during World War II.

Holy Roman Empire: A kingdom consisting of a loose union of German and Italian territories that existed from around the ninth century until 1806.

home rule: The governing of a territory by the citizens who inhabit it.

homeland: A region or area set aside to be a state for a people of a particular national, cultural, or racial origin.

homogeneous: Of the same kind or nature, often used in reference to a whole.

Horn of Africa: The Horn of Africa comprises Djibouti, Eritrea, Ethiopia, Somalia, and Sudan.

housing starts: The initiation of new housing construction.

human rights activist: A person who vigorously pursues the attainment of basic rights for all people.

human rights issues: Any matters involving people's basic rights which are in question or thought to be abused.

humanist: A person who centers on human needs and values, and stresses dignity of the individual.

humanitarian aid: Money or supplies given to a persecuted group or people of a country at war, or those devastated by a natural disaster, to provide for basic human needs.

hydrocarbon: A compound of hydrogen and carbon, often occurring in organic substances or derivatives of organic substances such as coal, petroleum, natural gas, etc.

hydrocarbon emissions: Organic compounds containing only carbon and hydrogen, often occurring in petroleum, natural gas, coal, and bitumens, and which contribute to the greenhouse effect.

hydroelectric potential: The potential amount of electricity that can be produced hydroelectrically. Usually used in reference to a given area and how many hydroelectric power plants that area can sustain.

hydroelectric power plant: A factory that produces electrical power through the application of waterpower.

IBRD *see* World Bank.

illegal alien: Any foreign-born individual who has unlawfully entered another country.

immigration: The act or process of passing or entering into another country for the purpose of permanent residence.

imports: Goods purchased from foreign suppliers.

indigenous: Born or originating in a particular place or country; native to a particular region or area.

Indo-Aryan language group: The group that includes the languages of India; also called Indo-European language group.

Indo-European language family: The group that includes the languages of India and much of Europe and southwestern Asia.

industrialized nation: A nation whose economy is based on industry.

infanticide: The act of murdering a baby.

infidel: One who is without faith or belief; particularly, one who rejects the distinctive doctrines of a particular religion.

inflation: The general rise of prices, as measured by a consumer price index. Results in a fall in value of currency.

installed capacity: The maximum possible output of electric power at any given time.

insurgency: The state or condition in which one rises against lawful authority or established government; rebellion.

insurrectionist: One who participates in an unorganized revolt against an authority.

interim government: A temporary or provisional government.

interim president: One who is appointed to perform temporarily the duties of president during a transitional period in a government.

internal migration: Term used to describe the relocation of individuals from one region to another without leaving the confines of the country or of a specified area.

International Date Line: An arbitrary line at about the 180th meridian that designates where one day begins and another ends.

Islam: The religious system of Mohammed, practiced by Moslims and based on a belief in Allah as the supreme being and Mohammed as his prophet. The spelling variations, Muslim and Muhammed, are also used, primarily by Islamic people. Islam also refers to those nations in which it is the primary religion.

isthmus: A narrow strip of land bordered by water and connecting two larger bodies of land, such as two continents, a continent and a peninsula, or two parts of an island.

Judaism: The religious system of the Jews, based on the Old Testament as revealed to Moses and characterized by a belief in one God and adherence to the laws of scripture and rabbinic traditions.

Judeo-Christian: The dominant traditional religious makeup of the United States and other countries based on the worship of the Old and New Testaments of the Bible.

junta: A small military group in power of a country, especially after a coup.

khan: A sovereign, or ruler, in central Asia.

khanate: A kingdom ruled by a khan, or man of rank.

kwashiorkor: Severe malnutrition in infants and children caused by a diet high in carbohydrates and lacking in protein.

kwh: The abbreviation for kilowatt-hour.

labor force: The number of people in a population available for work, whether actually employed or not.

labor movement: A movement in the early to mid-1800s to organize workers in groups according to profession to give them certain rights as a group, including bargaining power for better wages, working conditions, and benefits.

land reforms: Steps taken to create a fair distribution of farmland, especially by governmental action.

landlocked country: A country that does not have direct access to the sea; it is completely surrounded by other countries.

least developed countries: A subgroup of the United Nations designation of "less developed countries;" these countries generally have no significant economic growth, low literacy rates, and per person gross national product of less than $500. Also known as undeveloped countries.

leeward: The direction identical to that of the wind. For example, a *leeward tide* is a tide that runs in the same direction that the wind blows.

leftist: A person with a liberal or radical political affiliation.

legislative branch: The branch of government which makes or enacts the laws.

leprosy: A disease that can effect the skin and/or the nerves and can cause ulcers of the skin, loss of feeling, or loss of fingers and toes.

less developed countries (LDC): Designated by the United Nations to include countries with low levels of output, living standards, and per person gross national product generally below $5,000.

literacy: The ability to read and write.

Maastricht Treaty: The Maastricht Treaty (named for the Dutch town in which the treaty was signed) is also known as the Treaty of European Union. The treaty creates a European Union by: (a) committing the member states of the European Economic Community to both European Monetary Union (EMU) and political union; (b) introducing a single currency (European Currency Unit, ECU); (c) establishing a European System of Central Banks (ESCB); (d) creating a European Central Bank (ECB); and (e) broadening EC integration by including both a common foreign and security policy (CFSP) and cooperation in justice and home affairs (CJHA). The treaty entered into force on November 1, 1993.

Maghreb states: The Maghreb states include the three nations of Algeria, Morocco, and Tunisia; sometimes includes Libya and Mauritania.

maize: Another name (Spanish or British) for corn or the color of ripe corn.

majority party: The party with the largest number of votes and the controlling political party in a government.

mangrove: A tree which abounds on tropical shores in both hemispheres. Characterized by its numerous roots which arch out from its trunk and descend from its branches, mangroves form thick, dense growths along the tidal muds, reaching lengths hundreds of miles long.

manioc: The cassava plant or its product. Manioc is a very important food-staple in tropical America.

maquis: Scrubby, thick underbrush found along the coast of the Mediterranean Sea.

marginal land: Land that could produce an economic profit, but is so poor that it is only used when better land is no longer available.

marine life: The life that exists in, or is formed by the sea.

maritime climate: The climate and weather conditions typical of areas bordering the sea.

maritime rights: The rights that protect navigation and shipping.

market access: Market access refers to the openness of a national market to foreign products. Market access reflects a government's willingness to permit imports to compete relatively unimpeded with similar domestically produced goods.

market economy: A form of society which runs by the law of supply and demand. Goods are produced by firms to be sold to consumers, who determine the demand for them. Price levels vary according to the demand for certain goods and how much of them is produced.

market price: The price a commodity will bring when sold on the open market. The price is determined by the amount of demand for the commodity by buyers.

Marshall Plan: Formally known as the European Recovery Program, a joint project between the United States and most Western European nations under which $12.5 billion in U.S. loans and grants was expended to aid European recovery after World War II.

Marxism *see* Marxist-Leninist principles.

Marxist-Leninist principles: The doctrines of Karl Marx, built upon by Nikolai Lenin, on which communism was founded. They predicted the fall of capitalism, due to its own internal faults and the resulting oppression of workers.

Marxist: A follower of Karl Marx, a German socialist and revolutionary leader of the late 1800s, who contributed to Marxist-Leninist principles.

massif: A central mountain-mass or the dominant part of a range of mountains.

matrilineal (descent): Descending from, or tracing descent through, the maternal, or mother's, family line.

Mayan language family: The languages of the Central American Indians, further divided into two subgroups: the Maya and the Huastek.

mean temperature: The air temperature unit measured by the National Weather Service by adding the maximum and minimum daily temperatures together and diving the sum by 2.

Mecca (Mekkah): A city in Saudi Arabia; a destination of pilgrims in the Islamic world.

Mediterranean climate: A wet-winter, dry-summer climate with a moderate annual temperature range.

mestizo: The offspring of a person of mixed blood; especially, a person of mixed Spanish and American Indian parentage.

migratory birds: Those birds whose instincts prompt them to move from one place to another at the regularly recurring changes of season.

migratory workers: Usually agricultural workers who move from place to place for employment depending on the growing and harvesting seasons of various crops.

military coup: A sudden, violent overthrow of a government by military forces.

military junta: The small military group in power in a country, especially after a coup.

military regime: Government conducted by a military force.

military takeover: The seizure of control of a government by the military forces.

militia: The group of citizens of a country who are either serving in the reserve military forces or are eligible to be called up in time of emergency.

millet: A cereal grass whose small grain is used for food in Europe and Asia.

minority party: The political group that comprises the smaller part of the large overall group it belongs to; the party that is not in control.

missionary: A person sent by authority of a church or religious organization to spread his religious faith in a community where his church has no self-supporting organization.

Mohammed (or Muhammed or Mahomet): An Arabian prophet, known as the "Prophet of Allah" who founded the religion of Islam in 622, and wrote *The Koran,* the scripture of Islam. Also commonly spelled Muhammed, especially by Islamic people.

monarchy: Government by a sovereign, such as a king or queen.

money economy: A system or stage of economic development in which money replaces barter in the exchange of goods and services.

Mongol: One of an Asiatic race chiefly resident in Mongolia, a region north of China proper and south of Siberia.

Mongoloid: Having physical characteristics like those of the typical Mongols (Chinese, Japanese, Turks, Eskimos, etc.).

Moors: One of the Arab tribes that conquered Spain in the eighth century.

Moslem (Muslim): A follower of Mohammed (spelled Muhammed by many Islamic people), in the religion of Islam.

mosque: An Islam place of worship and the organization with which it is connected.

mouflon: A type of wild sheep characterized by curling horns.

mujahideen (mujahedin or mujahedeen): Rebel fighters in Islamic countries, especially those supporting the cause of Islam.

mulatto: One who is the offspring of parents one of whom is white and the other is black.

municipality: A district such as a city or town having its own incorporated government.

Muslim: A frequently used variation of the spelling of Moslem, to describe a follower of the prophet Mohammed (also spelled Muhammed), the founder of the religion of Islam.

Muslim New Year: A Muslim holiday. Although in some countries 1 Muharram, which is the first month of the Islamic year, is observed as a holiday, in other places the new year is observed on Sha'ban, the eighth month of the year. This practice apparently stems from pagan Arab times. Shab-i-Bharat, a national holiday in Bangladesh on this day, is held by many to be the occasion when God ordains all actions in the coming year.

NAFTA (North American Free Trade Agreement): NAFTA, which entered into force in January 1994, is a free trade agreement between Canada, the United States, and Mexico. The agreement progressively eliminates almost all U.S.-Mexico tariffs over a 10–15 year period.

nationalism: National spirit or aspirations; desire for national unity, independence, or prosperity.

nationalization: To transfer the control or ownership of land or industries to the nation from private owners.

native tongue: One's natural language. The language that is indigenous to an area.

NATO *see* North Atlantic Treaty Organization

natural gas: A combustible gas formed naturally in the earth and generally obtained by boring a well. The chemical makeup of natural gas is principally methane, hydrogen, ethylene compounds, and nitrogen.

natural harbor: A protected portion of a sea or lake along the shore resulting from the natural formations of the land.

naturalize: To confer the rights and privileges of a native-born subject or citizen upon someone who lives in the country by choice.

nature preserve: An area where one or more species of plant and/or animal are protected from harm, injury, or destruction.

neutrality: The policy of not taking sides with any countries during a war or dispute among them.

Newly Independent States: The NIS is a collective reference to 12 republics of the former Soviet Union: Russia, Ukraine, Belarus (formerly Byelorussia), Moldova (formerly Moldavia), Armenia, Azerbaijan, Uzbekistan, Turkmenistan, Tajikistan, Kazakhstan, and Kirgizstan (formerly Kirghiziya), and Georgia. Following dissolution of the Soviet Union, the distinction between the NIS and the Commonwealth of Independent States (CIS) was that Georgia was not a member of the CIS. That distinction dissolved when Georgia joined the CIS in November 1993.

news censorship *see* censorship

Nonaligned Movement: The NAM is an alliance of third world states that aims to promote the political and economic interests of developing countries. NAM interests have included ending colonialism/neo-colonialism, supporting the integrity of independent countries, and seeking a new international economic order.

Nordic Council: The Nordic Council, established in 1952, is directed toward supporting cooperation among Nordic countries. Members include Denmark, Finland, Iceland, Norway, and Sweden. Headquarters are in Stockholm, Sweden.

North Atlantic Treaty Organization (NATO): A mutual defense organization. Members include Belgium, Canada, Denmark, France (which has only partial membership), Greece, Iceland, Italy, Luxembourg, Netherlands, Norway, Portugal, Spain, Turkey, United Kingdom, United States, and Germany.

nuclear power plant: A factory that produces electrical power through the application of the nuclear reaction known as nuclear fission.

nuclear reactor: A device used to control the rate of nuclear fission in uranium. Used in commercial applications, nuclear reactors can maintain temperatures high enough to generate sufficient quantities of steam which can then be used to produce electricity.

OAPEC (Organization of Arab Petroleum Exporting countries): OAPEC was created in 1968; members include: Algeria, Bahrain, Egypt, Iraq, Kuwait, Libya, Qatar, Saudi Arabia, Syria, and the United Arab Emirates. Headquarters are in Cairo, Egypt.

OAS (Organization of American States): The OAS (Spanish: Organizaciûn de los Estados Americanos, OEA), or the Pan American Union, is a regional organization which promotes Latin American economic and social development. Members include the United States, Mexico, and most Central American, South American, and Caribbean nations.

OAS see Organization of American States

oasis: Originally, a fertile spot in the Libyan desert where there is a natural spring or well and vegetation; now refers to any fertile tract in the midst of a wasteland.

occupied territory: A territory that has an enemy's military forces present.

official language: The language in which the business of a country and its government is conducted.

oligarchy: A form of government in which a few people possess the power to rule as opposed to a monarchy which is ruled by one.

OPEC see OAPEC

open economy: An economy that imports and exports goods.

open market: Open market operations are the actions of the central bank to influence or control the money supply by buying or selling government bonds.

opposition party: A minority political party that is opposed to the party in power.

Organization of Arab Petroleum Exporting Countries see OAPEC

organized labor: The body of workers who belong to labor unions.

Ottoman Empire: An Turkish empire founded by Osman I in about 1603, that variously controlled large areas of land around the Mediterranean, Black, and Caspian Seas until it was dissolved in 1918.

overfishing: To deplete the quantity of fish in an area by removing more fish than can be naturally replaced.

overgrazing: Allowing animals to graze in an area to the point that the ground vegetation is damaged or destroyed.

overseas dependencies: A distant and physically separate territory that belongs to another country and is subject to its laws and government.

Pacific Rim: The Pacific Rim, referring to countries and economies bordering the Pacific Ocean.

pact: An international agreement.

Paleolithic: The early period of the Stone Age, when rough, chipped stone implements were used.

panhandle: A long narrow strip of land projecting like the handle of a frying pan.

papyrus: The paper-reed or -rush which grows on marshy river banks in the southeastern area of the Mediterranean, but more notably in the Nile valley.

paramilitary group: A supplementary organization to the military.

parasitic diseases: A group of diseases caused by parasitic organisms which feed off the host organism.

parliamentary republic: A system of government in which a president and prime minister, plus other ministers of departments, constitute the executive branch of the government and the parliament constitutes the legislative branch.

parliamentary rule: Government by a legislative body similar to that of Great Britain, which is composed of two houses—one elected and one hereditary.

parochial: Refers to matters of a church parish or something within narrow limits.

patriarchal system: A social system in which the head of the family or tribe is the father or oldest male. Kinship is determined and traced through the male members of the tribe.

patrilineal (descent): Descending from, or tracing descent through, the paternal or father's line.

pellagra: A disease marked by skin, intestinal, and central nervous system disorders, caused by a diet deficient in niacin, one of the B vitamins.

per capita: Literally, per person; for each person counted.

perestroika: The reorganization of the political and economic structures of the Soviet Union by president Mikhail Gorbachev.

periodical: A publication whose issues appear at regular intervals, such as weekly, monthly, or yearly.

petrochemical: A chemical derived from petroleum or from natural gas.

pharmaceutical plants: Any plant that is used in the preparation of medicinal drugs.

plantain: The name of a common weed that has often been used for medicinal purposes, as a folk remedy and in modern medicine. *Plaintain* is also the name of a tropical plant producing a type of banana.

poaching: To intrude or encroach upon another's preserves for the purpose of stealing animals, especially wild game.

polar climate: Also called tundra climate. A humid, severely cold climate controlled by arctic air masses, with no warm or summer season.

political climate: The prevailing political attitude of a particular time or place.

political refugee: A person forced to flee his or her native country for political reasons.

potable water: Water that is safe for drinking.

pound sterling: The monetary unit of Great Britain, otherwise known as the pound.

prefect: An administrative official; in France, the head of a particular department.

prefecture: The territory over which a prefect has authority.

prime meridian: Zero degrees in longitude that runs through Greenwich, England, site of the Royal Observatory. All other longitudes are measured from this point.

prime minister: The premier or chief administrative official in certain countries.

private sector: The division of an economy in which production of goods and services is privately owned.

privatization: To change from public to private control or ownership.

protectorate: A state or territory controlled by a stronger state, or the relationship of the stronger country toward the lesser one it protects.

Protestant Reformation: In 1529, a Christian religious movement begun in Germany to deny the universal authority of the Pope, and to establish the Bible as the only source of truth. (*Also see* Protestant)

Protestant: A member or an adherent of one of those Christian bodies which descended from the Reformation of the sixteenth century. Originally applied to those who opposed or protested the Roman Catholic Church.

proved reserves: The quantity of a recoverable mineral resource (such as oil or natural gas) that is still in the ground.

province: An administrative territory of a country.

provisional government: A temporary government set up during time of unrest or transition in a country.

pulses: Beans, peas, or lentils.

purge: The act of ridding a society of "undesirable" or unloyal persons by banishment or murder.

Rastafarian: A member of a Jamaican cult begun in 1930 as a semi-religious, semi-political movement.

rate of literacy: The percentage of people in a society who can read and write.

recession. A period of reduced economic activity in a country or region.

referendum: The practice of submitting legislation directly to the people for a popular vote.

Reformation *see* Protestant Reformation.

refugee: One who flees to a refuge or shelter or place of safety. One who in times of persecution or political commotion flees to a foreign country for safety.

revolution: A complete change in a government or society, such as in an overthrow of the government by the people.

right-wing party: The more conservative political party.

Roman alphabet: The alphabet of the ancient Romans from which the alphabets of most modern western European languages, including English, are derived.

Roman Catholic Church: The designation of the church of which the pope or Bishop of Rome is the head, and that holds him as the successor of St. Peter and heir of his spiritual authority, privileges, and gifts.

romance language: The group of languages derived from Latin: French, Spanish, Italian, Portuguese, and other related languages.

roundwood: Timber used as poles or in similar ways without being sawn or shaped.

runoff election: A deciding election put to the voters in case of a tie between candidates.

Russian Orthodox: The arm of the Orthodox Eastern Church that was the official church of Russia under the czars.

sack: To strip of valuables, especially after capture.

Sahelian zone: Eight countries make up this dry desert zone in Africa: Burkina Faso, Chad, Gambia, Mali, Mauritania, Niger, Senegal, and the Cape Verde Islands. *Also see* Club du Sahel.

salinization: An accumulation of soluble salts in soil. This condition is common in desert climates, where water evaporates quickly in poorly drained soil due to high temperatures.

Samaritans: A native or an inhabitant of Samaria; specifically, one of a race settled in the cities of Samaria by the king of Assyria after the removal of the Israelites from the country.

savanna: A treeless or near treeless plain of a tropical or subtropical region dominated by drought-resistant grasses.

schistosomiasis: A tropical disease that is chronic and characterized by disorders of the liver, urinary bladder, lungs, or central nervous system.

secession: The act of withdrawal, such as a state withdrawing from the Union in the Civil War in the United States.

sect: A religious denomination or group, often a dissenting one with extreme views.

segregation: The enforced separation of a racial or religious group from other groups, compelling them to live and go to school separately from the rest of society.

seismic activity: Relating to or connected with an earthquake or earthquakes in general.

self-sufficient: Able to function alone without help.

separation of power: The division of power in the government among the executive, legislative, and judicial branches and the checks and balances employed to keep them separate and independent of each other.

separatism: The policy of dissenters withdrawing from a larger political or religious group.

serfdom: In the feudal system of the Middle Ages, the condition of being attached to the land owned by a lord and being transferable to a new owner.

Seventh-day Adventist: One who believes in the second coming of Christ to establish a personal reign upon the earth.

shamanism: A religion of some Asians and Amerindians in which shamans, who are priests or medicine men, are believed to influence good and evil spirits.

shantytown: An urban settlement of people in flimsy, inadequate houses.

Shia Muslim: Members of one of two great sects of Islam. Shia Muslims believe that Ali and the Imams are the rightful successors of Mohammed (also commonly spelled Muhammed). They also believe that the last recognized Imam will return as a messiah. Also known as Shiites. (*Also see* Sunnis.)

Shiites *see* Shia Muslims.

Shintoism: The system of nature- and hero-worship which forms the indigenous religion of Japan.

shoal: A place where the water of a stream, lake, or sea is of little depth. Especially, a sand-bank which shows at low water.

sierra: A chain of hills or mountains.

Sikh: A member of a politico-religious community of India, founded as a sect around 1500 and based on the principles of monotheism (belief in one god) and human brotherhood.

Sino-Tibetan language family: The family of languages spoken in eastern Asia, including China, Thailand, Tibet, and Burma.

slash-and-burn agriculture: A hasty and sometimes temporary way of clearing land to make it available for agriculture by cutting down trees and burning them.

slave trade: The transportation of black Africans beginning in the 1700s to other countries to be sold as slaves—people owned as property and compelled to work for their owners at no pay.

Slavic languages: A major subgroup of the Indo-European language family. It is further subdivided into West Slavic (including Polish, Czech, Slovak and Serbian), South Slavic (including Bulgarian, Serbo-Croatian, Slovene, and Old Church Slavonic), and East Slavic (including Russian Ukrainian and Byelorussian).

social insurance: A government plan to protect low-income people, such as health and accident insurance, pension plans, etc.

social security: A form of social insurance, including life, disability, and old-age pension for workers. It is paid for by employers, employees, and the government.

socialism: An economic system in which ownership of land and other property is distributed among the community as a whole, and every member of the community shares in the work and products of the work.

socialist: A person who advocates socialism.

softwoods: The coniferous trees, whose wood density as a whole is relatively softer than the wood of those trees referred to as hardwoods.

sorghum (also known as Syrian Grass): Plant grown in various parts of the world for its valuable uses, such as for grain, syrup, or fodder.

Southeast Asia: The region in Asia that consists of the Malay Archipelago, the Malay Peninsula, and Indochina.

staple crop: A crop that is the chief commodity or product of a place, and which has widespread and constant use or value.

state: The politically organized body of people living under one government or one of the territorial units that make up a federal government, such as in the United States.

steppe: A level tract of land more or less devoid of trees, in certain parts of European and Asiatic Russia.

student demonstration: A public gathering of students to express strong feelings about a certain situation, usually taking place near the location of the people in power to change the situation.

subarctic climate: A high latitude climate of two types: *continental subarctic*, which has very cold winters, short, cool summers, light precipitation and moist air; and *marine subarctic*, a coastal and island climate with polar air masses causing large precipitation and extreme cold.

subcontinent: A land mass of great size, but smaller than any of the continents; a large subdivision of a continent.

subsistence economy: The part of a national economy in which money plays little or no role, trade is by barter, and living standards are minimal.

subsistence farming: Farming that provides the minimum food goods necessary for the continuation of the farm family.

subtropical climate: A middle latitude climate dominated by humid, warm temperatures and heavy rainfall in summer, with cool winters and frequent cyclonic storms.

subversion: The act of attempting to overthrow or ruin a government or organization by stealthy or deceitful means.

Sudanic language group: A related group of languages spoken in various areas of northern Africa, including Yoruba, Mandingo, and Tshi.

suffrage: The right to vote.

Sufi: A Muslim mystic who believes that God alone exists, there can be no real difference between good and evil, that the soul exists within the body as in a cage, so death should be the chief object of desire, and sufism is the only true philosophy.

sultan: A king of a Muslim state.

Sunni Muslim: Members of one of two major sects of the religion of Islam. Sunni Muslims adhere to strict orthodox traditions, and believe that the four caliphs are the rightful successors to Mohammed, founder of Islam. (Mohammed is commonly spelled Muhammed, especially by Islamic people.) (*Also see* Shia Muslim.)

Taoism: The doctrine of Lao-Tzu, an ancient Chinese philosopher (about 500 B.C.) as laid down by him in the *Tao-te-ching.*

tariff: A tax assessed by a government on goods as they enter (or leave) a country. May be imposed to protect domestic industries from imported goods and/or to generate revenue.

temperate zone: The parts of the earth lying between the tropics and the polar circles. The *northern temperate zone* is the area between the tropic of Cancer and the Arctic Circle. The *southern temperate zone* is the area between the tropic of Capricorn and the Antarctic Circle.

terracing: A form of agriculture that involves cultivating crops in raised banks of earth.

terrorism: Systematic acts of violence designed to frighten or intimidate.

thermal power plant: A facility that produces electric energy from heat energy released by combustion of fuel or nuclear reactions.

Third World: A term used to describe less developed countries; as of the mid-1990s, it is being replaced by the United Nations designation Less Developed Countries, or LDC.

topography: The physical or natural features of the land.

torrid zone: The part of the earth's surface that lies between the tropics, so named for the character of its climate.

totalitarian party: The single political party in complete authoritarian control of a government or state.

trachoma: A contagious bacterial disease that affects the eye.

treaty: A negotiated agreement between two governments.

tribal system: A social community in which people are organized into groups or clans descended from common ancestors and sharing customs and languages.

tropical monsoon climate: One of the tropical rainy climates; it is sufficiently warm and rainy to produce tropical rainforest vegetation, but also has a winter dry season.

tsetse fly: Any of the several African insects which can transmit a variety of parasitic organisms through its bite. Some of these organisms can prove fatal to both human and animal victims.

tundra: A nearly level treeless area whose climate and vegetation are characteristically arctic due to its northern position; the subsoil is permanently frozen.

undeveloped countries *see* least developed countries.

unemployment rate: The overall unemployment rate is the percentage of the work force (both employed and unemployed) who claim to be unemployed.

UNICEF: An international fund set-up for children's emergency relief: United Nations Children's Fund (formerly United Nations International Children's Emergency Fund).

universal adult suffrage: The policy of giving every adult in a nation the right to vote.

untouchables: In India, members of the lowest caste in the caste system, a hereditary social class system. They were considered unworthy to touch members of higher castes.

urban guerrilla: A rebel fighter operating in an urban area.

urbanization: The process of changing from country to city.

USSR: An abbreviation of Union of Soviet Socialist Republics.

veldt: In South Africa, an unforested or thinly forested tract of land or region, a grassland.

Warsaw Pact: Agreement made 14 May 1955 (and dissolved 1 July 1991) to promote mutual defense between Albania, Bulgaria, Czechoslovakia, East Germany, Hungary, Poland, Romania, and the USSR.

Western nations: Blanket term used to describe mostly democratic, capitalist countries, including the United States, Canada, and western European countries.

wildlife sanctuary: An area of land set aside for the protection and preservation of animals and plants.

workers' compensation: A series of regular payments by an employer to a person injured on the job.

World Bank: The World Bank is a group of international institutions which provides financial and technical assistance to developing countries.

world oil crisis: The severe shortage of oil in the 1970s precipitated by the Arab oil embargo.

wormwood: A woody perennial herb native to Europe and Asiatic Russia, valued for its medicinal uses.

yaws: A tropical disease caused by a bacteria which produces raspberry-like sores on the skin.

yellow fever: A tropical viral disease caused by the bite of an infected mosquito, characterized by jaundice.

Zoroastrianism: The system of religious doctrine taught by Zoroaster and his followers in the Avesta; the religion prevalent in Persia until its overthrow by the Muslims in the seventh century.

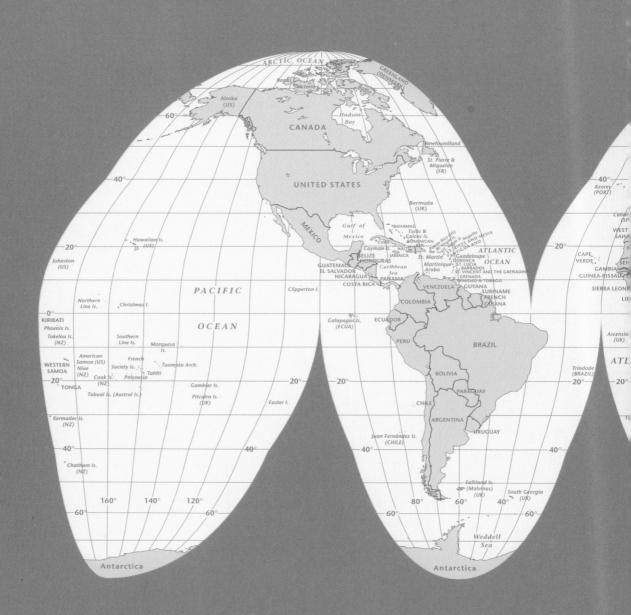